Studying Men and Ma

THE UNI''
WINC

..nuieth-century anxiety about a 'crisis in masculinity' still persists ,, particularly in English-speaking cultures. *Studying Men and Masculinities* offers an engaging and comprehensive overview of masculinity. Drawing on a wide range of cultural practices and texts from different genres and media, David Buchbinder examines the notion of patriarchy and the challenges to patriarchal power, including queer theory. The book considers whether crisis may in fact be built into the very structure of the masculine, and examines emergent masculinities post-9/11.

Theoretical positions within the field are clearly explained and applied to real-life case studies from literature, film, and television. Interspersed in each chapter are a series of questions and tasks aimed at encouraging the reader to engage her/himself in the study of masculinities in everyday life and popular culture.

This topical and thought-provoking book will be an invaluable resource for students of masculinities studies, sexuality studies, cultural studies, and gender theory.

David Buchbinder currently holds a Personal Chair in Masculinities Studies at Curtin University in Perth, Western Australia. His research interests include gender and masculinities studies, and literary and cultural studies. He has published *Masculinities and Identities* and *Performance Anxieties: Re-presenting Men*.

Studying Men and Masculinities

David Buchbinder

Routledge
Taylor & Francis Group

LONDON AND NEW YORK

First published 2013
by Routledge
2 Park Square, Milton Park, Abingdon, Oxon OX14 4RN

Simultaneously published in the USA and Canada
by Routledge
711 Third Avenue, New York, NY 10017

Routledge is an imprint of the Taylor & Francis Group

British Library Cataloguing in Publication Data
A catalogue record for this book is available from the British Library

Library of Congress Cataloging-in-Publication Data
Buchbinder, David, 1947-
 Studying men and masculinities / David Buchbinder. — 1st ed.
 p. cm.
 Includes bibliographical references and index.
 ISBN 978-0-415-57827-1 (hardback) — ISBN 978-0-415-57829-5 (pbk.) —
 ISBN 978-0-203-85222-4 (ebook) 1. Men. 2. Masculinity. 3. Patriarchy.
 4. Men's studies. I. Title.
 HQ1090.B853 2012
 305.31—dc23   2011050171

ISBN 13: 978-0-415-57827-1 (hbk)
ISBN 13: 978-0-415-57829-5 (pbk)
ISBN 13: 978-0-203-85222-4 (ebook)

Typeset in Times New Roman
by Cenveo Publisher Services

To my parents, Shula and Sam Buchbinder

Contents

Preface

"I dare do all that may become a man;/ Who dares do more is none," declares Macbeth to his lady in Shakespeare's play (I.vii. 46–47, Shakespeare, 1969), "become" here having the dual sense of "be appropriate to" and "enhance." In addition to being a historical play aimed at gratifying King James I as well as a narrative about overweening ambition and its social, political, and psychological consequences, *Macbeth* is also a play about being a man and how to be, or, to adapt Shakespeare's phrasing, to become a man. The text abounds in definitions of the masculine, whether in reference to a man's ability to kill another man in cold blood, his capacity to produce a line of descendants, or his maintenance of composure in the face of the terrifying and unthinkable.

The closing decades of the twentieth century and the opening decade of the present one have seen a great deal of anxiety and concern expressed about the role of boys and men in post-1960s culture and the changing definitions of masculinity. This book takes that anxiety as the starting point for an exploration of the masculine in the contemporary social and cultural context. It therefore differs from other texts that adopt a more traditional treatment of the topic, such as Jack S. Kahn's relatively recent *An Introduction to Masculinities* (Kahn, 2009), which examines different approaches to gender in general, and masculinity in particular, noting problems with the various theories and their approaches. Instead, I have chosen to inquire whether the perceived and much-debated "crisis in masculinity" is historically unique, and whether crisis may in fact be built into masculinity.

Therefore, I discuss various historical moments, although not chronologically; and I draw on a number of theories and theorists of the social, the cultural, and gender. (Although *society/social* and *culture/cultural* are sometimes used interchangeably, in this book I distinguish between them. "Society" and "social" I take to refer to social structures such as class, or interpersonal interaction, whereas by "culture" and "cultural" I intend common understandings, preoccupations, and activities.) I have quoted liberally from those theoretical works, for two reasons. First, I thought it important that their voices be heard directly, rather than filtered through summary and paraphrase of my own (although I have also summarized and paraphrased where, for example, the prose of the original might be thought to defeat many readers). In this way, the reader gains a sense of the original material, even if only in translation. Second, if it is true, as the Italian adage puts it, that the translator is a traitor (*Traduttore, traditore*), it may be equally the case that the commentator commits her or his own form of betrayal of the original. Providing direct quotation allows the reader to weigh her or his understanding of that original material against the commentary or application offered in this book.

I have drawn chiefly on popular culture for examples and "case studies" to illustrate the points made in each chapter. My reasons are twofold: in the first place, such texts are readily available and accessible to most, if not all, readers; and, in the second, most readers already have a stake in such material, because it constitutes a cultural environment in which they live. Accordingly, the theoretical material and the analyses of popular-cultural texts in *Studying Men and Masculinities* are intended to provide a model for readers by which to undertake their own analysis of such texts in their everyday lives. Interspersed throughout the chapters are sections titled "Activity." The questions and activities in each such section are indicative only: teachers (or, indeed, readers in general) might choose to supplement or substitute these with questions and activities of their own devising.

Some readers, especially those scholars working in the areas of gender or masculinities studies, may be disappointed or irritated by my omission of particular topics or theorists. I do not, for instance, consider the history and statistics of men's social, domestic, or military violence. The field of masculinities studies is a rich, complex one, and given the scope of an introductory text such as this, I have had to narrow the focus.

Other readers may take exception to some of the ideas expressed in this book because these may run counter to their own ideas or beliefs. However, this is as it should be: it was my intent, and it is my hope, that *Studying Men and Masculinities* will provoke its readers into agreeing or disagreeing with the ideas set out in this book. In this way, readers will be drawn to think about the issues, and arrive at insights and conclusions of their own, whether these entail rejecting the arguments set forth in this book, modifying them and supplementing them with other theories and ideas, or simply accepting what I have to say in the chapters following.

The suggestions for further reading at the end of each chapter are by no means intended to be exhaustive. Rather, they offer a variety of treatments of the topics, some supporting the points made in the chapter, others offering a different perspective. I have chosen to keep these suggestions to a minimum, lest the reader become dismayed by long lists of bibliographical entries. (Still further readings, of course, are to be found in the references at the end of the book, which record the sources of material I have quoted or alluded to in the preceding chapters.)

In writing this book, I have benefited greatly from the suggestions and emendations of readers of the early drafts of the manuscript. I want therefore to thank my colleagues Margaret Macintyre, Dr Ann McGuire, and Professor Jon Stratton, of the School of Media and Cultural Studies at Curtin University; my friends Sarah

Schladow and Sally Scott; and Professor Christopher E. Forth, of the Humanities and Western Civilization Program in the College of Liberal Arts and Sciences, Kansas University at Lawrence, Kansas. My thanks go also to Kris, who has tolerated with patience and good humor my thoughts, uncertainties, and anxieties while writing!

Acknowledgments

I would like to thank the University of Toronto Press for granting permission to use and adapt material from the following articles of mine, published in the *Canadian Review of American Studies*:

"Object or ground? The male body as fashion accessory," 34.3 (2004): 221–31.
"Enter the schlemiel: the emergence of inadequate or incompetent masculinities in recent film and television," 38.2 (2008): 227–45.

In addition, I am grateful to Professor Terri-Ann White, Director of the Institute of Advanced Studies and of UWA Publishing (University of Western Australia) for granting permission to use and adapt material from my chapter "'Past and future tense': the crisis in masculinity," in *Future Imaginings: Sexualities and Genders in the New Millennium*, edited by Delys Bird, Wendy Were and Terri-Ann White, 2003, Crawley, University of Western Australia Press, 27–40.

1 The end of masculinity?

After the release in 1999 of David Fincher's movie *Fight Club* (*Fight Club*, 1999), rumors began to circulate about the establishment of actual fight clubs, modeled on the principles of the fight club as outlined first in Chuck Palahniuk's novel (Palahniuk, 1996), on which the film was based, and then reiterated in the movie itself. Particularly disturbing were news items indicating that many of these fight clubs had developed among boys, especially teenage boys, in schools ranging geographically from the United States to as far away as Australia (see, for example "Police, D203 officials break up Jefferson 'fight club,'" 2011; Malkin, 2008; "Fight club draws techies for bloody underground beatdowns," 2006). Aside from concerns about a general increase in violence that such reports suggest, there arises also the following important question: to what in this younger generation of males did the movie speak, so as to encourage this mood of violence and the propagation of fight clubs?

Both the novel and the film offer several causes. We are told early on in both that "What you see at fight club is a generation of men raised by women" (Palahniuk, 1996: 50). This observation is compounded and supported by the fact that, after the age of about six, the narrator grew up with an absentee father, with whom he has maintained only a casual, sporadic relationship (Palahniuk, 1996: 50). Tellingly, of Tyler Durden, who turns out to be the narrator's alter ego, the narrator says, "Tyler never knew his father" (Palahniuk, 1996: 49). The implication here is that an earlier generation of men failed in their responsibilities towards their sons, who therefore perforce grew up in the care of women. The narrator remarks cynically, "I'm a thirty-year-old boy, and I'm wondering if another woman is really the answer I need" (Palahniuk, 1996: 51). He wonders further whether "Maybe self-destruction is the answer" (Palahniuk, 1996: 49).

To this assignment of blame by an entire generation of men is added the accusation that those elders have created for their successors a wasteland that is both physical (the destruction of natural habitats and consequently of the creatures that live in these, the creation of polluted and polluting cities, and so on) and ethical and spiritual. Thus, for example, the narrator has come to invest not only his money but his sense of self-worth and identity in purchasable objects, such as the IKEA furnishings that used to decorate his apartment before the blast that reduced everything in his personal urban habitat to splinters: "… you're trapped in your lovely nest, and the things you used to own, now they own you" (Palahniuk, 1996: 44). Durden's remedy is, first, to remasculinize the younger generation of men by toughening them up through fight club. This requires their complicity in keeping the very notion of a fight club secret, which in turn binds them as a group. Unlike professional boxing or wrestling and other forms of socially accepted aggressive activity, there are really no winners or losers in fight club:

> Fight club isn't about winning or losing fights. Fight club isn't about words. You see a guy come to fight club for the first time, and his ass is a loaf of white bread. You see the same guy here six months later, and he looks carved out of wood. This guy trusts himself to handle anything. There's grunting and noise at fight club like at the gym, but fight club isn't about looking good. There is hysterical shouting in tongues like at church, and when you wake up Sunday afternoon you feel saved.
>
> (Palahniuk, 1996: 51)

Fight club, then, is about restoring to men a sense of their own masculinity and a hardened male body no longer softened and sapped by the feminizing influences of the dominant culture of late capitalism.

The second aspect of Durden's solution to the dilemma faced by a younger generation of men is Project Mayhem, the aim of which is to conduct a campaign of terrorism focused on subverting and eventually destroying capitalist culture itself:

> … Tyler said, picture yourself planting radishes and seed potatoes on the fifteenth green of a forgotten golf course.
>
> You'll hunt elk through the damp canyon forests around the ruins of Rockefeller Center, and dig clams next to the skeleton of the Space Needle

leaning at a forty-five-degree angle. We'll paint the skyscrapers with huge totem faces and goblin tikis, and every evening what's left of mankind will retreat to empty zoos and lock itself in cages as protection against bears and big cats and wolves that pace and watch us from outside the cage bars at night.

(Palahniuk, 1996: 124)

Durden's vision, then, is to return both society and men to a pre-industrial, even primitive state, so that a proper balance can be restored both to nature and to gender, with a particular emphasis on the masculine.

Both the novel and the movie *Fight Club* emerged from a general sense developing toward the end of the twentieth century and into the twenty-first in many Western (and especially English-speaking) societies that masculinity has found itself in crisis. Yet, in *The Future of Men*, a slim, unassuming volume published in 1997, between the publication of Palahniuk's novel and the appearance of Fincher's film, Dave Hill surveys the changes in the cultural understandings of what it is to be a man, and of what masculinity is, and comes to relatively positive conclusions. He notes that many believe that there is "a crisis of male identity in the West" (Hill, 1997: 5), but proposes, toward the end of the volume, that there has in fact been a series of positive and desirable changes; for instance:

Never again will masculinity be as containable or as easy to describe in false terms as it has been during the last 150 years. Tomorrow's materially comfortable young men will have more freedom of identity on their hands than their grandfathers and even their fathers could have imagined. The luckiest will achieve the state of sustained independence which forebears enjoyed for a few years only before slipping into the state of mind called suburbia.

(Hill, 1997: 44)

He remarks that

Even present-day first impressions hint at how much more relaxed and elastic the category of masculinity is becoming: men do not look alike any more.

(Hill, 1997: 47)

Hill goes on to forecast that the new order of things

will involve men and women alike accommodating more flexible models of masculinity which acknowledge many features in common with femininity and which, largely as a result of this, are also able to accommodate those aspects of "masculinity" which do not do damage to children or women and do not denigrate either those men who do not exhibit the same "masculine" traits or those women who do. In this process men will be under the greater pressure to change, for they will need to share pieces of male territory with women with better grace than they have sometimes exhibited before.

(Hill, 1997: 52)

Thus, although Hill does note some problems (for example, that "The capacity of young and not-so-young men, including those who are highly educated and with considerable professional responsibilities, to remain puerile far into adulthood is already a depressing feature of contemporary life" [Hill, 1997: 50]), in the main his view is a largely positive and optimistic one of men changing and adjusting to new conditions of living in the culture. However, compared with the strident claims in the media of a crisis in masculinity and the publication of a spate of books on the topic, Hill's voice appears to be a minority one.

That "crisis in masculinity" (if this is indeed what it is) has been attributed to a number of causes; for example, second-wave feminism of the 1960s and 1970s (here we might remind ourselves of the narrator's observation in *Fight Club* that his is a generation of men raised by women), and the civil rights movements of the 1960s such as Black Liberation and Gay Liberation. Social, political, and other inequities and injustices were traced back to the dominance and power of white, middle-class, heterosexual males, who were then compelled to examine the power structures and dynamics of their societies, and their own roles in these. Changes brought about by these liberationist movements have included legal and political reform, as well as a greater social tolerance, if not always a simple acceptance as equals, of women, blacks, and gays and lesbians, especially in the public sphere, together with an increasing tolerance also of transgender and trans-sexual identities. There have also been shifts in language (for example, an aware-ness of the way assumptions about gender or race may be structured into the way we speak), which in turn have produced a more careful public use of language. Although this has often been dismissed as mere "political correctness," it has also brought about profound changes in the ways in which people think of, and speak to and about, one another.

Despite the evident belief of many that masculinity and femininity are unchanging and inevitable properties of male and female bodies, respectively, these attributes are in fact culturally specific and historically conditioned. If this were not so, men and women could be expected to behave identically every-where, in all cultures and at all times; but this is not the case, as much historical, anthropological, and sociological research indicates. Take, for example, the case of the Wodaabe people of West Africa, especially in Niger. Once a year, at the end of the rainy season in September, this nomadic people, split into various clans and families, gathers at an appointed site which has been kept secret until this point, in order that the young men participate in the week-long Gerewol (or Jeerewol), to dance and impress the marriageable women. The men paint their faces and decorate their bodies to accentuate their best features, paying particular attention to enhancing the whiteness of the eyes and teeth through the use of dark pigments; and it is the women who judge this male beauty pageant (see, for exam-ple, "Wodaabe" online video). Such a practice appears to invert the roles and relationships between men and women as we understand them in the West. Yet, within Wodaabe culture, the capacity of a young man to attract the attention of an eligible partner through his physical beauty and his ability to dance both is a sign of his masculinity and, at the same time, in part *constitutes* that masculinity. (For an anthropological account of the Wodaabe and the Gerewol, see Bovin, 2001: 37–54 and 58–61; for travellers' accounts, see Jones, 1998; Middleton, 2004.)

Activity 1.2

- The Wodaabe Gerewol is a ceremony designed to enable men to find wives, and women to find husbands; but it is the women who choose, on the basis of the men's physique, body decoration and looks. Whiteness of eyes and teeth constitute key elements in the men's attributes. Imagine in our own culture a similar beauty contest held in which women judge men:

  - In what, do you imagine, the characteristics of male attractiveness and beauty consist?
  - To what degree are these determined by current representations of ideal masculine beauty, and to what degree by other concerns, such as evident physical and mental health, earning capacity, temperament, etc.?

- Who determines the standards of male beauty in our culture, women or men?
- Who determines the standards of female beauty in our culture, women or men?
- These standards are obviously disseminated through the culture through such factors and media as advertising, film and television; can you think of any other ways they are circulated and reinforced (for instance, through parental or peer instruction)?

Modern Western notions of gender may be traced back only as far as the late seventeenth and early eighteenth centuries, the period known as the Enlightenment, and to the Industrial Revolution, to which the Enlightenment contributed. The shift from an agrarian economy to an industrial one had important consequences for people in society. Whereas in an earlier social and economic structure, work was centered in the home, whether in cottage industries such as weaving of cloth or in agricultural occupations, with the building of factories and the development of towns and cities around them, together with the emergence of mining centers, a new structure of work appeared that had an impact on family structures and on gender. It became normal for men to leave their homes to find and maintain employment, whereas women remained at home, keeping house and tending children. The public sphere thus came to be identified more strongly with men; the private, with women.

Although of course many members of a culture will refuse and resist changes in its structuring of gender, such transformations are inevitable. Cultures alter as their historical conditions alter. The so-called "crisis in masculinity" of the closing decade of the twentieth century and the opening decade of the twenty-first may thus be understood as a reaction to shifts occurring structurally in the culture, shifts that affect the way people understand and respond to notions of sex, sexuality, and gender. Moreover, given that historically men have wielded the most power in the culture, it is to be expected that it has also been men who have been most vocal about the perceived crisis in masculinity, because it is they who have the most to lose.

One way of understanding the notion of crisis is as a reaction of anxiety or even panic to cultural change. This usually alarming and undesired emotional response on the part of individuals is then projected outward as a generalized social response that redefines change as catastrophe. The "crisis" then ceases to be simply a reaction to perceived change. Instead, it is understood as a real threat. An important question we might ask, therefore, in relation to the perceived crisis in masculinity toward the end of the twentieth century is the following: is this the first time that such a crisis has occurred, or at any rate has been perceived? Certainly, much of the rhetoric around the notion of a crisis in masculinity implies that this has been a unique moment, historically speaking; yet some investigation into the history of masculinity suggests that this may not be the case. For example, during the late sixteenth and early seventeenth centuries in England a debate arose regarding the feminization of men and the masculinization of women in the upper middle class and nobility, signaled particularly in the fashions worn by each, and by the trend among women toward wearing spurs and carrying ornamental daggers. In 1620 a pamphlet, *Hic Mulier: or the Man Woman*, accused women of losing their femininity. Shortly after came a response, *Haec Vir* ("the womanish man"), justifying and explaining women's behavior by arguing that men had lost their masculinity, so that women had *had* to become masculine in place of the men (see, for example, Jardine, 1983: 154–58).

The causes of this acrimonious debate are numerous, including the longevity of Queen Elizabeth I's reign and the ambiguous sexuality of her successor, James I; and they need not detain us. Another, more recent example of a crisis in masculinity, as the historian Christopher E. Forth points out in his *Masculinity in the Modern West: gender, civilization and the body*, is the concern that arose toward the end of the nineteenth century about the "softening" and feminizing effects on men and their bodies of what was vaguely called "civilization." Whereas the Renaissance and the Enlightenment viewed the development of European societies as progressive, so that the export of European culture at the expense of indigenous ones to the Americas and, later, to Africa, Asia, and the Pacific was considered to enhance and improve the lot of non-European peoples in those regions, by the end of the nineteenth century "civilization" was thought to be exerting a negative effect on men and their bodies. There was, consequently, a fear that men would "degenerate," an idea linked to the new theories of evolution. That is, there was a concern that men would start to "de-evolve," returning to earlier evolutionary stages. Forth observes that there was "the feeling that the path toward remasculinization led away from the comforts and conveniences of the city toward more dangerous locales where death lurked at every step." He comments further that "this belief in the hygienic and therapeutic value of pain, violence and hardship has functioned in the West as a method of preserving men from the conditions of a civilized existence that, if left unchecked, threatened to render them soft, cowardly and effeminate" (Forth, 2008: 141). There were, in consequence, various calls to "toughen up" both boys and men, and various programs, including exercise regimens, to achieve this goal. The point to grasp in these examples is that crises in masculinity are perceived from time to time, and for various reasons.

The popular media persistently return to the issue of a contemporary crisis in masculinity, in different guises. These include its framing in terms of questions like "What is it that women want of men?" or "What is happening to men?" The emergence in the 1990s of the figure dubbed the "metrosexual" likewise occupied the media spotlight for a while, and still surfaces occasionally. The metrosexual (the coining of the term is credited to Mark Simpson, who used it to describe the British star soccer player David Beckham; see the various pieces collected on Simpson's webpage, www.marksimpson.com) is a male, usually relatively young (to his mid-30s), with sufficient disposable income to spend on grooming and dressing. A frequenter of the gym in order to keep his body in shape, the metrosexual is unafraid to use "product" on his face, hair, and body, or to visit a salon in order to undergo rubs, scrubs, and other treatments, including applications to depilate his body in order to remove unwanted body hair. For many, the metrosexual represents a feminized man, which in turn implies homosexuality, although metrosexuals themselves make it very clear that they are in fact heterosexual (with which the term "metrosexual" self-consciously rhymes). The metrosexual, then, embodies for many in the culture, especially men, an uneasiness around issues of gender, and particularly of masculinity.

The media were also responsible for summoning up a panic among the public around the issue of boys' performance in school. The anxieties evoked ranged from concern about boys' academic performance, in relation both to girls' improved academic performance and to the scholarly achievement of boys, historically considered, to boys' behavior both within and outside the classroom. Arguments ranged from the hypothesis that coeducational classrooms unfairly matched boys against *both* other boys *and* girls, to theories that boys require different kinds of pedagogy and pedagogical attention, whether because they are socialized differently from girls, or because their brains are wired differently (see, for example, "Boy-girl learning differences," 2001; Hall, 2003; Leo, 1999; Muggeridge, 2003; O'Beirne, 1998). However, as Michèle Cohen notes, concern about boys' education has a history that reaches back farther than the late twentieth century. For example, she cites the philosopher John Locke's considerations about the schooling of young men in his 1693 educational treatise *Some Thoughts Concerning Education* (Cohen, 1998: 21–23). Debbie Epstein et al. observe that

> the discourses in which debates about the schooling of boys have been framed are both narrow through the ways in which the terms "achievement" and "education" have been understood, and masculinist in style; that they lack a historical perspective; that it is unhelpful to set up a binary opposition between the schooling of girls and that of boys, according to which, if one group wins, the other loses; and that questions around equity and differences among boys and among girls as well as between boys and girls are key to understanding what is happening in schools.
>
> (Epstein et al., 1998: 4)

They discern three dominant strands in "the public debates about boys and achievement": "the 'poor boys' discourse; the 'failing schools' discourse; and the 'boys will be boys' discourse" (Epstein et al., 1998: 6). The "boys in school" problem thus becomes defined doubly as both *produced* by the crisis in masculinity and *contributing* to it.

Underlying this debate, from the perspective of those expressing concern for boys' scholastic performance, is what we might call a hydraulic model of such performance, or, in the words of Epstein et al., "if one group wins, the other loses." Thus, in addition to competing with other students simply on the basis of educational performance, the individual student has been made also the representative of her or his gender group in that competition. This is not, of course, the only model of understanding the issue that could be invoked. Although no doubt some women might adopt a possibly vengeful "It's our turn now – let's 'get' the boys" attitude, for most it is clearly a question simply of equity. This is particularly so in the light of the fact that "in the British context, the 11-plus examinations, by which children used to be selected for secondary schooling, were deliberately skewed so that girls had to achieve better results than boys in order to gain entry to selective grammar schools. To do otherwise would have meant that grammar schools would have been overwhelmingly populated by girls" (Epstein et al., 1998: 5). Such action suggests that more is at stake than simply a neutral assessment of children's scholastic ability.

In 1991 an extremely popular work, *Iron John: a book about men*, asserted that contemporary males suffer because they have been deprived of what the author calls "the deep masculine." Robert Bly, the author of this best seller, is a poet and the founder/leader of what has come to be known as the mythopoetic men's movement, characterized by their "wild man in the woods" camps, which received a good deal of media attention by the late 1980s. Bly infers the quality or attribute of the deep masculine from a range of stories, folk tales, myths, and an eclectic selection of anthropological information. He mines these in order to postulate that Western culture has lost continuity with traditional forms of masculinity, including the rites of passage by which a boy is inducted by adult males into manhood, together with all that this implies in terms of duties and responsibilities. The mythopoetic men's movement was founded in order to reclaim and restore that continuity, together with the deep masculine. The movement has spread worldwide, especially among English-speaking nations, with Bly finding many disciples outside the United States in countries like Australia and the United Kingdom.

In his preface Bly states, "I want to make clear that this book does not seek to turn men against women, nor to return men to the domineering mode that has led to repression of women and their values for centuries. The thought in this book does not constitute a challenge to the women's movement" (Bly, 1991: x). However, much of his argument in the book revolves around the responsibility of women, and particularly liberated, feminist women, for the sapping of this "deep masculine" in their menfolk. For example, only a few pages after the above statement Bly has the following to say:

> As men began to examine women's history and women's sensibility, some men began to notice what was called their *feminine* side and pay attention to it. This process continues to this day, and I would say that most contemporary men are involved in it in some way.
>
> There's something wonderful about this development – I mean the practice of men welcoming their own "feminine" consciousness and nurturing it – this is important – and yet I have the sense that there is something wrong. The male in the past twenty years has become more thoughtful, more gentle. But by this process he has not become more free. He's a nice boy who pleases not only his mother but also the young woman he is living with.
>
> In the seventies [that is, the period during which feminism consolidated gains made during the Sixties and developed further political power] I began to see all over the country a phenomenon that we might call the "soft male." Sometimes even today when I look out at an audience, perhaps half the young males are what I'd call soft. They're lovely, valuable people – I like them – they're not interested in harming the earth or starting wars. There's a gentle attitude toward life in their whole being and style of living.
>
> But many of these men are not happy. You quickly notice the lack of energy in them. They are life-preserving but not exactly life-giving. Ironically, you often see these men with strong women who positively radiate energy.
>
> (Bly, 1991: 2–3)

Although Bly may not say so explicitly, there is certainly the implication that somehow these young men have become "soft" under and because of the influence (for which, read "power") of women. Such men have apparently succumbed to the feminine discovered within themselves; they seek to please their mothers and their partners, and their "energy" has been eclipsed, if not indeed drawn off, by that of the women with whom they associate. That is, whereas on the one hand

Bly disavows antiwoman and antifeminist sentiments, on the other these are implicitly inscribed into the text he is writing.

Bly also remarks in his preface that

> Most of the language in this book speaks to heterosexual men but does not exclude homosexual men. It wasn't until the eighteenth century that people ever used the term homosexual; before that time gay men were understood simply as a part of the large community of men. The mythology as I see it does not make a big distinction between homosexual and heterosexual men.
>
> (Bly, 1991: x)

We may discern here the same ambiguity as is evidenced in the book towards women and their influence over men: whereas on the one hand Bly gestures towards the inclusion of gay men under the rubric of "men," on the other he divides heterosexual from homosexual men. In the first place, this is both the first and the last mention of homosexual men in the book, which in turn suggests that a homosexual orientation is less important than the fact of being sexed male, something that many gay men would no doubt contest. Indeed, Bly's gesture of inclusivity in fact ignores and erases the experience of homosexual men, historically speaking.

In the second place, his historical "perspective" is inaccurate in at least two ways. To begin with, the term "homosexual" was not coined until 1869, that is, the mid-*nineteenth* century (Dynes and Johansson, 1990: 555). This is an error of simple fact. The other inaccuracy is to be found in the statement "before that time gay men were understood simply as a part of the large community of men." As a number of historians have been at pains to point out, the presence of homosexual men in the social community has elicited, at best, an ambivalent response, and, at worst, forms of antagonism and violence against such men that would be readily recognized today as homophobia (see, for example, Boswell, 1980; Bray, 1982). Moreover, the social toleration of homosexuality in men was often conditional on factors such as class, power, and wealth, as well as religious feeling. Male–male sexuality might be willfully overlooked in the great and powerful in ways that did not operate to the advantage of the less powerful. One historical example is provided by the younger brother of King Louis XIV, Philippe de France, Duc d'Orléans (1640–1701), who, although married, scandalized the French court with his homosexual liaisons, but who was not persecuted on account of those liaisons, and who served as courtier and soldier (*Encyclopædia Britannica*, 2010). In other words, gay men were *not* perceived simply as "part of the large community of men," although certain accommodations could be reached in specific cases. The same is true of particular professions or occupations: "Bohemian" types, such as actors or artists, were often allowed some latitude because of the claim to artistic temperament.

Such historical inaccuracy results from the desire to identify a stable, permanent notion of the masculine. It can be seen also in the work of the Australian

Steve Biddulph, a family counselor and a disciple of Bly who has published a number of extremely popular books. In his 1994 best seller *Manhood: an action plan for changing men's lives* (which went into a second edition only a year after its first appearance), Biddulph remarks:

> The Industrial Revolution is usually seen in terms of what we gained – and we gained a good deal (or you would have just spent the day hoeing turnips in the rain!). But we have yet to take stock of what we lost. For the first time in half a million years of human existence, men stopped working alongside women and children in their villages and farms and went to work apart, in factories, and mines. And in a break with eternal tradition, boys began being raised by women. For aeons of time before this, boys grew up with the sweetness of male teaching from several older men who took pride and placed great store in their maturation. Unless the tribe or village raised good men, everyone's life was endangered.
>
> (Biddulph, 1995: 30)

Here Biddulph lays the responsibility for the implied demasculinization, or at any rate the faulty masculinization, of boys at the feet of women, although without attributing the Industrial Revolution itself to anyone, although it was of course men who brought it about. Moreover, there is a globalization of a culturally specific notion of masculinity in the final sentence: the introduction of "the tribe or village" suggests that Biddulph is speaking of a universalizing (that is, a generic) idea of the masculine, rather than situating "masculinity" as a culturally and historically specific quality.

Furthermore, the Industrial Revolution is identified as a critical moment in vast temporal spans ("half a million years," "eternal tradition," "aeons of time"), yet nowhere is there a sense that cultures change through time, and that notions of gender and gender-appropriate behavior (or how people learned these) might likewise change. Somehow, therefore, masculinity was passed on unaltered from father to son, until the critical moment of the Industrial Revolution, at which point everything shifted radically. Although many historians of various stripes agree on the importance of the Industrial Revolution and its lasting impact on the cultures that succeeded that period, no historian would advance so nostalgic and, above all, so historically naïve a depiction of the structuring and dynamics of gender at the time.

Biddulph's portrait of the period is also class-blind. What of the masculinity (or, better, masculinities) of the nobility and the middle class? These are simply swept into invisibility in Biddulph's creation of an idealized working-class male who somehow imbibed his masculinity at his father's knee, and who would pass it on to his own son. The details remain vague about what that masculinity might have been like, except that it was warm and comforting, and different from the warmth and comfort offered by the mother to her son.

In addition, Biddulph seems to imagine that the family has been structured identically in all cultures and at all times, although his last-minute inclusion of "tribe" and "village" suggests a belated realization that this might not indeed have been the case. Nevertheless, his idealized vision of an imaginary father–son pair, happily working side by side in the fields or at the cottage loom, fails to take account of other historical possibilities, for example, those fathers of the nobility who sent their young sons to be squires in royal households, or whose children were seized as royal wards in order to forge or prevent political alliances. Or, indeed, those youthful middle-class sons dispatched to other households both foreign and domestic to learn a commercial trade and to make important social and business connections. Nor does Biddulph consider the possibility expressed by many historians of the family that for the working class (itself an anachronistic term if referring to pre-Industrial Revolution culture), "family" was not a simple and heart-warming notion of hearth and home. It was a way of surviving in a feudal or semifeudal social structure, and of ensuring, via multiple offspring, one's own survival, as an aging and increasingly incapacitated dependent, in a culture that lacked any conception of public welfare.

Identifying such historical vagueness in such accounts is not mere scholarly pedantry. Rather, that inaccuracy is central to the project of the work of such writers as Bly and Biddulph. By creating a picture of the past that lacks nuance, they are able to mythicize that past and so render it universal, applicable to all cultures in all places and at all times. Simultaneously, they are able to invoke a moment when things changed, and not necessarily for the better. Historical accuracy and detail would not only dull the edge of this strategy, whose principal objective is to identify women as the cause of men's problems; they would introduce elements and raise questions that might render that aim ineffective.

Bly's ambivalent handling both of women and homosexual men suggests that he feels profoundly uneasy at having to address these two groups in a postliberationist context, but at the same time is compelled to do so in order to appear politically balanced and objective. Clearly gay men are the more problematic group, because they are dismissed in the preface as being simply included under the umbrella of "men," even although the history of homosexual men and homophobia makes it clear that they have *not* been regarded by the dominant heterosexual male community as belonging to and participating in the "real" or "complete" masculine. Women pose a different problem. By effectively ignoring and excluding gay men and their experience, Bly foregrounds heterosexual masculinity, which necessarily means that he must engage with women as a factor in the shaping of masculinity. The thrust of his book, indeed, is an attempt to find a way of defining and constructing the masculine independently of women.

Another example of a popular response to the felt crisis in masculinity may be found in the establishment in 1990 of the Promise Keepers, a conservative Christian organization intended to transform men into more devout members of society. This objective, on the face of it, would appear to be laudable and apolitical. Nevertheless, there *are* political underpinnings to their ideology, which is suggested by the multiplicity of meanings and levels of importance attributed to this organization:

> What to make of the Promise Keepers? In the current world of electronic 24-hour news media with around-the-clock deadlines and instant analysis, the early answers have been concise, often unitary, and capable of being captured in a sound bite. Promise Keepers are a reactionary reassertion of patriarchal authority; they are a pawn of Christian Right political operatives; they are another sign of our current evangelical religious revival; they are part of a new phenomenon – men coming to terms with their own vulnerabilities and responsibilities. Promise Keepers is a new phenomenon; it is another example of that old-time religion; it is political; it is religious.
>
> (Williams, 2001: 1)

Rhys H. Williams suggests that

> PK [Promise Keepers] becomes a kind of Rorschach test, allowing observers to read on to it what they expect to find in modern society and its religion. And, reactions to PK also reflect the ambivalences, tensions, even contradictions that Americans bring to the intersection of religion and politics.
>
> Thus, an "undercover" *MS.* magazine investigation finds PK to be what I might paraphrase as "patriarchy with a human face." Men are being told to be nice masters, but masters just the same. Messner's (1997) study of the politics of masculinity puts PK in the center of antifeminist backlash. Those convinced that the nation is absorbed by a "culture war" often view PK and its adherents as shock troops for what is still called the "Christian Right" and therefore cannot believe that PK is not political before all else. And religion writers from such papers as the *Charlotte News-Observer* and the *Dallas Morning-News* find sincere, religiously motivated "average Joes" trying to figure out how to be better husbands, fathers, and Christians; in addition, they duly note that many of the participants' wives report being thrilled that their husbands are getting involved with this type of religious group.
>
> (Williams, 2001: 1–2)

This ambiguity about what the Promise Keepers means as an organization does not, in itself, signify therefore that it has no political ideology or agenda. As Williams and others in *Promise Keepers and the New Masculinity: private lives and public morality* suggest, it is more likely, rather, that the loose structure and belief system of Promise Keepers allow for variations in ideology and agenda, although the latter is bounded by particular precepts and goals.

Bryan W. Brickner, in his mostly carefully neutral study of the Promise Keepers, characterizes its relation to politics thus:

> When Bill McCartney asks men to make a personal commitment to Jesus Christ and to accept him as their Savior, it does not concern politics.

When Dr. Tony Evans tells men not to *ask* for the leadership of their family back, but to *take it back*, it is not about politics. When Charles Colson warns men that American culture is collapsing and that "it is of life-and-death importance to this nation," it is not about politics. When Pastor Raleigh Washington tells men "to establish committed relationships across racial lines," it is not about politics.

According to the Promise Keepers, all of these issues may have been politicized, but they are not political. This is how Promise Keepers defend their movement as being nonpolitical. Politics is about issues that are open to discussion; issues that are debatable. Politics is *not* about the immutable. More accurately, politics should not debate that which is timeless: God's word.

(Brickner, 1999: 2–3; original emphasis)

The referring of such issues to the word of God as irrefutable and beyond question is a tactic that immediately forecloses any debate about their nature and merit, political or otherwise. "The leadership of their family" *implies* a certain politics, as does Dr Evans's urging of his membership to seize that leadership. That this is the case is highlighted by Brickner's account a little later of the discussion in a group of members belonging to the Promise Keepers:

Once, Joseph [a member of a Promise Keepers group] said that women have taken over the leadership of the family; he implied that women were to blame for the disintegration of traditional family values. Almost in unison, the group challenged him, upholding the view usually stated by Promise Keepers that women have only stepped into the leadership role because men have abdicated it [sic]. Men have failed, the others emphasized, women have only taken on more responsibility because of men's failures.

(Brickner, 1999: 26)

This is not, then, an argument simply about an abstract or hypothetical notion of leadership, but also about power, about who controls the family – which means that it *is* about politics. Implicit in this is the idea that "American culture is collapsing" not simply because it is more secular and materialist than the Promise Keepers would have, but also because men's ascendancy has been challenged and diminished.

A similar juggling with meaning is to be found in the suggestion offered by the Ambassador Training Level One manual with regard to answering questions about the Promise Keepers' attitude toward homosexuality:

2. Example 2: "Isn't Promise Keepers really anti-homosexual?" You might answer, "Our statement of faith clearly states that we believe the Bible is the Word of God, so in areas where the Bible clearly speaks to an issue, we must agree with it. Our purpose statement says clearly that we are committed to uniting men; therefore men who are struggling with homosexuality are welcome at our gatherings."

(Brickner, 1999: 5)

Brickner summarizes this: "Promise Keepers is not antihomosexual; they are pro-Bible. Because the Bible is clear (according to Promise Keepers) about the sin of homosexuality, it is not a political issue. Men who are 'struggling with homosexuality' and 'committed to uniting with men' are welcome at Promise Keepers gatherings in the same way as are other sinners" (Brickner, 1999: 5). However, the history, from early modern Europe onwards, of homosexual men and women shows that they have *not* been treated in the manner of "other sinners," who (setting aside murderers and the like) in general were not legally outlawed as a matter of course, persecuted both within and outside the law, and made to suffer physical violence and death at the hands of law-enforcement officers and of self-appointed vigilantes because they were petty thieves, adulterers, or seducers. The Promise Keepers "welcome" only those gay men "who are struggling with homosexuality," that is, those who cannot accept their own sexual orientation, often *because of* the history of the persecution and denigration of nonheterosexual people. Thus, the net *effect* remains the same as for an avowedly antihomosexual group.

What emerges from Brickner's account is that the Promise Keepers, whatever their professed religious faith and social ideology, remain a men's organization charged with the task of reclaiming and retaining male power and privilege. Unsurprisingly, therefore, that organization has been criticized by, among others, feminist groups for the way in which it attempts to impose on women a traditional, subordinate role. We may infer from this that the women's movements of the 1960s are held responsible by the Promise Keepers for causing a fundamental imbalance in gender relations, the proper nature of which is comprehended as conservative, traditional, and patriarchal.

However, in the final chapter of his book, Brickner departs from his objectivity in the rest of his account. He remarks, having commented on the openness of the men he interviewed and the meetings at which he participated:

> I also found them to be pathetic, weak, tormented, and pained. How is that possible you might ask? We differ on metaphysical principles, I suppose. I would often see a Promise Keeper as a bewildered other – a victim – a slave – a weak man in need of comfort and direction, in need of a concierge. The interesting point is that they embrace these characterizations. They recognize they are victims of Adam's sin, slaves to this world, and weak men in need of the loving grace of Jesus. These "negative" characterizations are espoused as signs of strength, as God's will.

As an example of something good to say about the group, Brickner paints an image of a father and son at breakfast; but, tellingly, as an example of something bad about Promise Keepers, he remarks on their acceptance of

> the Bible as literal truth, [and] the reliance/acceptance of a moral order based on original sin, which happens to be caused by a woman, or the convenience of a masculine holy trinity.

> (Brickner, 1999: 124)

Ironically, then, Brickner finds the membership of the Promise Keepers not masculine *enough*, despite its being all-male and focused on issues that, at some level, connect with masculine power and control. This, in turn, suggests that there is another model of masculinity against which the author measures the Promise Keepers. However, we should be wary of assuming that it is therefore necessarily a more radical or liberal model.

Equally, it would be a mistake to assume that neither the mythopoetic men's movement nor the Promise Keepers group has anything of real benefit to offer its respective memberships. Clearly, many men feel that they *have* benefited from belonging to one or the other of these groups. Our purpose in considering their beliefs and attitudes critically has been, rather, to show, first, that they are founded in anxiety about men's place in the contemporary world and, second, that that anxiety proceeds from the sense that men have lost power to women.

Many theorists of gender, and of masculinity in particular, are more cautious than Dave Hill about the future for men, although for reasons that are not necessarily grounded in a historically or culturally localized panic about the crisis in masculinity. For example, Roger Horrocks, a psychotherapist, opens his tellingly titled *Masculinity in Crisis* with the following:

> This book argues that masculinity in Western society is in deep crisis. The masculine gender has all kinds of benefits, but it also acts as a mask, a disguise, and what in psychotherapy is called a "false self." But who are we behind the false self?
>
> But more than this, I shall suggest that masculinity *is a crisis* for men today – that the masculine gender is a precarious and dangerous achievement and is highly damaging to men.
>
> (Horrocks, 1994: 1; original emphasis)

For Horrocks, then, *crisis is already structured into the masculine.* However, his notion of "crisis" is perhaps better described as a radical and fundamental instability within the masculine, and may be thought of as an issue for the men of yesterday as well as today.

Like Horrocks, Anthony Clare, a doctor and psychiatrist, sees the crisis in masculinity as, in a sense, of men's own making. *On Men: masculinity in crisis* considers various aspects of what it is to be a man, from the biological, including an understanding of genetics, to the social. Clare points out a number of ironies, such as that men's scientific ambition to intervene in and engineer the reproductive process, resulting in such technologies as *in vitro* fertilization (IVF), has resulted in the increasing irrelevance of men, to women, to children, and to society as a whole (Clare, 2000: 101–28). He observes that "At the heart of the crisis in masculinity is a problem with the reconciliation of the private and public, the intimate and the impersonal, the emotional and the rational" (Clare, 2000: 212). Unlike Hill's, Clare's prognosis is pessimistic:

> Unless men wake up to what is happening all around them they will find themselves in even greater trouble. The omens are not good. Richard Scase is

but one of a number of social analysts who believes that current trends spell disaster for men. In his recently published book, *Britain Towards 2010*, Scase predicts that there will be more single persons, fewer children, persistently high rates of divorce and a "churning" of partners (repeated changing rather than any consistent commitment). Most of the single people will be male – one in three men will be living alone by 2010. Some one and a half million men will be permanently excluded from the workforce, either because of early retirement or because they just will not have the education and skills necessary for employment. And given the growing demand for skilled people able to work creatively and collaboratively rather than in a hierarchical, competitive and status-obsessed fashion, men may find themselves redundant in the job recruitment market.

(Clare, 2000: 220–21)

In *Male Trouble: masculinity and the performance of crisis*, a study of both film and drama in relation to the idea of "male trouble," Fintan Walsh observes that "recent studies have revealed how throughout the twentieth century, national crises and trauma (translated as emasculating) have been quickly followed by periods of remasculinization." He goes on to summarize some of these:

George Mosse, for example, identifies the rise of Fascism in 1920s Germany as the assertion of a fanatical, militaristic masculinity in response to national humiliation at the Treaty of Versailles following the First World War. Leon Hunt understands the "uncertain maleness" of 1970s Britain as an effective working through the disintegration of the Fordist heavy industries, deteriorating labour relations, the impact of First Wave Feminism, and the rise of the gay movement. Susan Jeffords identifies a rise in macho-masculinity in the United States throughout the 1980s, as exemplified in the figure of Rocky. Jeffords equates this development in the form of masculinization in response to 1960s hippy culture, and the allegedly weak leadership of President Jimmy Carter.

Walsh remarks: "What seems important to note here is that there is nothing new about troubled masculinity" (Walsh, 2010: 9).

Other scholars and writers take a longer historical perspective on the question of whether masculinity is indeed in crisis, and if so, what the causes might be. For example, in *The End of Masculinity*, John MacInnes, a sociologist, develops the thesis that the European Enlightenment, in substituting the notion of a social "contract" for the divine right of kings, led to a notion of gender difference that contained within it the cause of its own confusion. He observes,

It has become a cliché to argue that masculinity is in crisis. But although men's privilege is under unprecedented material and ideological challenge, the briefest historical survey will show that masculinity has always been in one crisis or another. ... This is because the whole idea that men's natures can be understood in terms of their "masculinity" arose out of a "crisis" for all men: the fundamental incompatibility between the core principle of modernity that all human beings are essentially equal (regardless of their sex) and the core tenet of patriarchy that men are naturally superior to women and thus destined to rule over them.

(MacInnes, 1998: 11)

For MacInnes, the logic of a gender system which sought simultaneously to extend equal rights to both sexes but also to preserve the dominance of the male sex necessarily contained within itself, as Christopher Forth puts it, "the seeds of its own undoing" (Forth, 2008: 237); and it was that collapse that was being witnessed toward the end of the twentieth century.

Forth lengthens the view still further, seeing historical continuities rather than ruptures. He explores the competing and often contradictory impulses and consequent tensions that have constructed masculinity in the Anglo-European world since the sixteenth century and that have in effect constituted a perpetual state of crisis for men in that world. He observes that,

Judging from the widespread academic and media claims today about a "crisis of masculinity" in the Western world, one might guess that inadequacy and defensiveness are common feelings among many men, though the pervasiveness of and rationale for this anxiety are the subject of considerable disagreement. Most scholars concur that the very term "crisis" is simply inadequate. If there is no stable or non-critical period to be found prior to the disturbance in question (and historians have not found one), then the very idea of a crisis makes little sense.

(Forth, 2008: 3)

Forth adds:

Put differently, the recurrence of "crisis" as a means of describing masculinity at various historical moments is to some extent made possible by the paradoxes that lurk at the heart of modernity's relationship with masculinity and the male body. After all, modernity is continually troubled by what Ulrich Beck describes as "counter-modernity," a discourse that "absorbs, demonizes and dismisses the questions raised and repeated by modernity" by positing "constructed certitudes" in the face of the liquefying tendencies of modernization. Arising with and in reaction to modernity, counter-modern impulses seek to renaturalize many of the things that modernity sends into motion, often by imagining a new modernity purged of its unhealthy or "feminizing" components. ... Insistence upon an essential, embodied and recuperable masculinity lurking beneath the veneer of civilization is one of the most durable examples of a counter-modernity that asserts itself within and against modernity.

(Forth, 2008: 5)

Forth regards the various "crises" through which masculinity has historically made passage as precipitated by a fundamental conflict between and mutual contradiction of understandings of the male body and the workings of civilization. He ascribes to the latter what he calls the "*double logic of modern civilization*": "a process that promotes and supports the interests of males while threatening to undermine those interests by eroding the corporeal foundations of male privilege. Civilization, in short, both supports and dismantles the 'natural' rationale for male dominance" (Forth, 2008: 5; original emphasis). Echoing Horrocks's observation that "masculinity *is* a crisis," Forth remarks that, "Founded upon the central paradoxes of modernity, a 'crisis of masculinity' is a recurring, even structural feature of life in our world" (Forth, 2008: 15). He concludes his study by observing:

> Although sometimes perceived as being an extension and facilitator of "patriarchal" gender relationships, modernity continues to function as a double-edged sword that, among its many paradoxical effects, extends and supports male dominance while creating the conditions that subvert the "natural" basis for that dominance. The same civilization that bolsters male dominance also contains the seeds of its own undoing, which is one reason why this concept has elicited such diverse reactions throughout the modern era. Yet history is not necessity, and the negative patterns of the past might be undone if people are prepared [to] break with modes of thought and behavior that have outlived their usefulness. ... By probing the durable and entrenched aspects of this tension between masculinity and modernity, this book illustrates both the possibility and the difficulty of moving beyond the constraints of history.
>
> (Forth, 2008: 237)

A literary scholar, Sally Robinson, in *Marked Men: white masculinity in crisis*, identifies the crisis as emanating, in America, from the liberationist movements of the 1960s, and as affecting chiefly white men who constitute (or who are represented, or who represent themselves, as constituting) the "mainstream." However, she notes that

> The "mainstream" is, in fact, a far more volatile space than is usually acknowledged in literary or cultural criticism, as most critics assume that the action is found on either end of a high-low cultural, and class, divide. The middle, as I see it, is an essentially *defensive* cultural and political formation, one characterized by suspicion, even paranoia, about the passing of a now delegitimized cultural order.
>
> (Robinson, 2000; original emphasis)

That is, the "mainstream," which continues to be invoked as though it were an identifiable and stable population majority, is in fact a site of uncertainty and of contestation. Robinson remarks:

> Announcements of crisis, both direct and indirect, are *performative*, in the sense that naming a situation a crisis puts into place discursive conventions

and tropes that condition the meanings that event will have. A crisis is "real" when its rhetorical strategies can be discerned and its effects charted; the reality of a particular crisis depends less on hard evidence of actual social trauma or do-or-die decision-making than on the power of language, of metaphors and images, to convincingly represent a sense of trauma and turning point. … The language of crisis imposes a certain narrative logic on an event or, more nebulously, a social trend or cultural formation. And while we might assume that logic to be governed by a teleological drive toward resolution and closure, the rhetoric of crisis actually functions to defer that closure. The rhetorical power of "crisis" depends on a sense of prolonged tension; the announcements of crisis are inseparable from the crisis itself, as the rhetoric of crisis performs the cultural work of centering attention on dominant masculinity. The question of whether dominant masculinity is "really" in crisis is, in my view, moot: even if we could determine what an actual, real, historically verifiable crisis would look like, the undeniable fact remains that in the post-liberationist era, dominant masculinity consistently represents itself as in crisis.

(Robinson, 2000: 10–11; original emphasis)

Robinson's point here is that a language of crisis in fact *produces* the perception of crisis. The two things (language and perception) are inextricably linked. For her, post-1960s masculinity has always been, that is, has always represented itself as, in crisis.

In what, then, does this crisis for men consist? Robinson's argument is that, until the liberationist movements of the 1960s, white men (and particularly white middle-class men) enjoyed a measure of power that was linked to their being "unmarked." That is, because "gender" appeared to refer to and mean "women," and "race," "black" and other people of color, to be male and white constituted not only a norm but also a "natural" kind of identity. The effect of this was to erase white masculinity from the social picture, so that white masculine power appeared to recede into the background, if not, indeed, to vanish entirely. One effect of the liberationist movements around gender and race was to make white masculinity visible by insisting on the gendering and "racing" of white men. This in turn raised both questions and criticisms about the power that white men have traditionally exercised in the culture, while at the same time concealing it under a mask of normativity and naturalness. In addition, and importantly, the marking of white men in this way also brought into visibility the white male body, hitherto an assumed cultural norm that was beyond question. Such materialization of the white male body also made it vulnerable, that is, literally capable of being wounded, in terms of what could be said about it in the culture.

Robinson persuasively argues that the reaction of white men has been to lay claim to a form of identity politics, the tactical strategy adopted in the 1960s and afterwards by minority groups or groups treated as minorities, in order both to establish a political position with regard to the politics of the dominant, and to acquire a voice that would be heard in political debate. Because such identity politics commence from the position of belonging to an oppressed and silenced, and hence victimized, social group, white men as a group began to lay claim to an equal (if not, indeed, greater) marginalization and oppression. Images both literal and metaphoric of "wounded" masculinity and of "wounded" white men began to appear in both popular and more highbrow cultural texts, and, as Robinson demonstrates in her readings of various texts, such wounding is linked to the "marking" and rendering visible of white men as both gendered and racialized identities. In this way, the symbolic vulnerability of the white male body made visible and material became the motive for a claim of victimhood.

Robinson's focus on white masculinity does not mean, of course, that men of color may not equally have experienced a sense of crisis around being men. However, the reasons for any such sense are likely to have been different. For example, negative shifts in the national economy are likely to affect most immediately those (of whatever ethnicity) in the lower socioeconomic bracket, making it difficult to hold down jobs, keep families, and so on. Moreover, Caucasian and non-Caucasian masculinities define one another within a complex system of race, gender, and sexuality. Indeed, there would be no point in having a term like "Caucasian" unless there was at least one other, oppositional (but not necessarily contradictory) term to give it some boundary of meaning. That "meaning" is not purely linguistic or categorical: it includes a range of social and cultural values, understandings, and assumptions. Accordingly, therefore, a shift, or "crisis," in the one necessarily entails a complementary shift in the other.

If we return to the examples with which we began this chapter, namely, Palahniuk's novel *Fight Club* and Fincher's film version of it, we might note an important (indeed, critical) discrepancy between the two. The tone of Palahniuk's narrator is ironic, which should alert the reader to the need to evaluate the statements he makes with care. Moreover, we need to bear in mind that Tyler Durden is a projection of the narrator's own mental and emotional state. This, in turn, suggests that we need to judge whether fight club and Project Mayhem represent an intrinsic and foundational masculinity emerging to claim its own presence and status, as the narrative proposes, or are, rather, simply the plausible effects of an unsettled mind. The novel closes with some ambiguity: the narrator is in a mental institution, but is furtively treated by some members of the hospital staff as "Mr Durden," with encouragements as "'Everything is going according to the plan,'" "'We're going to break up civilization so we can make something better out of the world,'" and (perhaps chillingly) "'We look forward to getting you back'" (Palahniuk, 1996: 208). However, the film strips the strong sense of irony out of the narrative by making Tyler a separate, independent character. It also omits the mental-institution ending. As a result, the story of the narrator is presented as something to be taken seriously, a genuine comment on the state of masculinity at the end of the twentieth century. It is presumably this to which young males respond in their emulations of Tyler Durden's fight club.

Crisis (whether real or only perceived) and masculinity, it would appear, have gone hand in hand historically, although the immediate causes for any sense of crisis have often differed. As we have seen, the growing cultural anxiety towards the end of the twentieth century and into the twenty-first about a crisis in masculinity can be connected to other anxieties about the waning of masculine power and the emergence of new or hitherto ignored or suppressed ways of being men. In order to explore these ideas further, we need now to understand the terms and concepts within which debates about gender, and about masculinity in particular, are conducted.

Activity 1.3

- Begin keeping a journal and/or scrapbook of items about the current state of men and masculinity that you encounter in your reading, listening or viewing.
- After you have collected a sufficient number of these, examine them, and see if you can determine:
  - particular "themes" or preoccupations;
  - recurring suggestions and recommendations as to how the "crisis in masculinity" might be solved.
- Reflect critically on this material.
  - While of course the rhetoric will suggest that it is boys and men who are losing their masculinity, to their detriment, in reality whose interests are threatened by the "crisis in masculinity," and to whose real benefit are the solutions suggested?
- In the chapter you have just read, for example, these matters are made almost explicit with regard to the Promise Keepers: for this group, the "crisis in masculinity," presented as a failure of religious faith, is less about how boys and men find their identity in a changing social and cultural world than it is about how males may retain their familial and social power in that world.
  - Can you similarly analyze the material you are collecting?

Suggested further reading

Foster, T.A. (ed.) (2011) *New Men: manliness in early America*, New York and London: New York University Press.

Garcia, G. (2008) *The Decline of Men: how the American male is getting axed, giving up, and flipping off his future*, New York: Harper Perennial.

Kimmel, M. (1996; 3rd edn 2011) *Manhood in America: a cultural history*, New York: Oxford University Press.

——, (2005) *The History of Men: essays on the history of American and British masculinities*, Albany: State University of New York Press.

——, (2009) *Guyland: the perilous world where boys become men*, New York: Harper.

Messner, M.A. (2000) *Politics of Masculinities: men in movements*, Walnut Creek, CA: AltaMira press.

Nelson, D.D. (1998) *National Manhood: capitalist citizenship and the imagined fraternity of white men*, Durham and London: Duke University Press.

Rotundo, E.A. (1993) *American Manhood: transformations in masculinity from the Revolution to the modern era*, New York: Basic Books.

Sax, L. (2007) *Boys Adrift: the five factors driving the growing epidemic of unmotivated boys and underachieving young men*, New York: Basic Books.

Schwalbe, M. (1996) *Unlocking the Iron Cage: the men's movement, gender politics, and American culture*, New York and Oxford: Oxford University Press.

2 Thinking (through) gender

In order to begin to understand masculinity, we need to frame it within a more general understanding of gender, otherwise we are left simply with a shopping list of features, characteristics, and behaviors. Alternatively, we find ourselves looking at a kind of do-it-yourself kit for constructing a predetermined notion of "man," or a self-help book offering us ways to become more recognizably and acceptably masculine. The title of this chapter is intended to suggest several possible simultaneous meanings and strategies.

"*Thinking* gender" suggests something along the lines of "having gender in mind," but also "a notion of gender that is self-conscious and self-reflexive." In addition, "Thinking *through* gender" implies first a careful consideration of both the idea of gender and how gender operates socially and culturally. Second, "thinking through gender" suggests that gender provides a lens or lattice by means of which we both perceive and think about the world, and through which we interact with it. Third, "thinking through gender" invites us to transcend gendered ways of thinking – to think *beyond* gender as familiar, comfortable, and, for the most part, invisible because it is simply a part of the way things just *are*.

Gender, sex, and sexuality

We begin with the term "gender" itself. Although this word occurs fairly regularly in everyday usage (for example, it is to be found frequently in official and semi-official questionnaires), its exact sense and implications are not always well understood. "Sex" and "gender" are often used interchangeably, although, as we shall see, there are key meanings that distinguish each from the other. Furthermore, particular formations of "gender" are thought to flow automatically from "sex." That is, there is an assumption that the body is an irreducible physical, material fact, so that its anatomical configuration (as male or female) necessarily entails the behaviors appropriate to a particular configuration, namely, masculine or feminine behaviors.

We need instead to think of gender not as a freestanding concept, but rather as related in a complex way to two other key concepts: sex and sexuality. One way of thinking of the relationship between sex and gender is to see it as rather like that between raw material and processed product. Thus, in Western cultures it is generally understood that we may be *born either* male *or* female, that is, with differing genital configurations (namely, with a penis or a vagina) and reproductive capacities and functions. However, as we shall shortly see, not all cultures subscribe to a two-sex notion of the human body and reproduction process (often called *dimorphism*: having two forms). Nevertheless, we have to *live as* boys/men *or* girls/women. Put another way, we each must learn the behavior and manners, the gestures and attitudes that the culture deems appropriate to each sex. It is through learning these that we become socialized and *gendered*, moving from the raw fact of our individual anatomical sex (being male or female) to a processed social product (behaving as a man or a woman). The social and cultural expectations of a man and the manner and degree to which he acknowledges and lives up to them we understand as *masculinity*; those applicable to a woman, together with her compliance with them, we think of as *femininity*.

One way of understanding this is to think of the terms "male" and "female" as overdetermined, and indeed overwhelmed, by the concept of gender. That is, although we commonly think of "male" and "female" as the prior biological-anatomical bedrock on which gender ("masculinity" and "femininity") is founded, it is difficult to separate anatomical difference from gender difference. (This is an idea we will return to later in chapter 3, in a discussion of Judith Butler's notion of gender performativity.) The terms "man" or "woman" are thus in a sense ambiguous. They each encode a double meaning: the first signifies anatomical sex difference; the second, the ensemble of social and cultural expectations of each sex (namely, its gender) and the degree to which the individual of a particular sex measures up to and meets those expectations.

However, we should note that there is no *necessary* connection between the morphology of sex (male or female) and the combination of behavior and attitude that we call gender (masculinity or femininity). It is possible for a man to impersonate the feminine, just as a woman may impersonate the masculine. However, the culture ensures through a number of measures that its members believe in and subscribe to such a connection. These include the marginalizing or masking of other possibilities, and the ridiculing, humiliation. or even punishment of those who do not comply with those cultural expectations. Thus, because it is in our own interests, in order to survive and function in the culture, that we understand as seamless the connection between anatomical sex and culturally and socially imposed gender, we make simple equations: female body and genital characteristics = woman = femininity; male body and genital characteristics = man = masculinity. These assumptions (for that is in effect merely what they are) then become *naturalized*. That is, they appear to us to be in the natural order of things, logical, necessary, and the way things have always been, everywhere, for everyone.

So, when we encounter any disruption in these apparently natural chains of equivalences, we may tend to react with horror, revulsion, nausea, anger, contempt, or violence, among other responses. This is the case not only often with women whose behavior is perceived to be "mannish" or with men who seem to be effeminate, but also with individuals whose bodily morphology may not easily fit into the two-sex, two-gender system that has developed in most Western societies. For example, the hermaphrodite, now usually called an *intersex* person, is someone born either with indeterminate sexual characteristics (for instance, a rudimentary penis or vagina) or with ambiguous ones (both a penis and a vagina, although commonly one may be less developed than the other). Such an individual is not easily classified within the existing sex/gender system. Accordingly, then, infants who are identified as hermaphrodite or intersex are often subjected to surgical "correction" or "gender reassignment," their sex often determined by parental choice as well as the reliance on the judgment and experience of the medical team in attendance. This, in turn, often means a compliance with cultural assumptions about what constitutes "boyness" or "girlness," which refers us back, in a loop, to cultural notions of masculinity and femininity.

To take another example, the condition in males known as androgen insensitivity syndrome (AIS) may cause the body to fail either to trip the necessary hormonal signals at puberty or to respond to those signals as the hormones flood the body. Those males with AIS may find that their voices do not break at puberty; one or both of their testes may fail to descend from the body into the scrotal sac; they may not develop facial or body hair; they may develop female-looking breasts; and so on. The condition is usually treated with injections of androgens (male hormones), especially testosterone. The point to grasp here is that *our two-sex, two-gender system does not allow for such individuals,* any more than it accommodates the intersex individual: indeed, *these identities disrupt the system itself.* Defined as anomalies and therefore as "abnormal" or "unnatural," their very anomalousness serves to confirm the authority of the two-sex, two-gender system in place.

To our understanding of that system we must add another component: sexuality. Just as the words "man" or "woman" embrace both the genital and reproductive configuration of individuals as well as the set of behaviors and attitudes expected of either sex, so "sexuality" as a term is ambiguous. It too covers a range of possible meanings. Chief among these are sexual orientation and sexual behavior. The latter in turn includes such factors as the degree of sexual activity in an individual's life, and the sexual practices that an individual finds erotically arousing as well as emotionally and psychologically satisfying.

Of the various possibilities available to men and women in the culture, the overriding assumption about sexual orientation is that it is, or should be, heterosexual, namely, oriented toward the opposite sex. The poet Adrienne Rich has called this "compulsory heterosexuality" (Rich, 1993: 227–54). After all, male and female genitals are formed as anatomically complementary with each other. Moreover, there is both an instinctual and a cultural need to propagate young, in order to ensure the future of the family, the community (or nation), and, beyond both of these, the species. Thus, not only is heterosexuality "natural," in the sense

of being the means, shared by most living things, by which offspring are generated, but it also structures social and cultural relationships between men and
women.

The fact that women are the child-bearers, for example, has meant that
women have traditionally been in addition assigned particular social roles,
which include that of homemaker. However, as the anthropologist Gayle Rubin
notes:

> Although every society has some sort of division of tasks by sex, the
> assignment of any particular task to one sex or the other varies enormously.
> In some groups, agriculture is the work of women, in others, the work of
> men. Women carry the heavy burdens in some societies, men in others. There
> are even examples of female hunters and warriors, and of men performing
> child-care tasks.
>
> (Rubin, 1997: 39)

Thus, from the perspective of the cultural mandating of heterosexuality (Rubin
calls it "obligatory heterosexuality"; see, for instance, Rubin, 1997: 40), nonheterosexual orientations, inclinations, and practices are marked as "unnatural."
Yet, as Rubin observes,

> Hunger is hunger, but what counts as food is culturally determined and
> obtained. ... *Sex is sex, but what counts as sex is equally culturally deter-
> mined and obtained.* Every society also has a sex/gender system – a set of
> arrangements by which the biological raw material of human sex and procre-
> ation is shaped by human, social intervention and satisfied in a conventional
> manner, no matter how bizarre some of the conventions may be.
>
> (Rubin, 1997: 32; emphasis added)

She earlier defines "sex/gender system" as "the set of arrangements by which
human society transforms biological sexuality into products of human activity
and in which these transformed sexual needs are satisfied" (Rubin, 1997: 28). The
relationship, therefore, between sex and gender is a complicated and nuanced
one, and, moreover, varies from culture to culture, according to the social structure and social needs of each.

We should, therefore, be cautious about the idea of "normality." This term
refers to the attitudes, practices, inclinations, and so on observed as shared by
most members of the culture; a norm is simply a standard. However, in practice
the *normal* tends to become the *normative*, that is, the requirement that *everyone*
meet the relevant norm or standard. This shift from observation to requirement is
not necessarily self-evident. Because the normative is often hedged with various
threats and punishments to be meted out to nonconformists, it easily becomes the
normal, as people in the culture move toward compliance rather than confront the
consequences of noncompliance.

Activity 2.1

- Think about some instances in your own life, whether gained through observation, direct experience, the reading of books or the viewing of movies and TV, in which you have been able to detect a difference between normality and normativity.

  ○ On what criterion (or criteria) of behavior did the distinction depend (for example, a norm of gender behavior or sexual practice)?

Essentialist versus constructionist views

We need, therefore, to be careful about assuming a simple relationship between the human sex–gender–sexuality triad and the sex–sexuality dyad of other creatures in our world. In the first place, gender appears to be chiefly a social and cultural phenomenon, in so far as it is not governed simply by instinct, implanted by the process of evolution. Gender requirements and assigned behaviors differ not only across cultures, but may also change across historical periods within a single culture.

If we look beyond Western cultures, we find that other cultures may have more complex sex/gender systems. For example, some Native American peoples structure into their sex/gender system a third gender, the so-called *berdache* or Two-Spirit person, that is, someone anatomically of one sex who identifies with the other gender. Many Native Americans object to the term "berdache," used widely in anthropological work on North American indigenous peoples (see, for example, Greenberg, 1988: 40–56). The term originates in a Spanish word that suggests male effeminacy and/or sexual submissiveness. For the cultures concerned, "Two-Spirit individual" is the preferred term, and does not necessarily define the individual so described by sexual orientation or role (Stryker, 2004). Although Two-Spirit persons may have sometimes been made objects of ridicule or contempt (often ritualized) within their particular cultures, at the same time they have also been regarded as revered shaman figures who have escaped the division into one sex or another, or who have embodied both sexes in the one body and identity. Likewise, in Greco-Roman culture, hermaphrodites may have been reviled by those around them, but they also inspired awe because of the twinned sex identities that they literally embodied.

A still more nuanced gender-system exists in Sulawesi, in the Indonesian archipelago, where among the Bugis people there are "three sexes (female, male, intersex), four genders (women, men, calabai [false woman], and calatai [false man], and a fifth meta-gender group, the bissu [literally 'transvestite priest,' but in fact hermaphroditic]" (Graham, 2001). In addition, such complexity implies an equal richness in cultural notions of and possibilities for sexual orientation and activity, whereas historically in most Western cultures heterosexuality has been the only officially sanctioned erotic orientation. If gender were indeed innate and the inevitable result of anatomical sex, such variations as we have considered among Native Americans and the Bugis people ought to be simply impossible.

Theories of gender and gender behavior that argue from nature, natural history, and the observed behavior of animals may be grouped under the category of *essentialist* theorizations. That is, they assume an essence of sex and gender that is reproduced genetically. Such theories frequently invoke Charles Darwin's important and influential idea of the evolution of species, as well as archeological and anthropological findings; and they underlie popular notions such as the idea that man is the hunter whereas woman is the gatherer, or that in engaging in the often ruthless cut-and-thrust of modern business, men simply replicate what their ancestors did on the African savanna in prehistoric times. These characterizations are founded on the idea that our collective archaic past as human beings and the way people lived in those days are hardwired into our brains and bodies. For instance, aggressive or violent male behavior is accordingly explained by such bodily factors as the larger, more muscular male physique and the effect of the powerful male hormone testosterone, and their function in protecting territory and clan or primitive community from intruders or invaders.

Essentialist theories of gender also often draw parallels between humans and animals in terms of social and sexual behaviors and social organization. Data gathered from experiments with animals or the observation of animals in their natural habitats may be applied to humans, in order to explain human practices, responses, or ways of behaving. The argument that human beings are also "just" animals overlooks or willfully ignores such facts as that people have not lived in identical kinds of society. For example, it is difficult to discern whether democracy, as a way of organizing society, has much meaning for or in animal groups as diverse as, say, ants and wolves, whereas humans have gone to war in order to preserve the notion of democracy or to impose it on societies deemed unjust, according to the lights of democracy as a set of beliefs about how societies should be organized.

Perhaps the paradigmatic case is that of same-sex sexual behavior. Historically, the condemnation of homosexuality (especially male homosexuality) in Western cultures has been justified by reference to the Bible, the founding Judeo-Christian scriptural text of those cultures. Although several passages in both the Old and New Testaments speak disapprovingly of homosexual relations and forbid them, the key passages are generally taken to be in the Book of Leviticus. Leviticus 18:22 states, in the King James Version (1611), "Thou shalt not lie with mankind, as with womankind: it is abomination," and Leviticus 20:13 commands, "If a man also lie with mankind, as he lieth with a woman, both of them have committed an abomination: they shall surely be put to death. Their blood shall be upon them." The Hebrew *to'evah* is here translated as "abomination," implying not only transgression but something that both contravenes and revolts nature as well as God, whereas the rendering "sin" in more recent translations is somewhat more anodyne, and suggests an offence to God only. John Boswell argues that the

Hebrew word "does not usually signify something intrinsically evil, like rape or theft (discussed elsewhere in Leviticus), but something which is ritually unclean for Jews, like eating pork or engaging in intercourse during menstruation, both of which are prohibited in these same chapters." He infers from this that "Leviticus 18 is specifically designed to distinguish the Jews from the pagans among whom they had been living, or would live … ." Boswell goes on to argue that the injunction against male homosexuality was therefore intended to preserve the ritual cleanliness of the Jews as a people, rather than being simply a moral condemnation of sexual transgression (Boswell, 1980: 100–101).

Nevertheless, by the Middle Ages, homosexuality came to be understood as *peccatum contra naturam*: *the* (not merely *a*) sin against nature (Boswell, 1980: 103, note 42), a sense perpetuated by the King James English translation of the Bible, the standard in English-speaking cultures for several centuries. However, Boswell cautions us to treat the notion of "nature" with care, because the term is a philosophical as well as semantic minefield. It may refer, among other things, to that which is the essence of something, and hence characteristic of it. It may signify a generalization for the "observable universe"; or for that which "does or would occur without human intervention" (Boswell, 1980: 11). Boswell notes that the condemnation of homosexuality as unreproductive and therefore unnatural is selective:

> Nonreproductivity can in any case hardly be imagined to have induced intolerance of gay people in ancient societies which idealized celibacy or in modern ones which consider masturbation perfectly 'natural,' since both of these practices have reproductive consequences identical with those of homosexual activity. This objection is clearly a justification rather than a cause of prejudice.
>
> (Boswell, 1980: 12)

He also points out that the assumption that homosexual behavior is absent among animals

> is demonstrably false: homosexual behavior, sometimes involving pair-bonding, has been observed among many animal species in the wild as well as in captivity. This has been recognized since the time of Aristotle and, incredible as it seems, has been accepted by people who *still* objected to homosexual behavior as unknown to other animals.
>
> (Boswell, 1980: 12; original emphasis)

Boswell argues further that this assumption

> is predicated on another assumption – that uniquely human behavior is not "natural" – which is fundamentally unsupportable in almost any context, biological or philosophical. Many animals in fact engage in behavior which is unique to their species, but no one imagines that such behavior

is "unnatural"; on the contrary, it is regarded as part of the "nature" of the species in question and is useful to taxonomists in distinguishing the species from other types of organisms. If man were the only species to demonstrate homosexual desires and behavior, this would hardly be grounds for categorizing them as "unnatural." Most of the behavior which human societies most admire is unique to humans: this is indeed the main reason it is respected. No one imagines that human society "naturally" resists literacy because it is unknown among other animals.

(Boswell, 1980: 12–13)

Essentialist theorizations of sex and gender, and the relationship between these, have contributed a good deal to our understanding of this complex set of terms and concepts, and the behaviors to which they refer. Such theorizations are, because of their scientific nature, grounded in Enlightenment notions of knowledge, chiefly the idea that the world and all that it contains can be measured, weighed, quantified, and analyzed according to a restricted set of methods and procedures. However, as we have seen, for example in Boswell's critique of ideas of "nature" and same-sex behaviors, the application of other methods and procedures may highlight weaknesses or blind spots in this scientific method.

Moreover, essentialist arguments can be used as political devices or weapons. For example, essentialist notions of "woman" and "femininity" have been used to argue against feminism and the increasing presence in the public sphere of women, and essentialist arguments from "nature" have justified attacks both verbal and physical on homosexual men and women. Indeed, one key difficulty with essentialist theory is that, effectively, it renders futile any hope of social change. If it were true that today we are simply replaying and reenacting the scripts by which our remotest ancestors survived, the best we can hope for is the containment, rather than the change and development, of attitudes and behaviors deemed antisocial – although how these latter can be thought of in that way becomes problematic, if they are indeed the foundation of who we are.

Constructionist (or constructivist) theories of gender argue, to the contrary, that, rather than *structuring* social relations, *gender is the product of the way a society develops*. Whereas essentialist theories situate gender in the material body and relate it to both physiological factors (such as hormones) and a history of species development, constructionist theories postulate that there are social and cultural influences that operate in and around such material factors as the body, whatever its evolutionary history. Those influences precede our individual entry into the world. Consequently, we must, from our earliest years, learn how to accommodate ourselves to them and how to find our place within the structures that they create. In other words, *we cannot construct our gender for ourselves*: it is predetermined for us by a vast, complex, and (at least in our very early years) irresistible array of forces, pressures, and persuasions.

Thus, even before an infant is born, one of the first things its parents often want to know is its sex. Once this has been determined, an almost invisible machinery starts up, setting in place patterns of expectation and compulsion, beginning with such apparently innocuous items as the kinds of color deemed appropriate for the baby's clothing, the sorts of toys that it will be given to play with, and the like. Even when the child has parents who are sensitive to issues of gender and who seek to neutralize conventional expectations of boys and girls, social and cultural influences still play a powerful role, through playgroups, friendships, schooling, television programs, advertising, and so on. Later, of course, the individual who was the child might decide to contest the way in which she or he has been gendered. However, that contestation is not an absolutely new formation. It is, rather, a reaction to and a resistance of a structure of gender that was always-already in place and that has already situated and formed the individual in important and indelible ways.

Nevertheless, constructionist theories do make space for such re-formations of gender to occur, unlike essentialist theories, which tend to see gender as embedded in the body and as in effect immutable. Moreover, because constructionism addresses social histories and configurations as well as cultural practices, its theorizations of gender and sexuality, and the relation between them, are more fluid. Put another way, essentialist theory seeks to fix sex, gender, and sexuality as both unchanging and universal, whereas constructionist theory perceives these as historically and culturally specific.

However, this does not mean that constructionist theory bypasses or ignores questions of the body and its workings: to do so would be foolhardy, because, for example, it is clear that biochemical functions such as the production of hormones *can* affect behavior. Rather, constructionism seeks to understand how the culture makes meaning of such behavior and how it valorizes (gives value to) it. For instance, rather than simply accepting that male aggression or violence is inevitable because of the presence of high levels of testosterone in the male body, constructionist theorists ask such questions as: "What value or values in this culture, at this time, are attributed to male aggression and violence?" "Is it possible that male aggression and violence are socially and culturally encouraged, and if so, in what ways, and toward what ends?" "Is aggressive and violent male behavior always produced simply by hormonal influences, or can those influences be triggered by social situations and circumstances?"

Activity 2.2

- Explore and examine the articles and the advertisements in women's or men's magazines:
    - Can you identify any elements of these that can be categorized as generated by either an essentialist or a constructionist understanding of gender?
    - How does such identification affect your understanding of the "gender project" of the publication in question?

The essentialist/constructionist debate is sometimes reductively characterized as the opposition between nature and nurture. The discussion above indicates that the issues are more complex than a simple opposition between body and upbringing. However, these two extremely important factors cannot be overlooked or neglected in a consideration of the ways in which gender is understood and explained by different kinds of theory. The debate itself can be thought of in terms of a tension chiefly between understanding as *ideological* or as *discursive*.

Theories of ideology and of discourse may appear at first sight to be alternate versions of the same thing. Both kinds of theory are *materialist*; that is, both look to social and historical forces as the causes of human behavior and ideas, rather than ascribing these to individual choice, divine Providence, or some other cause external to the social. Both are concerned with the central question of how and why we understand in particular ways the social world we inhabit and our relations with others in that world; and both operate with the key concepts of language, knowledge, and power. However, they think through these issues in significantly different ways, and they have different aims. Finally, both have been powerfully influential in contemporary theorizations of social structures and dynamics, power and its distribution, and, especially for our purposes, gender: much feminist theory, for example, has drawn on Marxist and/or Foucauldian thought.

Contemporary theories of ideology, which derive from the work of Karl Marx, the nineteenth-century German philosopher, historian, and political economist (among other intellectual functions) who took up residence in England, have as their ultimate goal the betterment of society for everyone. This requires an understanding of the way modern, Western social, political, and economic systems work, in order to devise a more equitable distribution of wealth and socioeconomic function. Marx identified capitalism as an oppressive and unjust organization of labor, wealth, and social structure, and believed that revolution that overthrew the entire system was the only remedy.

Current theories of discourse derive from the writings of Michel Foucault, the twentieth-century French philosopher and historian (indeed, he was a philosopher *of* history). Compared with Marxist theorizations and analyses, the Foucauldian elaboration of discursive formations seems less optimistic, even defeatist: concerned with the way power circulates through the social structure and determines our understanding of ourselves and our world, Foucault appears to advocate a resigned acceptance of its workings. However, this is to misunderstand Foucault's project, which is really to alert us to the operations of power upon us, and thereby to encourage us to resist these.

The theorizations of both ideology and discourse are both extensive and complex, and a full account of either is beyond the scope of the present book. Instead, what is presented below is a very much reduced presentation of each, intended as a way of working with an introduction to the theory of masculinity – a sort of "Super-Lite" version of both ideology and discourse. Readers are therefore strongly encouraged to explore ideology and gender further for themselves (see, for instance, "Suggested further reading" at the end of this chapter).

Ideology and gender

"Ideology" is often misunderstood as signifying a system of belief that is outmoded, clumsy, or different from or opposed to one's own set of beliefs. So, whereas one's own belief system appears self-evident, natural, and "correct," in the sense that all right-thinking people would "of course" agree, the belief system of another person (especially someone of a different background, race or ethnicity, religion, or political affiliation) seems wrong-headed, out of touch with reality, deluded, and/or perverse. However, the theorization of ideology argues not only that the ideology and the structure of *any* society or group are closely connected, but also that *it is impossible to escape ideology*. The very ways we observe and understand, think and talk are not only ideologically saturated but also themselves articulate and circulate ideology.

Catherine Belsey, for example, observes that

> ideology is both a real and an imaginary relation to the world – real in that it is the way in which people really live their relationship to the social relations which govern their conditions of existence, but imaginary in that it discourages a full understanding of these conditions of existence and the ways in which people are socially constituted within them. It is not, therefore, to be thought of as a system of ideas in people's heads, nor as the expression of a higher level of real material relationships, but as the necessary condition of action within the social formation.
>
> (Belsey, 1986: 46)

Put otherwise, ideology develops out of the reality of people's relation to the social: to social classes, their dynamics and relationship to one another; structures of employment and labor; patterns of social interaction; and so on. However, at the same time, ideology overlays and masks that relation so that contradictions, inconsistencies, and inequities are smoothed over and naturalized: "Ideology obscures the real conditions of existence by presenting partial truths. It is a set of omissions, gaps rather than lies, smoothing over contradictions, appearing to provide answers to questions which in reality it evades, and masquerading as coherence ..." (Belsey, 1986: 46). Thus, the existence of the members of a society is constituted by the structure of the society and the conditions of existence permitted by that structure, but is framed by "a system of representations (discourses, images, myths) concerning the real relations in which people live" (Belsey, 1986: 46).

However, Belsey warns:

> It is important to stress ... that ideology is in no sense a set of deliberate distortions foisted upon a helpless working-class by a corrupt and cynical

bourgeoisie (or upon victimized women by violent and power hungry men). If there are groups of sinister men in shirt-sleeves purveying illusions to the public these are not the real makers of ideology. Ideology has no creators in that sense, since it exists necessarily.

(Belsey, 1986: 46)

Ideology, then, emerges out of social structure and the relations of people to that structure, but it *disguises* those relations in order to ensure its own smooth operation. It becomes naturalized, and in turn naturalizes for us our conditions of social existence. It "exists in commonplaces and truisms as well as in philosophical and religious systems. It is apparent in all that is 'obvious' to us," so that the way things appear to be are understood as the way things simply *are*, and have always been (Belsey, 1986: 46).

One powerful agent of ideology is advertising. It ensures continuing sales and thereby also maintains production, of course, but it also preserves and furthers ideology by circulating it through the culture. The aim of the advertising industry is not merely to inform us about what is on offer in the marketplace by way of goods or services for sale, but in fact *to create a need in us as consumers* for these things. Accordingly, therefore, we are made to feel anxious about our looks, our health, our sex appeal, our ability to appear presentable in terms of the latest fashions, our possession of "labor-saving" devices, our apparent wealth (or lack of it), and so on, so that we focus, not on the *real* value of these goods and services in terms of actual need or of the gap between what it cost to produce them and what it costs us to acquire them, but rather on our desire for them, *a desire that is represented to us as real need.*

Advertising operates through *interpellation*, an idea developed by the twentieth-century French Marxist theorist Louis Althusser. He suggests that ideology works by interpellating (that is, "hailing" or addressing) us. However, the "us" (or "me") that ideology addresses must be understood less as an actual identity or individual than a *subject*, an important term in studies in sociology, culture, and gender. Whereas it seems only common sense to understand ourselves as autonomous, unique individuals who, possessing both will and agency, act freely in and on the world around us, theories of ideology (and, as we shall see later, also of discourse) by contrast postulate *that our sense of ourselves* (as autonomous agents possessed of free will) in fact *is shaped for us* by forces beyond our control and, indeed, even beyond our awareness of them. Accordingly, we imagine our own uniqueness and autonomy to be beyond question. However,

subjectivity isn't a property that we own, but on the contrary we are subjects *of* various agencies. Our individual identity, then, is determined, regulated and reproduced as a structure of relationships. For instance, we may be subjects of (subjected to) parental affection/authority; legal protections/compulsion; commercial enterprise/exploitation; national or cultural characteristics/stereotypes; and so on.

(Hartley, 1994b: 309–10)

Althusser specifies this still further. To summarize and clarify his rather tortuous language: the subject comes into existence through ideology, but at the same time ideology is brought into being through the subject, for ideology cannot exist in a void, without a subject. It is, therefore, a reciprocal relationship and existence, and for this reason "ideology has no history" because in effect its history can be only that of the subjects that it constitutes and that constitute it. This means, in turn, that there is no subjectivity outside ideology – no "self" or "identity" that is not already ideological, because it has been formed entirely within ideology (Althusser, 1976: 44–45).

In a famous metaphor, Althusser likens ideology to a policeman on the street who shouts, "Hey, you!" and, because we recognize that each of us is always "you" to someone else, we turn round in response:

> By this mere one-hundred-and-eighty-degree physical conversion, he [the person hailed] becomes a *subject*. Why? Because he has recognized that the hail was "really" addressed to him, and that "it was *really him* who was hailed" (and not someone else). Experience shows that the practical tele-communication of hailings is such that they hardly ever miss their man: verbal call or whistle, the one hailed always recognizes that it is really him who is being hailed. And yet it is a strange phenomenon, and one which cannot be explained solely by "guilt feelings," despite the large numbers who "have something on their consciences."
>
> (Althusser, 1976: 48; original emphasis)

That call of "Hey, you!" is issued to us every day in different situations and contexts. We may, for example, be interpellated as children or parents, students or teachers, young people or adults, workers or bosses, and so on.

Gender, too, is an instance of interpellation: we are "hailed" as men or women, and we respond by engaging in the behavior appropriate to the nature of that "hailing." Indeed, if we think about it, we are interpellated in terms of gender in different ways all the time. For example, a male may be interpellated as a son, a father, a partner, a friend, an employer, an employee, a sportsman, and so on. It is unlikely that his behavior in all these instances of interpellation remains consistent. As a simple instance, amongst his close friends or in the changing room of a sports facility, he is likely to use language and behavior that are different from the way he is likely to speak and behave when in the company of his parents, his children, or his boss. From this, we may infer that "masculinity" (and, of course, "femininity" for women) is actually fragmented and multiple for each individual male. In other words, one might exhibit various masculinities during the course of a single day, but ideology smooths over any inconsistencies or possible contradictions among these masculinities, so that it appears to that subject that he behaves throughout in a consistently regular manner as a man (see also Aboim, 2010).

An interesting and more concrete example is furnished by both Jeff Lindsay's *Dexter* novels by (Lindsay, 2004, 2005, 2007, 2009, 2010) and the TV series based on them (*Dexter*, 2006–). A serial killer who sees it as his task to kill other serial killers, Dexter Morgan must nevertheless function (and function plausibly) as a normal member of society, and of the Miami police force. Because, as a serial killer, he occupies an extremely marginal position, if not indeed a position entirely outside the range of what constitutes centrality/marginality, Dexter is more aware than most of the ways in which he is interpellated: adopted brother to Deborah Morgan, who also works in the police force; colleague to figures like Vince Masuoka; subordinate to Lt Migdia (Maria, in the TV series) LaGuerta; boyfriend and later husband to Rita; "mentor" to her daughter Astor and son Cody, both damaged by the violent relationship of their parents and with more than a slight inclination toward murder themselves; and, not least, figure of judgment and vengeance to his victims. Dexter must perform "Dexter," a unified, integrated subject; and much of the tension in the narratives is brought about by the threat not only of the revelation of his true nature, but also of the unraveling of these variously interpellated identities.

Advertising interpellates us as particular kinds of consumer: it isolates specific identities and backgrounds, whether defined by gender, ethnicity or race, class, age, and so on, and it defines particular needs, real or imaginary. For example, advertisements for laundry detergents have traditionally targeted (interpellated) women as the people responsible for the well-being of the domestic household. Accordingly, women are represented in such commercials as loving, concerned for the cleanliness of the members of the household, especially the children, and as efficient and competent in the maintenance and smooth running of the house. It follows, "therefore" (the scare quotes are intended to draw attention to the fact that this is an artificial logic), that such women would "of course" (naturally, obviously) want the product that cleaned clothes the best. In turn, the public spectacle of the family members arrayed in bright, clean outfits would then reflect on the female consumer of laundry products as demonstrating her concern for her family's comfort and well-being, as well as her "natural" competence as wife and mother.

In thus targeting the women in households across the nation, such commercials also define the gender roles appropriate to those women. To say, if one is a woman, "I don't buy this or any other laundry product, because I have better things to do than wash clothes" is to court condemnation: one would be censured not only as a housewife and mother, *but also as a woman*. Yet the same statement issuing from the mouth of a man would be less likely to attract such criticism.

Advertising of laundry products often draws also on "science," whether this is represented by men and women in lab coats in what appears to be a laboratory, seemingly testing the product to ensure that it does its job better and more effectively than rival brands of the same kind of product, or by invoking chemical terminology ("Now with added X," where "X" is a chemical-sounding word – for instance, "radianite" – whether or not it signifies an actual chemical compound). Such a tactic indicates the function of "science" as ideological. This is not to say that science is purely imaginary, but rather that it can be used in ideological ways.

That science is ideologically valorized in our culture can be tested by imagining a laundry detergent that was sold on the basis that it cleaned better than its competitors because its contact with water released thousands of little fairy folk who specialized in cleaning garments. Our culture no longer credits explanations of phenomena that invoke supernatural events or figures; they are not "scientific."

Activity 2.3

- Consider the ways in which you might be interpellated during an average day.

  o   How many social "identities" are you required to assume through these interpellations?

- Now consider how many versions of "masculinity" or "femininity" you might perform during the course of a day.

  o   What consistencies or inconsistencies among those versions do you notice?

- Think about some of the movies or TV shows that you have watched, and the ways in which a character has been interpellated by the other characters.

  o   How does this affect the way in which you understand the construction of that character?

- Now consider the way or ways in which you have been interpellated by the movie or TV program: as neutral observer, gendered spectator, moral or ethical judge, etc.

  o   How does this affect the way in which you now understand the movie or program?

- Imagine that you are employed by an advertising company to market a laundry detergent to men.

  o   What would be the features to which you would draw attention that would make it appealing to male consumer; that is, how would you interpellate that subject?

  o   What does that suggest about the ideological construction of masculinity, for example, in terms of what aspects of the male subject are "natural" (essential, biological, anatomical), and which may be classed as "cultural" (constructed, determined by assumption, practice, history, etc.)?

- Now imagine that you have been commissioned to develop an advertising campaign to sell to female consumers an item traditionally identified as purchased by men; for example, power tools.

  - First, consider how such an item is (re-)presented to men, and how that (re-)presentation draws on, highlights, or otherwise invokes "masculinity." How would you reframe this in order to sell the product to women? What does this suggest about the ideological construction of femininity in relation to masculinity?

Gender may also be understood as ideological in that anatomical, sexual difference is transformed into a system of values that are then presented to us as inevitable and natural. Our complicity with that system is engineered in different ways: for instance, for men, through the offer of sexual and social power; for women, in the promise of support, security, and protection via love and marriage (or its equivalent). In an important way, the gender system interpellates each of us according to our anatomical sex, although there is no *necessary* connection between the latter and the way each of us is interpellated. A fairly clear example of how ideology works in relation to gender can be seen in as simple a sentence as "Boys line up to the right; girls to the left." Such a statement interpellates those to whom it is addressed in terms of gender; and in a two-gender system in which men tend to be privileged over women, the distinction between "boys" and "girls" is marked: *the very terms incorporate gender difference*, paralleling the assumption of gender difference literally incorporated in the body. The alignment to right or left also carries implications of privilege. As the French feminist Hélène Cixous observes, in pairings like man/woman, right/left, sun/moon, the term on the left of the slash is usually the dominant, privileged term, the one on the right, the subordinate, unprivileged one (Cixous, 1994: 37–38).

However, if we recast the above sentence as "Young people with penises line up on one side; young people with vaginas on the other," we can see a significant ideological as well as semantic shift. The key term now becomes "young people," which does not distinguish between male and female, and which therefore interpellates the addressees differently from the earlier instruction. "With penises" or "with vaginas" now becomes simply an attribute, akin to "with brown eyes" or "with blue eyes," "with green shirts" or "with red shirts": this formulation does not distinguish between biological males and females, on the one hand, and, on the other, transsexual or intersex individuals. Moreover, "on one side … on the other" does not give value to and hierarchize spatial position in the same way as "to the right … to the left" seems to do.

Discourse and gender

Whereas theories of ideology see both power and the meaning it generates as arranged hierarchically, from the top down, theories of discourse by contrast perceive the entire social structure and its activities as suffused with power. That is, for Foucault and those who have used and developed his theorization of discourse, power does not emanate from any *single* source or structure. Indeed, Foucault postulates that power and knowledge function simultaneously and together: he calls this "power/knowledge." This means more than the fairly commonplace idea that knowledge *is* power. This is certainly true; for example, think of how helpless one might feel in a strange city or country, where one does not know the layout of the town (where does one go to purchase a particular item? Whom does one ask for directions?, etc.) and may not be able to speak the local language (how does one ask for something in a shop? Does a word that looks familiar mean the same thing there? Do people there use a word one is familiar with for a common item?, etc.). However, rather than seeing power as oppressive, as theories of ideology tend to do, Foucault understands power as *productive*. That is, it *creates* identity, difference, relationships, and the like. Knowledge, in this light, functions alongside power by distinguishing between what is known and what is not known, who knows and who does not know, and how such knowledge organizes the world, society, and the relationship of one subject to others. Put another way, knowledge *positions* one, and that positioning is itself at once both a cause and an effect of power. Thus, power produces knowledge, and knowledge produces power: the two work in reciprocal and complementary ways.

However, power/knowledge also operates through discourse in a deeper, subtler manner. In general, the notion of discourse suggests speech, dialogue, or some other verbal interaction. For example, to many linguists, "discourse" signifies a passage of language longer than a single sentence. However, for Foucault, although this sense is not lost, it is extended and broadened, and made more complex. "Discourse" encompasses not only what people say and write to each other, but also what sorts of cultural preoccupations or themes are most commonly spoken of – *or are permitted to be spoken of.* Moreover, discourse should be understood as embracing social and cultural practices and behaviors of all kinds as a form of indirect speech. Not only do such practices and behaviors tell us something about the people who undertake them, but, like speech or writing considered discursively, they also define cultural preoccupations and themes.

Discourses do not simply provide topics of conversation. Rather, *they determine what can be spoken of and in what way or ways*, as well as what cannot or should not be articulated, and therefore must remain inferiorized, marginalized, or simply silenced. There are, therefore, rules to any discourse, although as members of the culture we are not necessarily aware of these (Foucault calls these rules *regularities*). Moreover, discourses are not necessarily limited to particular social contexts or sites. Indeed, often the discourse may be detected through analysis of a number of different aspects of cultural activity (in Foucault's terms, these are *discursive formations*). As with ideology, then, it is impossible to evade discourse, *because not only what we do or think but also who we are* (or believe ourselves or one another to be) *emerge only in and through discourse.*

Foucault's theory of discourse comes out more fully in his later writings; in his earlier work, he explores the notion of the *episteme*, from the Greek *epistēmē*, a term that is related to the word "epistemology," which means "the study of meaning." Foucault considered how, over time, particular ideas might change significantly in meaning, although the terms by which those meanings were denoted might have remained the same (for example, he investigated the notions of "madness" or "the madman"). He concluded that there were structures by which we understand both language and phenomena in particular ways in specific cultures, at specific historical moments. This type of structure he called the episteme; and he argued that it changes over time, and in relation to historical events in the culture, including interaction with neighboring or more exotic cultures.

For example, if you were asked to write a brief descriptive essay about the snake, as a generic term, you would probably think back to your lessons in biology and remember that all life forms are classified in a descending hierarchy from domain through kingdom, phylum, class, order, family, down to genus and species. You would then no doubt situate the snake within that system, noting, for example, that it is a reptile, vertebrate, cold-blooded, and so on. You would probably point out also that some snakes, like the rattlesnake or the cobra, are venomous, whereas others, like the boa or the python, kill by constriction; and you might also add that some snakes, like the grass snake or the pine snake (the latter goes by a number of names), are harmless, at least to humans.

However, if you looked in a medieval bestiary, or book of beasts, you would find the snake described rather differently from what you might expect. Here is what a thirteenth-century English bestiary has to say about the snake:

> The snake has three habits; the first of these is that when it grows old its eyes grow dim and if it wants to renew them, it starves itself and fasts for many days until its skin grows loose. Then it looks for a narrow crevice in the rocks. It wriggles into it and sloughs its old skin. And we through many tribulations put off the old Adam for Christ's sake and seek Christ the spiritual rock, and find a narrow fissure, that is, the strait gate. ¶Its second habit is that when it comes to a river to drink water, it does not take its poison with it, but leaves it behind in a pit. When we come together to hear the heavenly word of God in church, we must leave behind our earthly body, that is, earthly and evil desires. ¶Its third habit is that if it sees a naked man, it is frightened, but if it sees him clothed, it attacks him. In spiritual terms, the serpent was unable to attack the first man, Adam, as long as he was naked in paradise, but when he was clothed, that is, his body became mortal, then it attacked him.

(Barber, 1999: 196)

This may strike us as a rather fanciful and, from a scientific or biological point of view, not very helpful description. However, as Richard Barber, the translator of this particular bestiary, observes, "the object of the bestiary is not to document the natural world and to analyse it in order to understand its workings. The writers of bestiaries knew the laws of nature before they began their work, and were concerned only to expound them":

> They knew that everything in Creation had a purpose, and that the Creator had made nothing without an ulterior aim in mind. And they knew, too, what that purpose was: the edification and instruction of sinful man. The Creator had made animals, birds and fishes, and had given them their natures or habits, so that the sinner could see the world of mankind reflected in the kingdom of nature, and learn the way to redemption by the examples of different creatures. Each creature is therefore a kind of moral entity, bearing a message for the human reader.
>
> (Barber, 1999: 7)

That is, the episteme in the England (and, more generally, Europe) of the thirteenth century was different from that which determines how we understand the world, humans, and human society today. Medieval thinkers took the universe to be a *Liber Mundi*, or Book of the World, "written" by God and full of meaning. It was the purpose of human learning to read this text and to arrive at an understanding of the secret meanings of all of its parts and interactions. This is substantially different from our episteme today, after the Enlightenment and the waning influence of religious thought, when the purpose of the examination of physical objects and phenomena is to understand them in and of themselves. The episteme, then, is not simply a particle of knowledge, or factual item; rather, *the episteme determines what counts as knowledge.*

To bring the notion of the episteme closer to the question of gender, let us consider an idea that remained influential from as early as classical Greece to as late as the seventeenth century: that the entire universe was made up of only four elements: earth, air, fire, and water. This concept underlay and supported a number of other systems of knowledge. For example, in astrology one or another of these elements is attributed to each of the zodiacal signs. In medicine and notions of health, the theory of the four "humors" (melancholic, choleric, sanguineous, and phlegmatic) assumed that the human body was constituted by the four elements in varying combinations, and that these had particular seats in the body, melancholy, for instance, being produced because of an excess of black bile. Thus, someone diagnosed as possessing a sanguineous humor, whose symptoms were such traits as courage, optimism, and "amorousness" (which could mean anything from a tendency to fall in love easily to outright lecherousness), was dominated by the blood in his or her body, which meant that there was a preponderance of moistness (attributable to the element of water) combined with heat (the element of fire).

The theory of the four elements, then, is part of an episteme that affected not only how the world was *understood*, in terms of analytical knowledge, but also how the world was *perceived*. Even the question of sexual difference and gender could be attributed to this episteme, as Thomas Laqueur shows, in his *Making*

Sex: body and gender from the Greeks to Freud. He demonstrates how scholars, doctors, and other thinkers understood genital difference (that is, penis and vagina) to be the result of a difference of heat in the body. Because life was thought to need heat, it was assumed that semen contained the heat necessary to generate new life. Thus, the male body, and male genitals in particular, were understood to be filled with this vital heat (but only a finite quantity of it, hence the belief that each ejaculation of semen depleted a man's body of its vitality). Indeed, the male genitals were understood to have been "exploded" out of the body cavity because of this very heat. By contrast, because woman was understood to be simply the passive receptacle for this seed/heat of life, the womb was thought of as maintaining only as much heat as was required to sustain the new life being conceived, but not enough to expel the genital organs within her body. Thus, the female reproductive system, according to this episteme, was simply the inverse of the male one (see, for example, Laqueur, 1990: 24–62). Laqueur goes on to demonstrate that, despite the discoveries about human anatomy during the Renaissance and the interest of Enlightenment scientists in the workings of the body, the two-sex/single-genital model of the human reproductive system continued to be taught and published in medical textbooks as late as the early nineteenth century, despite the significant shift in episteme brought about by the Renaissance and the Enlightenment.

We might wonder why this was so; and here we may see the difference between episteme and ideology. Although there was clearly plenty of evidence that the archaic anatomical model did not correspond with what could be observed when the human body was dissected, equally clearly something else operated to keep that model in place in such official sites as medical schools and textbooks. Such willful blindness was generated by an *ideological commitment* to continue to see the female reproductive system as the inverse of the male one, and therefore secondary (and inferior) to it. There was, of course, no *intrinsic* reason why the polarities should not have been reversed, and the male genitals seen as secondary and hence inferior to the female ones ... except that, of course, the entire theory was devised by men, who "naturally" took their own bodies to be the norm. (The word "naturally" is placed between scare quotes in order to signal, once again, that there is nothing natural about this assumption, that it, too, is derived ideologically and, as we shall see, discursively.)

Activity 2.4

- How have you typically thought of "knowledge"?
- Reflect on the epistemic shift brought about by the technological revolution and the broader access to computers, the Internet, and the World Wide Web. Has the idea of "knowledge" changed?
- Research traditionally has consisted of investigation along both a horizontal axis (what have various scholars had to say about the

topic?) and a vertical one (what has been the historical genesis of ideas relevant to the topic, and what have been the "family relationships" among those ideas?).

   ○ Has the World Wide Web, with its array of hyperlink connections, suggested "similar items," and so on, changed the way we think today about research? If so, in what ways?

• Again, research traditionally has required the researcher to evaluate the material she or he encounters in terms of value and authority, through the weighing of the nature of the documentation, the situating of the authors of such documentation (whether academic, popular, journalistic, etc.), the context of the documentation (whether it is published, say, by a university press or a scholarly journal, or rather by a publisher of popular works), and so on. The World Wide Web offers free access to anyone, anywhere, to post material of any description.

   ○ How has this affected the idea of the value and authority of researched material – and how does one assess such qualities in research gathered from the Web?

We have considered Foucault's earlier reliance on the notion of the episteme because it explains the way in which his theory of discourse developed. Although in his later work he quietly dropped the idea of the episteme, it nonetheless underpins his theorization of discourse, to which the notion of power/knowledge became central. For Foucault, the various topics or themes of discourse do not preexist discourse itself, but rather *are created by discourse*. Or, to put it another way, discourse *brings into view* those topics or themes, and in so doing positions us as discursive subjects in relation to these, which in turn means a distribution of power. As a discourse, gender does not simply assign already existing terms like "masculine" and "feminine," but instead *creates the possibilities for their existence and application*. If gender were truly natural, we ought to be able to talk about animals as being masculine or feminine in attitude and behavior; however, this clearly would make little sense, despite our awareness that animals, like humans, are sexed. For example, could we say of a bull that it behaves in a masculine way – or, conversely, that a cow had a feminine air about her? We can, of course, talk about aggressive behaviors in male animals or submissive ones in female ones; but it is only when these behaviors are imported into the human and social frame that they become tagged "masculine" or "feminine."

We may think of discourse, in the first place, as *multiple* and, in the second, as *completely permeating the human, social world*, saturating it as various discourses converge or intersect, creating new possibilities through the combination (or subtraction) of specific discourses. Our subjectivity, or sense of self, is thus produced discursively, through the intersection of such discursive strands as sex, gender, sexuality, age, race or ethnicity, class, and so on. Indeed, we can imagine the social world as a sphere the surface of which is threaded through and through with electrical filaments, each pulsating with power. Those filaments represent discourses; and where they meet, cross each other, or pass by one another, they produce and bring into visibility particular identities, beliefs, situations, ideas, and even events.

It is important, when considering Foucault's notion of discursive power, to bear in mind, first, that he does not think of power as purely coercive (that is, as forcing individuals or groups to act in certain ways or perform certain deeds) or as purely repressive (that is, as prohibiting the actions or deeds of individuals or groups). He remarks:

> power is tolerable only on condition that it mask a substantial part of itself. Its success is proportional to its ability to hide its own mechanisms. Would power be accepted if it were entirely cynical? For it, secrecy is not in the nature of an abuse; it is indispensable to its operation. Not only because power imposes secrecy on those whom it dominates, but because it is perhaps just as indispensable to the latter: would they accept it if they did not see it as a mere limit placed on their desire, leaving a measure of freedom – however slight – intact? Power as a pure limit set on freedom is, at least in our society, the general form of its acceptability.
>
> (Foucault, 1981: 86)

Foucault clarifies his idea further:

> By power, I do not mean "power" as a group of institutions and mechanisms that ensure the subservience of the citizens of a given state. By power, I do not mean, either, a mode of subjugation which, in contrast to violence, has the form of the rule. Finally, I do not have in mind a general system of domination exerted by one group over another, a system whose effects, through successive derivations, pervade the entire social body.
>
> (Foucault, 1981: 92)

For Foucault, then, power does not function in the way that Marxist theory conceives it: as operating from the top down through a hierarchy that imposes its will upon those with less access to power. In Foucauldian thought, power is

> the moving substrate of force relations which, by virtue of their inequality, constantly engender states of power, but the latter are always local and unstable. The omnipresence of power: not because it has the privilege of consolidating everything under its invincible unity, but because it is produced from one moment to the next, at every point, or rather in every relation from one point to another. Power is everywhere; not because it embraces everything, but because it comes from everywhere. ... power is not an institution, and not a structure; neither is it a certain strength we are

endowed with; it is the name that one attributes to a complex strategical situation in a particular society.

(Foucault, 1981: 93)

Where Marxist theory tends to formulate and conceive of power as functioning in a static social structure dominated by a few who wield power over the rest, Foucauldian theory identifies power as something dynamic, arising out of inequalities that shift, turn, and change, and in so doing produce different relations among people and institutions, which in turn produce knowledges of different kinds. Importantly, for Foucault, power is not vested in the hands of the few but is omnipresent, "not because it embraces everything, but because it comes from everywhere."

Importantly, Foucault declares, "Where there is power, there is resistance, and yet, or rather consequently, this resistance is never in a position of exteriority in relation to power" (Foucault, 1981: 95). That is, power can exist *as* power only in the presence of resistance, whether actual or only possible. Without resistance, power functions in a vacuum, and therefore ceases to *be* power; there is nothing for it to be exercised upon. Power, therefore, *presupposes* resistance, and seeks to annul, contain, repress, or silence it directly or in anticipation. Foucault emphasizes "the strictly relational character of power relationships":

> Their existence depends on a multiplicity of points of resistance: these play the role of adversary, target, support, or handle in power relations. These points of resistance are present everywhere in the power network. Hence there is no single locus of great Refusal, no soul of revolt, source of all rebellions, or pure law of the revolutionary. Instead there is a plurality of resistances, each of them a special case: resistances that are possible, necessary, improbable; others that are spontaneous, savage, solitary, concerted, rampant, or violent; still others that are quick to compromise, interested, or sacrificial; by definition, they can only exist in the strategic field of power relations.
>
> (Foucault, 1981: 95–96)

Just as power is everywhere, so is resistance, or it least its possibility. This is why Foucault states that "there is no single locus of great Refusal," and why he is dubious about revolution as a means of substantially changing discursive formations. Instead, there exists "a plurality of resistances," many of which no doubt occur on a regular, even daily, basis.

He continues:

> But this does not mean that they are only a reaction or rebound, forming with respect to the basic domination an underside that is in the end always passive, doomed to perpetual defeat. Resistances do not derive from a few heterogeneous principles; but neither are they a lure or a promise that is of necessity betrayed. They are the odd term in relations of power; they are inscribed in the latter as an irreducible opposite.
>
> (Foucault, 1981: 96)

In thus rejecting the idea of power as monolithic and irresistible, Foucault creates a space within which change is possible. That space also allows for our positioning as subjects in relation to particular discourses and therefore also in relation to the particular forms of power for which specific discourses act as relays.

Let us see how this works by returning to our earlier example of the advertisement for laundry detergent. Where an ideological analysis commences with the assumption that the housewife and mother's gender identity is already established and fixed, framed by particular ideologies, a discursive analysis might ask how the various discourses invoked by such an advertisement *produce* the figure of "housewife-and-mother." Such discourses include those of gender and the family, which in turn create a discursive formation that we might call domesticity. A happy housewife and mother will create a contented home, which in turn will make her family content: this is the underlying "message" that makes the promotion of this laundry product workable; it has little to do with actual biochemical interactions in the washing machine, or with the chemical structure of the laundry powder itself. The image of the happy housewife draws on a fairly familiar discourse of gender that constructs woman as homemaker and nurturer. Her proper place, therefore, is in the home; this is where she best fulfills her role, even if she is also a worker outside the home. Indeed, the implication in some forms of this kind of commercial is that the product and the technology of such white goods as washing machines and electric dryers *permit* the woman to work outside the home and yet to maintain the role which is hers, apparently by right.

However, when we ask such questions as "Why doesn't the husband and father deal with the laundry?" or "Why isn't at least one of the children detailed to take care of the washing of clothes?", we begin to perceive how the discourses work. They *produce* the adult parents as each occupying a role defined by gender, and the children as dependent beings who not only should *not* be put to work, but who are not really even *capable* of work. Yet this is clearly untrue: in developing countries very young children are often employed as a means of bringing some income into the family coffer; even in Western countries in the not-too-distant past young children were similarly occupied, until labor laws made it illegal to employ children under a certain age. (This, in itself, points to a discourse about children as innocent and helpless beings until they reach a particular age, often arbitrarily defined; yet "the child" as such a figure is of relatively recent appearance, historically speaking.) There are other questions one might ask, for example: "What's the deal with washing clothes regularly anyway? Why not wear them until they become rags and fall off the body, and then buy new ones?" Such interrogations are indices of areas of possible resistance to the discourses that are at work in such an advertisement. However, the text of the advertisement itself is created and framed in such a way as to deflect our attention from such possible points of resistance, thereby encouraging us to remain attentive and obedient to the familiar discourses being rehearsed.

Let us also briefly revisit the *Dexter* narratives, and consider them now in relation to discourse. Such a reading shows that Dexter shifts among various discourses, for instance, those of the family, domesticity, morality, and so on.

A serial killer intent on protecting his subjectivity *as* a serial killer, Dexter must make himself aware of the discursive formations (although of course these are not presented as such in the narratives) and become adept at negotiating them. It is that consciousness, as much as his murderous identity, that sets him apart from the other characters (aside, of course, from the other serial killers).

Must one make a choice between ideology and discourse as ways of framing, analyzing, and understanding cultural texts and phenomena – and, for our purposes, the workings and meanings of gender? Sara Mills observes that, "For some, discourse is the larger term within which there exist [sic] a range of different ideologies, whilst for others ideologies are made manifest through a variety of different discourses," and she notes: "It is part of the history of the usage of the term discourse that it has been constituted in reaction to the meanings associated with the term ideology, and that struggle with the concept ideology is still a part of its current range of meanings" (Mills, 1997: 46).

It is no doubt possible to speak of *gender* as an ideology, if what we have in mind is that gender tends to privilege and serve the interests of a particular group in the culture. From this perspective, anatomical sex becomes the basis on which is erected the superstructure of gender. Accordingly, much feminist critique of gender, especially in the 1960s and 1970s, was grounded in a Marxist theorizing of gender, and therefore tended to construct men as the oppressors and women as the oppressed. This necessarily meant that more attention was paid to the position of women in such a power structure, and was inclined to neglect the possibility that there were power differentials also among men.

Moreover, it left unanswered the question of whether it was indeed possible for women to overthrow that structure in order to produce a more equitable set of gender relations. Rather, it seemed, women were instead committed to a tactics of fringe warfare, challenging masculine power and the social situations that it created. By contrast, a discursive analysis seeks to undo gender structures and relations at all levels and in all dimensions, in the process interrogating *both* masculinity *and* femininity. That said, we should note that it is possible to talk about masculine ideolog*ies*, rather than *an ideology* of masculinity. Such ideologies might include such characteristics of the masculine as stoicism as an ideal, strength and courage as desirable traits, and so on.

Nonetheless, it is important to bear in mind that these characteristics, however desirable, are not necessarily grounded in the body. That is, they are not naturally *inherent* in maleness. The question, therefore, arises as to how they have come to be assumed as key elements of masculinity. To address this issue, we turn in the next chapter to the work of Judith Butler, who uses Foucauldian theory to explore the nature of gender.

Suggested further reading

Beasley, C. (2005) *Gender and Sexuality: critical theories, critical thinkers*, Los Angeles: Sage.

Fulcher, J. (2004) *Capitalism: a very short introduction*, Oxford: Oxford University Press.

Glover, D. and Kaplan, C. (2000) *Genders*, London and New York: Routledge.

Gutting, G. (2005) *Foucault: a very short introduction*, Oxford: Oxford University Press.

Kimmel, M.S. and Plante, R.F. (eds) (2004) *Sexualities: identities, behaviors, and society*, New York: Oxford University Press.

Pascoe, C.J. (2007) *Dude, You're a Fag: masculinity and sexuality in high school*, Berkeley: University of California Press.

Seidman, S., Fischer, N. and Meeks, C. (eds) (2011) *Introducing the New Sexuality Studies*, London and New York: Routledge.

3   Doing/undoing gender

Although Foucault does not directly address issues of gender and the structured inequalities between men and women, his work has proved very productive for other theorists who do focus on gender. Chief among these has been the philosopher Judith Butler, who has sought, to adapt the title of one of her books, to trouble gender and our familiar assumptions about it. In so doing, she brings a new and exciting and, some might say, liberating approach to questions of sex, sexuality, and gender. Butler unsettles naturalized "commonsense" assumptions about gender. Arguing that not only gendered behaviors but also the very notion of sex itself are learned, she proposes that we "do" our genders unconsciously yet faithfully on a daily basis. Her project, therefore, is to "undo" the seeming naturalness of gendered behavior.

Sex and gender

In *Gender Trouble: feminism and the subversion of identity*, Butler uncouples the apparently logical relationship between sex and gender. She observes:

> If gender is the cultural meanings that a sexed body assumes, then a gender cannot be said to follow from a sex in any one way. Taken to its logical limit, the sex/gender distinction suggests a radical discontinuity between sexed bodies and culturally constructed genders. Assuming for the moment the stability of binary sex, it does not follow that the construction of "men" will accrue exclusively to the bodies of males or that "women" will interpret only female bodies. Further, even if the sexes appear to be unproblematically binary in their morphology and constitution (which will become a question), there is no reason to assume that gender ought also to remain as two. The presumption of a binary gender system implicitly retains the belief in a mimetic relation of gender to sex whereby gender mirrors sex or is otherwise restricted by it. When the constructed status of gender is theorized as radically independent of sex, gender itself becomes a free-floating artifice, with the consequence that *man* and *masculine* might just as easily signify a female body as the male one, and *woman* and *feminine* a male body as easily as a female one.
>
> (Butler, 1990: 6; original emphasis)

She goes on to suggest that "perhaps this construct called 'sex' is as culturally constructed as gender; indeed, perhaps it was always already gender, with the consequence that the distinction between sex and gender turns out to be no distinction at all." She argues that, "As a result, gender is not to culture as sex is to nature; gender is also the discursive/cultural means by which 'sexed nature' or 'a natural sex' is produced and established as 'prediscursive,' prior to culture, a politically neutral surface *on which* culture acts" (Butler, 1990: 7; original emphasis). Another way of conceiving this is to understand that *the very existence of a dimorphic sex system may depend on the prior existence of a gender system that makes sense of genital difference*, rather than seeing it, as we usually do, the other way around: gender as dependent on sexual configuration.

Activity 3.1

- Imagine a world in which there was no such thing as gender:

    ○ What would be the implications for individual and institutional behaviors in such a society?
    ○ Would there remain a need for people to differentiate themselves from one another, and on what basis might such differentiation exist and function? By what other forms of category and class than "male/female" or "man/woman" might people in this hypothetical world understand themselves and others?

- If you experience difficulty imagining such a state of things, think about why that might be, and how that very difficulty might indicate the deeply ingrained assumptions in the culture about sex and gender, and the relationship between them.
- Do you think that recent developments in fertility and the conception of infants (for example, IVF [*in vitro* fertilization], surrogate motherhood and the like) have affected cultural notions of the relation of sex to gender?
- Has this activity encouraged you to think about sex and gender differently?

    ○ If so, then in what ways?
    ○ If not, consider the reasons for maintaining the familiar understandings of the dominant sex/gender system.

For Butler, the question of gender and its relation to sex is a complex, many-layered issue, leading her, in *Bodies That Matter: on the discursive limits of "sex"*, to interrogate the apparently self-evident distinction between essentialism and constructionism, although she tends more to the latter. She is interested in, among other things, the conditions under and by which the subject (the "I" which we all use unreflectingly, as a matter of sheer, unquestioned fact) is able to emerge and function (Butler, 1993: 7). She observes:

> Consider the medical interpellation which (the recent emergence of the sonogram notwithstanding) shifts an infant from an "it" to a "she" or a "he," and in that naming, the girl is "girled," brought into the domain of language and kinship through the interpellation of gender. But that "girling" of the girl does not end there; on the contrary, that founding interpellation is reiterated by various authorities throughout various intervals of time to reenforce or contest this naturalized effect. The naming is at once the setting of a boundary, and also the repeated inculcation of a norm.
>
> (Butler, 1993: 7–8)

The drawing of a boundary through a gendered naming to which Butler alludes does not consist simply of the distinction between male and female, masculine and feminine, boy and girl. For her, such a boundary also distinguishes the human from the nonhuman:

> We see this most clearly in the examples of those abjected beings[1] who do not appear properly gendered; it is their very humanness that comes into question. Indeed, the construction of gender operates through *exclusionary* means, such that the human is not only produced over and against the inhuman, but through a set of foreclosures, radical erasures, that are, strictly speaking, refused the possibility of cultural articulation. Hence, it is not enough to claim that human subjects are constructed, for the construction of the human is a differential operation that produces the more and less "human," the inhuman, the humanly unthinkable. These excluded sites come to the "human" as its constitutive outside, and to haunt those boundaries as the persistent possibility of their disruption and rearticulation.
>
> (Butler, 1993: 8; original emphasis)

From her perspective, then, those sex/gender "anomalies" that we discussed in chapter 2 may be understood as marking the boundaries not only between sex and gender, but also between the human and the nonhuman ("inhuman," in Butler's terms). They also therefore, by extension, establish the line between the cultural and the noncultural, the understood and accepted, on the one hand, and, on the other, the strange and rejected, the unknown and the unthinkable.

Those boundaries are maintained discursively, suggests Butler, because it is only by observing and operating within these boundaries that we come to know ourselves as subjects, that is, as beings existing in a culture and acknowledged by others in that culture. In order to shore up the tenuous relationship between anatomical sex and cultural gender, we are required discursively to announce ourselves repeatedly as men or women. Butler calls this the iteration or citation of gender (see, for example, Butler, 1993: 15):

The category of "sex" is, from the start, normative; it is what Foucault has called a "regulatory ideal." In this sense, then, "sex" not only functions as a norm, but is part of a regulatory practice that produces the bodies it governs, that is, whose regulatory force is made clear as a kind of productive power, the power to produce – demarcate, circulate, differentiate – the bodies it controls. Thus, "sex" is a regulatory ideal whose materialization is compelled, and this materialization takes place (or fails to take place) through certain highly regulated practices. In other words, "sex" is an ideal construct which is forcibly materialized through time. It is not a simple fact or static condition of a body, but a process whereby regulatory norms materialize "sex" and achieve this materialization through a forcible reiteration of those norms.

(Butler, 1993: 1–2)

Butler here argues that the "materialization" of the body (that is, the way in which we understand our own bodies and those of others to exist physically and to manifest certain characteristics) is not a simple matter of nature or of common sense. Rather, materialization occurs through the filtering process of discursive practices and their resulting norms. Put more starkly and in an oversimplified way, without the discourse of gender, there would be no point to identifying one or another body as male or female.

What Butler intimates here, and goes on to develop further in *Bodies That Matter* and her later book, *Undoing Gender* (Butler, 2004), is that, contrary to the idea that sex is primary and natural, and the foundation for gender as cultural identity and behavior, gender is in fact a highly coded set of behaviors *intended to assert sex*. To put it differently, one is discursively *compelled* to behave in a masculine or feminine way *in order to be taken for* a male or female. Refusal or inability to iterate or cite one's gender and hence, by implication, one's sex in this fashion are likely to put one outside the boundary dividing the known from the unknown, the cultural from the noncultural, the human from the nonhuman.

However, Butler goes on to remark:

That this reiteration is necessary is a sign that materialization is never quite complete, that bodies never quite comply with the norms by which their materialization is impelled. Indeed, it is the instabilities, the possibilities for rematerialization, opened up by this process that mark one domain in which the force of the regulatory law can be turned against itself to spawn rearticulations that call into question the hegemonic force of that very regulatory law.

(Butler, 1993: 2)

There is, then, always a gap, a lag, a failure in the way bodies obey the requirements for their "materialization." That very hesitancy, as Butler points out, can serve to open up a space where not only does the "rematerialization" of bodies become possible, but so does an interrogation of the apparently irrefutable and irresistible law that regulates how we perceive and understand the relation of sex and gender.

Butler goes on to propose:

> a return to the notion of matter, not as site or surface, but as *a process of materialization that stabilizes over time to produce the effect of boundary, fixity, and surface we call matter*. That matter is always materialized has, I think, to be thought in relation to the productive and, indeed, materializing effects of regulatory power in the Foucaultian sense. Thus, the question is no longer "How is gender constituted as and through a certain interpretation of sex?" (a question that leaves the "matter" of sex untheorized), but rather, "Through what regulatory norms is sex itself materialized? And how is it that treating the materiality of sex as a given presupposes and consolidates the normative conditions of its own emergence?"
>
> (Butler, 1993: 9–10; original emphasis)

That is, rather than conceive of sex as a simple material characteristic or given of the body, as we generally and "naturally" tend to do, Butler invites us to interrogate that very assumption: how is it, exactly, that we not only perceive sexual difference, but understand it in ways that simply naturalize it? To what advantage (or disadvantage) do we do so? And, more pertinently for our purposes, by what processes do we do so?

Gender as performative

The constant pressure on us as members of a culture to cite our gender produces what Butler calls the performativity of gender. However, she is careful to distinguish gender *performativity* from gender *performance*:

> For if I were to argue that genders are performative, that could mean that I thought that one woke in the morning, perused the closet or some more open space for the gender of choice, donned that gender for the day, and then restored the garment to its place at night. Such a willful and instrumental subject, one who decides *on* its gender, is clearly not its gender from the start and fails to realize that its existence is already decided *by* gender.
>
> (Butler, 1993: x; original emphasis)

Such an enactment of gender as Butler describes is a performance of gender, as we might see undertaken by female or male impersonators, or by drag queens or kings. Rather, gender performativity is a constraint imposed discursively on members of the culture.

The idea of performativity itself Butler borrows and adapts from the work of the linguist J.L. Austin. Butler summarizes Austin's theory thus:

> Performative acts are forms of authoritative speech: most performatives, for instance, are statements that, in the uttering, also perform a certain action

and exercise a binding power. Implicated in a network of authorization and punishment, performatives tend to include legal sentences, baptisms, inaugurations, declarations of ownership, statements which not only perform an action, but confer a binding power on the action performed.

(Butler, 1993: 225)

Thus, for instance, when one makes a promise and says, "I promise to do X," the *saying* of the promise is also the *undertaking* of the promise: it becomes binding. This is what Austin means when he calls such speech acts performatives (as opposed to constatives, which we may think of as descriptive statements about the world around us and the conditions obtaining in that world). For Butler, gender is performative in that *it is an undertaking*, as it were, *by the individual to enact the gender discursively (and hence culturally) assigned as appropriate to that individual's sexual (that is, genital) configuration.* To vary a point made a little earlier in this chapter, one does not act in a masculine or feminine manner *because* one is male or female; rather, one acts in such a manner *in order to be seen (by oneself as well as by others) as* male or female.

Passing

The implications of this are both interesting and complex. In the first place, Butler's theory suggests that gendered behavior purports to function as a gage or guarantee of sex identity in a social and cultural condition in which no such guarantee can have any meaning, or at any rate no stability of meaning. In other words, we all undertake to believe the performative nature of gender behavior *as though* it were a true, stable, and universal indicator of the sex of the subject. This has a further ramification: namely, it places us all in the situation of having to "pass" as male or female.

We are perhaps more familiar with the idea of passing in terms of a person of color who is taken for, or who wishes to be taken for, white; a Jewish person who is taken for, or who wishes to be taken for, non-Jewish; or a gay man who is taken for, or wishes to be taken for, a straight one. However, passing is not as rare or contained a phenomenon as one might think. As Brooke Kroeger observes, "There is gender passing, class passing, and age passing. ... There is even what is erroneously termed 'reverse passing,' as in straight for gay or white for black, along with dozens of acts of racial, ethnic, and national claim or camouflage" (Kroeger, 2003: 5). Although gender passing has chiefly been associated with gay-passing-for-straight and with transvestism or cross-dressing of some kind, in the light of Butler's observations, we might understand that *all of us seek, under pressure from the culture, to pass* as belonging to one sex grouping or the other. The point to grasp here is that the culture *requires* men and women to perform this act of passing on a daily basis, or to face the consequences: marginalization, ridicule, and humiliation through verbal or physical abuse, even, in a worst-case scenario, death.

The implications of this are significant. Gender behavior becomes in effect a form of protective mimicry, providing a camouflage for the subject as a social entity. The "passing" of persons of color as white, Jews as non-Jews, and gays as straight has taken place within the context of the desire of members of an oppressed, persecuted, or otherwise marginalized minority to employ a stratagem that allows them to find safety, peace, and the opportunity to better themselves. However, although notion of "passing" in terms of gender implies that we are all minority "Others" *unless we can learn to "pass" as the dominant*, that is, as fully masculine or fully feminine, by obeying the behavioral imperatives laid down for each sex.

If this is so, then it is the case that we are all discursively (but not necessarily successfully) coerced into masquerading as the dominant, while at the same time retaining some degree of awareness that it *is* a masquerade. Small wonder, then, that the culture reacts to any exposure of gender as a cultural fantasy about appropriate behavior. Such a revelation destabilizes the entire gender system, and reveals it to be a colossal confidence trick. And small wonder, too, that many individuals prove extremely reluctant (sometimes even violently so) to accept the idea of gender behavior as a form of "passing." Not only would this require radically rethinking oneself and one's place in the social world, but there is also the implicit suggestion that one has somehow been taken in, and therefore made in some measure to look foolish.

A further implication of Butler's notion of gender as performative is that that *performativity requires, whether literally or symbolically, an audience* of some kind. Gender behavior, that is, needs to be *witnessed*. It cannot be performed in a vacuum of solitude. This suggests that not only is gender performativity a spectacle to be *viewed* by others but it is also a performance to be *understood* and *judged* by those others, as we will see in the application in chapter 4 of Foucault's imagined panopticon to the notion of masculinity. Consequently, even when by ourselves, we usually do not abandon all efforts at gender performance and become something else, something *un*gendered: rather, *we continue to act as though we remained under observation by an unseen audience.*

What of those who may, whether through choice or circumstance, deny the imperatives and refuse the masquerade – refuse to "pass"? Is it possible for such individuals to remain *un*gendered? Or do they, rather, persistently resist the imperatives, in a sort of inversion of the repetitious iteration of gender? And what of the subject who *cannot* meet those norms, despite all good will and eagerness to do so? Some such subjects may be assigned to the opposite gender category through social uncertainty, ridicule, or opprobrium; for instance, the "girly" or "faggy" male homosexual. However, others simply fail to make the grade, and their bodies and behaviors are read accordingly as ludicrous, pathetic, or in some other way marginalized.

By undoing the naturalized assumptions about the relationship between sex and gender and challenging earlier theories of gender, Butler demonstrates how both "sex" and "gender" come into view and hence take on substance only through discourse, understood as reaching from language to cultural phenomena, attitudes, and behaviors. The title of her book *Bodies That Matter* thus signifies multiple meanings: this is a book that not only discusses the way bodies *have* matter, or are materialized and given substance, but also explores the way only certain bodies *do* matter, or have meaning and importance in the culture. Butler's work has been influential in enabling theorists to rethink questions of sex, gender, and relation between these. It has been central also in the development of queer theory, which has sought to undo traditional binaries such as male/female and heterosexual/homosexual, in order to make more spacious and inclusive the context within which we discover ourselves as subjects.[2]

However, we should not understand that the challenging of traditional norms of sex and gender has been a motif only of the latter part of the twentieth century. We noted in the previous chapter, for instance, that questions about masculinity and femininity as they applied to male and female bodies were already current in the late sixteenth and early seventeenth centuries. Shakespeare's comedy *As You Like It*, believed to have been composed between 1598 and 1600, may be read as in part reflecting the emerging crisis in gender of the time. It features a female character, Rosalind, played, as was the custom then, by a boy actor, who disguises herself as a male who then dresses up as a woman. Part of the delight of this play for Shakespeare's contemporary audiences, then, would no doubt have lain in the unraveling of the various layers of gender in watching a boy play a woman play a boy play a woman.

In the twentieth century, the relationship between anatomical difference and social or cultural gender is explored interestingly in three novels: Virginia Woolf's satirically humorous *Orlando: a biography* (1928), Ursula K. LeGuin's science-fiction narrative *The Left Hand of Darkness* (1969), and Jeanette Winterson's partly autobiographical *Written on the Body* (1992). It is no doubt significant that all three were authored by women, two of whom (Woolf and Winterson) refused the cultural imperative of heteronormativity (that is, the directive towards heterosexuality). Speaking, therefore, from the margins of a society that privileges both men and heterosexuality, these authors are well positioned to explore and challenge that privilege.

Orlando, in Woolf's novel, is born male in England during the reign of Queen Elizabeth I (1533–1603) and, remaining comparatively young, survives into the early twentieth century. At the age of 30, Orlando changes sex spontaneously, becoming a woman around the time of the beginning of the Enlightenment. She notes (Woolf uses both masculine and feminine pronouns to refer to Orlando at this point in the narrative) the differences between being a man and being a woman. These shift from simple behavioral differences, such as how to walk, the degree of leg that may be shown in public, and so on, to temperamental or "innate" differences, such as feeling submissive towards, and requiring the support and protection of, a man. Because of Orlando's ambiguity of sex and gender, there is a certain self-consciousness and a level of calculation in the way in which she behaves now towards both men and women. Nor is the ambiguity of gender limited to Orlando him/herself: for example, when Orlando (as a young man) initially sees the woman who becomes his first great love, the Russian Sasha (the name itself is ambiguous in gender, because it is a Russian diminutive of either "Alexander" or "Alexandra"). She appears androgynous, possessing "a figure ... whether boy's or woman's" (Woolf, 1992: 36).

Orlando him/herself is pursued by the Archduchess Harriet Griselda "of Finster-Aarhorn and Scand-op-Boom in the Roumanian territory" (Woolf, 1992: 110). The Archduchess turns out, upon Orlando's return, as a woman, from Turkey, to be in fact the Archduke Harry, who fell in love with the then male Orlando and disguised himself as a woman in order to be close to him (Woolf, 1992: 173–74). (In the movie *Orlando*, the issue of the ambiguity of gender in this work is pointed up early by the performance of the role of Queen Elizabeth I by a male actor, the flamboyantly and unapologetically gay Quentin Crisp [Orlando, 1992].)

In a passage that strangely prefigures Butler's reversals of and challenges to the common assumptions about the relationship of sex to gender, the narrator of Woolf's novel discusses the importance of clothing:

> She [Orlando] was becoming a little more modest, as women are, of her brains, and a little more vain, as women are, of her person. Certain suscepti-bilities were asserting themselves, and others were diminishing. The change of clothes had, some philosophers will say, much to do with it. Vain trifles as they seem, clothes have, they say, more important offices than merely to keep us warm. They change our view of the world and the world's view of us. For example, when Captain Bartolus saw Orlando's skirt, he had an awning stretched for her immediately, pressed her to take another slice of beef, and invited her to go ashore with him in the long-boat. These compliments would certainly not have been paid her had her skirts, instead of flowing, been cut tight to her legs in the fashion of breeches. And when we are paid compli-ments, it behoves us to make some return. Orlando curtseyed; she complied; she flattered the good man's humours as she would not have done had his neat breeches been a woman's skirts, and his braided coat a woman's satin bodice. *Thus, there is much to support the view that it is clothes that wear us and not we them; we may make them take the mould of arm or breast, but they mould our hearts, our brains, our tongues to their liking.*
>
> (Woolf, 1992: 179–80; emphasis added)

Here, Woolf addresses the critical notion that clothing functions, in the culture, as costume whose purpose it is to signify gender to others. After all, there is no more reason why men should not wear skirts than why women should not (and in fact do) wear pants or trousers, *except for the very good reason that in Western cultures skirts signify femininity, and therefore also femaleness.* Woolf takes this one step further, ironically and paradoxically suggesting that *the signs of gender produce the facts of sexual difference.* Just as Orlando becomes more female the more she wears feminine attire, so, Woolf invites us to consider, our understand-ing of own gender may be dependent on such "vain trifles" as the kind of clothing we choose (or are compelled by the culture) to don. In Butler's terms, Orlando enacts the gender behavior appropriate to the sex to which she currently belongs or is assigned.

Unlike Archduke Harry, who remains male even when impersonating a female in the guise of the Archduchess Harriet, Orlando's physical transformation requires a profound shift in his/her performance of gender. That such a shift may have seismic social and legal as well as personal consequences is indicated in the questioning of Orlando's claim to property:

> No sooner had she returned to her home in Blackfriars than she was made aware by a succession of Bow Street runners and other grave emissaries from the Law Courts that she was a party to three major suits which had been preferred against her during her absence, as well as innumerable minor litigations, some arising out of, others depending on them. The chief charges against were (1) that she was dead, and therefore could not hold any property whatsoever; (2) that she was a woman, which amounts to much the same thing; (3) that she was an English Duke who had married one Rosina Pepita, a dancer; and had had by her three sons, which sons now declaring that their father was deceased, claimed that all his property descended to them. Such grave charges as these would, of course, take time and money to dispose of. All her estates were put in Chancery and her titles pronounced in abeyance while the suits were under litigation. Thus it was in a highly ambiguous condition, uncertain whether she was alive or dead, man or woman, Duke or nonentity, that she posted down to her country seat, where, pending the legal judgement, she had the Law's permission to reside in a state of incognito or incognita, as the case might turn out to be.
>
> (Woolf, 1992: 160)

Orlando, then, is a kind of sex/gender nomad, wandering from one category and its associated requirements and restrictions to another. Like a true nomad, after her transformation into a woman, he/she becomes an outsider who understands the workings of society in ways that "true" or "real" men and women may not, because they have assimilated and are obedient to the dictates of the cultural sex/gender system. Woolf's Orlando therefore is a maverick figure in an otherwise recognizable and familiar context of social mores and gendered behaviors.

By contrast, Ursula LeGuin, the daughter of an anthropologist, evokes in *The Left Hand of Darkness* an alien society the sexual and gender structures of which are very different from ours, and which is observed and described to us by several nonnative narrators who share our own understandings and prejudices about sex and gender. The world of the planet Gethen, called Winter by the Ekumen or council of planetary worlds and societies represented by the Envoy Genly Ai, is populated by a species of human who are ambisexual, that is, who individually contain within them both male and female sexual and reproductive organs. The narrative is made up of a number of journal entries, indigenous folk tales and myths, and reports from previous expeditions to Gethen.

One report makes up chapter 7, "The Question of Sex." In it the Investigator of the first Ekumenical landing party, Ong Tot Oppong, speculates that perhaps Gethen was originally populated by the early Colonizers by way of an experiment. After explaining the phases of *somer* (sexual inactivity or latency) and *kemmer* (estrus, or sexual desire and reproductive fertility), the report goes on to detail how the latter phase causes some of the inhabitants of the planet to manifest femaleness and others, maleness, in sexual reproductive terms. However, such manifestations are not stable: a member of this society who becomes female in one phase of *kemmer* may become male in the next. The Investigator's account goes on to say:

> The structure of their societies, the management of their industry, agriculture, commerce, the size of their settlements, the subjects of their stories, everything is shaped to fit the somer-kemmer cycle. Everybody has his holiday once a month; no one, whatever his position, is obliged or forced to work when in kemmer. No one is barred from the kemmerhouse [an institution permitting people to meet for sex when not pair-bonded], however poor or strange. Everything gives way before the recurring torment and festivity of passion. That is easy for us to understand. What is very hard for us to understand is that, four-fifths of the time, these people are not sexually motivated at all. Room is made for sex, plenty of room; but a room, as it were, apart. The society of Gethen, in its daily functioning and in its continuity, is without sex.

> (LeGuin, 1969: 84)

The effective blanking out among the Gethenians of both sex and gender, except for a monthly period, has profound implications for the way in which their society is structured and functions – and foregrounds how our own society necessarily takes into account issues of both sex and gender. The Investigator remarks:

> Consider: Anyone can turn his hand to anything. This sounds very simple, but its psychological effects are incalculable. The fact that everyone between seventeen and thirty-five or so is liable to be … "tied down to childbearing," implies that no one is quite so thoroughly "tied down" here as women, elsewhere, are likely to be – psychologically or physically. Burden and privilege are shared out pretty equally; everybody has the same risk to run or choice to make. Therefore nobody here is quite so free as a free male anywhere else.
>
> Consider: A child has no psycho-sexual relationship to his mother and father. There is no myth of Oedipus on Winter.
>
> Consider: There is no unconsenting sex, no rape. As with most mammals other than man, coitus can be performed only by mutual invitation and consent; otherwise it is not possible. Seduction certainly is possible, but it must have to be awfully well timed.
>
> Consider: There is no division of humanity into strong and weak halves, protective/protected, dominant/submissive, owner/chattel, active/passive.

In fact the whole tendency to dualism that pervades human thinking may be found to be lessened, or changed, on Winter.

(LeGuin, 1969: 84–85)

LeGuin's novel, then, imagines a world in which "Our entire pattern of socio-sexual interaction is non-existent. ... They cannot play the game. They do not see one another as men or women. This is almost impossible for our imagination to accept. What is the first question we ask about a newborn baby?" (LeGuin, 1969: 85).

Winterson's novel, written from the first-person point of view, is about an intensely passionate and emotional extramarital affair. In its aftermath, the narrator has broken up with the married lover because the latter has been diagnosed with leukemia and her husband, a doctor, has claimed that he can cure her, but only if the narrator relinquishes any claim on his wife. The "default" reading position that we normally adopt would assume heterosexuality on the part of the narrator, which would in turn make this figure male. However, Winterson is careful never explicitly to disclose the sex and/or gender of her narrator. Consequently, as readers we are unable to determine whether the narrator behaves in a gender-appropriate manner or not, nor whether the narrator's various sexual liaisons are heterosexual, homosexual, or of some other category. The knowledge that Winterson is lesbian would, of course, predispose many readers to assume as a consequence that the narrator is female. Nevertheless, even such a supposition as this, based on biographical knowledge about the author (itself a questionable form of literary criticism), may be destabilized by the several mentions throughout the narrative of earlier boyfriends (Winterson, 1994: 92–93, 143, 152). Does this mean that the narrator is a heterosexual male who engages occasionally in homosexual encounters, or is he in fact bisexual? Or is the narrator a lesbian female who indulges in sporadic heterosexual affairs – or is she, rather, bisexual? The narrative's refusal to position the narrator within clear categories of sex, gender, and sexuality means that the reader is likely to feel unsettled by such questions, which remain unanswered.

The *Dexter* narratives, at which we glanced in chapter 2, offer another example of the unsettling effect of the blurring of gender boundaries, or the refusal to acknowledge these (Lindsay, 2004, 2005, 2007, 2009, 2010; *Dexter*, 2006–). The first four novels – *Darkly Dreaming Dexter* (2004), *Dearly Devoted Dexter* (2005), *Dexter in the Dark* (2007), and *Dexter by Design* (2009) (Lindsay, 2004, 2005, 2007, 2009) – all commence with an evocation of (if not also an invocation to) the moon. (*Dexter in the Dark* actually opens with a prologue titled "In the Beginning," but the first chapter returns us to the moon as a central image.) Moreover, they recurrently mention and describe the moon. The moon has, of course, traditionally been associated with madness (the word "lunacy" is derived etymologically from *luna*, the Latin for "moon"), and with monstrosity (think, for example, of the werewolf, who transforms from human to beast at the full moon, according to folk tale and cultural myth). Dexter, who narrates the events, refers to himself frequently as a monster, and sometimes wonders whether he is crazy. Thus, for instance, he describes himself early in the first of the series of novels, *Darkly Dreaming Dexter*, as "a very neat monster" (Lindsay, 2004: 11). Later in the same novel, Dexter ponders:

> I might be losing all, or many, of my marbles. What if I had been slipping into insanity a piece at a time for years, and this new killer had simply triggered the final headlong fall into complete craziness? How could I hope to measure the relative sanity of somebody like me? … But if I was losing my hold on sanity as I had built it, it was all my problem, and the first part of the problem was that there was no way to know for sure.
>
> (Lindsay, 2004: 80)

Later still, the metaphor of the lost marbles returns: "I had assumed I was simply going crazy, dropping several handfuls of marbles into the recycle bin" (Lindsay, 2004: 185).

However, the moon has also been culturally identified with woman and the feminine. Greco-Roman deities associated with the moon have usually been female, for instance, and menstruation is tied closely in the cultural imagination with the lunar cycle. Grotesquely, Dexter too is at the mercy of that cycle: his Dark Passenger, the entity or alter ego who motivates him to kill, is at his most powerful as the moon passes through its full phase. Indeed, Dexter's "femininity" is pointed up when his sister Deb (herself rather masculine in behavior) irritably tells him, "You're chattering like a schoolgirl" (Lindsay, 2004: 202).

Although Dexter is, by his own profession, reasonably attractive, he is (at least in this first volume) reasonably asexual. Damaged psychologically since childhood, Dexter, who frequently refers to himself in the third person, describes himself as "Quirky, funny, happy-go-lucky, dead-inside Dexter" (Lindsay, 2004: 13), and remarks:

> Whatever made me the way I am left me hollow, empty inside, unable to feel. It doesn't seem like a big deal. I'm quite sure most people fake an awful lot of everyday human contact. I just fake all of it. I fake it very well, and the feelings are never there. But I like kids. I could never have them, since the idea of sex is no idea at all. Imagine doing those things – How can you? Where's your sense of dignity?
>
> (Lindsay, 2004: 14)

Yet Dexter has a girlfriend, Rita. She is part of his disguise of normality. Attractive, the mother of two, Rita becomes the "perfect date." "[A]lmost as badly damaged as I am" (Lindsay, 2004: 52), she, too, is uninterested in sex – at least, at the outset. Indeed, Dexter describes her as "merely my beard, a silly kid's costume I wore on weekends …" (Lindsay, 2004: 127). The use of the word "beard" as a metaphor for "disguise" is interesting, because loaded: it is the term often used by closeted gay men to describe the women who accompany them in order to provide the illusion of heterosexuality. However, Dexter is not gay. Rather, he is simply uninterested in sex.

Lindsay has thus constructed a character in Dexter whose alienness and hence distance from us, the readers, are measured not only by his sociopathology and psychopathology as a serial killer but also by the ambiguity of his gender status and sexuality. This is suggested also in the TV series as early as the opening credits sequence. Although of course all the images of the penetration and slicing of flesh in that sequence refer to Dexter's nature as a serial killer, some of those images carry other possible meanings. For example, the penetration of Dexter's arm by the mosquito suggests a violation of the male body, which is commonly constructed as *im*penetrable, unlike the female one. A male body open to the entry of another body thus may suggest the feminization of that male body. Moreover, the shaving nick and oozing blood to which Dexter applies a tissue produces an image that might evoke in some viewers the suggestion of the sanitary pad used by women at times of menstruation.

In addition, many viewers are no doubt aware that the actor playing Dexter, Michael C. Hall, also played the gay character David Fisher in the TV series *Six Feet Under* (2001–5), and so might view his interpretation of Dexter through the lens of that earlier, gay character. The final image in this sequence, showing Dexter leaving his apartment, smiling and nodding acknowledgment to some unseen person, may be read, after the other images, as a deliberate performance that disguises the violence and bloodshed implicit in the earlier shots, even although these have offered images of the ordinary and quotidian. Thus, rather than exploring the ways in which gender boundaries may be interrogated and/or blurred, Lindsay has used such blurring and interrogation in order to create a character in Dexter who unnerves us, not only because we are asked, through the narrative point of view, to empathize with a serial killer, but also because his character is created in such a way as to disturb our assumptions about gender and sexuality.

Activity 3.2

- Have you read any novels, or viewed any movies or TV programs that challenged your assumptions or understandings of sex, gender, and the relation between these?

  ○ What was the nature of the challenge?
  ○ Reflect on your response or reaction: were you repelled? Intrigued? Excited by the possibilities? Frightened of them?
  ○ Has the material explored in this chapter helped you in some measure to understand that response or reaction?

Suggested further reading

Brady, A. and Schirato, T. (2011) *Understanding Judith Butler*, Los Angeles: Sage.

Ginsberg, E.K. (ed.) (1996) *Passing and the Fictions of Identity*, Durham and London: Duke University Press.

Lloyd, M. (2007) *Judith Butler: from norms to politics (key contemporary thinkers)*, Cambridge, UK and Malden, MA: Polity Press.

4   Regarding patriarchy

An important question that needs to be asked, in any discussion of gender issues, is the following: what are the conditions for the formation of (gendered) subjectivity? We have addressed this matter to some extent in exploring gender in terms of ideology and discourse, which in turn has brought into consideration the historical and material factors affecting the development of the gendered subject. However, one key element that we have not addressed directly (although in referring to the social dominance of men and the privileging of masculinity we have glanced at it obliquely) is the notion of *patriarchy*. One sense of "regarding" in the title of this chapter, then, is "concerning" or "about" patriarchy.

Activity 4.1

- Before continuing with this chapter, answer the following questions:

    ○   Are you acquainted with the word "patriarchy"?
    ○   If so, what do you understand by it?

Although it is a key concept, "patriarchy" is a problematic term in the discussions and debates around gender. That this is the case is reflected in the absence of handbooks about and introductions to the notion of patriarchy itself, although one can find many works that discuss patriarchy in relation to women, men, feminism, and so on. However, there is (at least at the time of writing of the present work) no *Complete Idiot's Guide to Patriarchy*, no *Patriarchy for Dummies*, nor is there a volume titled *Patriarchy* in Routledge's New Critical Idiom series. Of course, both authors and publishers are doubtless wary of producing a text that might seem to promote and confirm patriarchy as a positive structuring of gender, subjectivity, and, more broadly, society – or that might invite men, especially young men, to become better or more effective "patriarchs." This would surely irritate and anger women, especially feminists, as well as the many men who support feminist ideals or harbor their own misgivings about or criticisms of patriarchy. It would also seem historically regressive after the achievements of feminism and the various women's movements of the past 40 years. There are, of course, books that do promote such a backward-looking intellectual, philosophical, and social position; but they rarely, if ever, feature on their front covers the word "patriarchy."

What is "patriarchy"?

Much of the discussion centered on gender is embedded in a strong sense of historical and cultural specificity. However, "patriarchy" by contrast tends, especially in nonscholarly contexts, to be used as a free-floating, transhistorical, and transcultural term and point of reference. Thus, although cruder forms of feminist critique may imply that "patriarchy" or, sometimes, "the patriarchy" has always been around and has always oppressed women, what has been more rarely addressed are questions such as: has patriarchy always taken the same forms, historically and socially speaking? If patriarchy has indeed always oppressed women, has it always been in the same ways? In other words, universalizing and generalizing the concept of "patriarchy" can be helpful only in broad-brush representations of gender politics and issues. Any closer inspection of such representations inevitably reveals flaws and gaps in the history, the logic, and the argument.

Moreover, we need to distinguish between what we might call a *formal* patriarchy and a *symbolic* or *informal* one. The word "patriarchy" itself means "rule of (or by) the father." Formal patriarchies are those social structures in which the power held and wielded by a male individual over all other members of the community is commonly acknowledged as deriving from his position as the sire of his people either literally (that is, he has fathered many, if not indeed most, members of the community) or symbolically (he is regarded as the father-figure of his people). There are many examples of such social structures in the ancient world: to take an instance from the founding text of Judeo-Christian culture, in the Bible the dynasty that establishes the Hebrew people is that of Abraham, Isaac, and Jacob, who are referred to commonly as "the patriarchs." In such a structure, the patriarch's rule may be absolute. Moreover, often he controls the sexuality of his people, and particularly that of other men who might conceivably become rivals to his power, by the taking of women into his own household, or the distributing of women among selected and favored males within the tribe or clan.

A much later variation of this form of control can be seen in the medieval practice of the *jus primae noctis* (Latin for "the law of the first night"), known in French as the *droit du seigneur* ("the lord's prerogative"), by right of which the lord of a domain or territory might take the virginity of the bride of any of his serfs or peasants. Such a practice, of course, asserted the nobleman's power over those he owned by right of title or by seizure of land, but it also established the possibility of producing a population through whose veins ran the blood of the noble master, consolidating still further his claim to power over the peasantry and to their allegiance and loyalty.

A symbolic or informal patriarchy, by contrast, is a social structure or community within which power is dispersed among the male subjects. Such power is not necessarily vested self-evidently and officially in a single male individual, although often, of course, we do find men heading large organizations and corporations as well as governments. However, we are left with the troubling question: where does this power originate? It cannot be simply the sum of the power possessed and wielded by all men. Power, especially in the Foucauldian sense, does not work like that. Moreover, this does not explain the apparent unequal access to and sharing of power among men. Rather than see masculine power as something *owned* by individual males, therefore, it is more productive to think of such power as *something held out as promised* to men, and as *always only provisionally held* by individual males. Thus, although individual men may indeed run and control organizations and communities ranging from the family through to complex multinational corporations, and although they may accrue varying levels of power thereby, they nevertheless remain implicated in an overarching system of power *that remains finally beyond their own control.*

A more nuanced understanding of the way a symbolic patriarchy works, then, is to see it as a discursive formation by means of which sex, sexuality, and gender become intelligible and legible within a particular economy of power. "Economy" is here to be grasped as a system of checks and balances that regulates the flows of power to and among individuals. As with the national financial economy, with which we are more familiar, in an economy of power there are connections and interrelations among the various social systems (for example, religion, government, commerce, or education) that constitute the sources of power in the society. These in turn produce the various cultural discourses that characterize a society at a specific historical moment. An economy of power generates not only benefits but also costs. The advantaging of some necessarily implies the disadvantaging of others – indeed, often, the disadvantaging of the many in favor of the few.

We may understand an informal patriarchy, then, as a particular kind of economy that ranges across the multiple, interrelated institutional systems to whose organization we give the name "society." The power inherent in those systems not only governs the activities and practices of the individual system itself but may also be harnessed in the service of giving meaning to sex difference, and hence also to gender and sexuality. Take, for instance, the case of a high-born woman in the medieval feudal system. In this system land ownership, together with the ownership of the peasants or serfs resident on one's land, was central. It defined one's social and political position. A noblewoman, no matter her personal attributes, such as intelligence, beauty, or social grace, was thus the vector of dynastic concerns, chief among which were the transfer of property from generation to generation, and from family to family, and the provision of offspring who would be the inheritors of that property.

Under the burgeoning capitalism and colonial expansionism of the later eighteenth and nineteenth century in Britain, the question of dynastic wealth and power remained, but this time as a middle-class concern; this is one of the themes in as early a work as Samuel Richardson's novel *Clarissa, or the History of a Young Lady* (1747–48) (Richardson, 2004). The decay, in Britain at least, of the hereditary aristocracy and its power, together with the increasing wealth of the middle class, who sought not only to acquire the property of the old nobility but also to emulate their manners and customs, meant that traditional class boundaries were becoming more permeable, opening the way for a particular understanding of the principle of individualism. It is at this time that the figure of the self-made man, the individualist who struggles with and overcomes all odds, begins to populate not only the pages of novels in both Europe and the United States, but also the actual social world. The counterpart to this outgoing, thrusting, ambitious and (presumably eventually) successful male was the nurturing female, whether mother or wife. She preserved the family hearth and home, and ensured for her man a safe haven away from the pressures of the social and financial world when he returned. The private and the public worlds thus came to be defined and distinguished from one another in gendered ways that would have seemed somewhat foreign 200 years earlier.

The patriarchal order and the patriarchal economy

"Patriarchy," then, is today less an overt, explicit social structure than a rather nebulous set of discursive strands that constitute for people in the culture an order and way of thinking of themselves as subjects within a sexed and gendered economy. Even so, we should not make the error of believing that, because we may think of "patriarchy" as an abstract thing, it has no material effects in the real social world. Because it is a way of organizing and directing how we think of ourselves and others, and the ways we behave both towards and against others, the discursive formations of patriarchy exert a powerful influence in our lives. Those formations, moreover, change and adapt to changing sociohistorical contexts. Thus, even when it may appear that gender identity and behavior remain stable historically, it is likely that the discursive formations have adjusted to changing conditions in order to preserve and maintain that identity and behavior.

Of course, it is not difficult to see that, in general, men have fared better historically, in terms of the access to and the wielding of power, than have women. From this we may infer that, at any given historical moment, the patriarchal economy aligns itself with current institutional systems and their characteristic flows of power. However, we must recall that even among men the access to power is unequal. From this we may infer further that, by distributing power differentially and unequally among *both* men *and* women, the patriarchal economy produces subjectivities for both *groups* (men and women considered in broad terms, such as gender, sexuality, race, class, age, and the like) and *individuals* (men and women considered in particular terms, such as a black middle-aged working-class woman, a young Hispanic upper-middle-class man, an elderly wealthy white gay male, and so on).

Activity 4.2

- Think about the three specific examples given parenthetically at the end of the last paragraph.

    o Where do you think each is positioned in relation to power and privilege, and which traits or characteristics do you consider to be the most empowering or most disempowering?

- Imagine two or three other subject types in terms of gender, sexuality, race, class, and age (you may, of course, add other traits), and perform the same exercise as in the activity above.

- Have these exercises enabled you to think of subjectivity and power in ways different from how you have usually thought of them in relation to one another?

    o If so, analyse those differences in conceptualizing the connection between the subject and power.

So, rather than imagine patriarchy as a static, transhistorical monolith and thereby reify it (that is, turn it into an actual, physical thing or object: "*the* patriarchy"), we should instead understand it as functioning under two closely interrelated aspects. The first of these is as a social and conceptual *structure* that is capable of adapting to current social, economic, and cultural conditions. As a structure, therefore, patriarchy organizes sexual and social identity both differentially and preferentially. It thus produces gendered subjectivity within an order of rank and precedence that establishes not only the privileging of men over women but also the privileging of some men over others, on such grounds as race, social class, physique, or sexual orientation. We may think of this as the *patriarchal order*: a social structure that advantages men, as a class, over women, as a class; and that privileges men who possess or demonstrate certain characteristics over those who do not.

The second aspect of patriarchy concerns the ways in which the patriarchal order generates and distributes the flows of power within both social and institutional organizations. This we may call the *patriarchal economy*. Its connection to the patriarchal order is so close that one defines the other, such that they operate complementarily and synchronously. The patriarchal economy determines the nature and the extent of the power available to men and women, both as a class and as individuals. Although it may be impossible to disentangle the patriarchal order from the patriarchal economy, it is useful to be able to distinguish at least conceptually between them. That way we are less likely to make overbroad generalizations about the history and nature of patriarchy.

Two brief examples, both drawn from British history, may help to demonstrate a more nuanced understanding of "patriarchy." Queen Elizabeth I, who reigned in England 1558–1603, and Margaret Thatcher (later Baroness Thatcher), Prime Minister of Britain 1979–90, were both women with considerable political, economic, and social power. Yet neither noticeably advanced the cause of gender equality, whether by addressing (and redressing) the status of women in general, or by promoting women to positions of subordinate power. In the case of Elizabeth, "In order to maintain her position in a culture which conferred power chiefly upon men, [she] employed a number of strategies designed either to appropriate power under the sign of monarchy itself, or else to erase as far as possible the signs of her own femininity, and thus to assert her claim to masculine power" (Buchbinder, 1989). Thatcher, by contrast, established herself almost in rivalry with Queen Elizabeth II, and adopted by turns both hectoring and nanny-ing strategies with regard to her ministers and public servants, and, indeed, to the public at large. She thereby represented herself as a kind of austere, disciplinarian maternal figure who remained nonetheless curiously unfeminine. Indeed, she became known as the Iron Lady. A feminist might argue that, given the pervasive effect of patriarchy, the only way a woman could rise to a position of power was to minimize her femininity and thus become symbolically masculinized. Although this is no doubt true, the point here is that these two powerful women preserved the patriarchal *order* while manipulating and benefiting from the patriarchal *economy*. The distinction between these aspects of patriarchy, then, suggests a second meaning of the term "regarding" in the title of this chapter, namely, the idea of looking at or observing patriarchy.

Activity 4.3

- Think about powerful female figures today, whether in political or institutional structures (Condoleezza Rice, under the George W. Bush administration, or Hillary Clinton, under the Obama administration, are examples of women in power within a political structure):

  - To what degree do such women foreground or background their status and identities as women in order to achieve their positions and administer power?
  - How do they negotiate the patriarchal order?
  - What power flows to them in the patriarchal economy?

Men, women, and the patriarchal order

As we have already begun to see, it would be mistaken to assume that, because men tend to benefit from the power afforded by a patriarchal order, all men there-fore share equally in the wielding of power. To make such a claim would be to represent gender relations and politics in an extremely simplified form, reduced to an understanding of women as locked in a permanent and perpetual hostile tension with men, and vice versa. Moreover, such a representation implies that women are, by definition, absolutely *excluded* from the patriarchal order. Yet, clearly, women are critically necessary to that order – otherwise, how is it to define itself, and to work? There is no parallel or complementary matriarchal order against which to distinguish itself, and by which a different structuring of power operates to the benefit of women.

A subtler way of understanding how a symbolic patriarchal economy works is to see it as hierarchical, so that *both* women *and* men must function within a structure that distributes power *differentially and unequally.* This is not to say, of course, that the empowerment or disempowerment of men is identical to the empowerment or disempowerment of women within a patriarchal economy; nor, for that matter, that, in most Western societies, the empowerment or disempower-ment of white men is equivalent to that of men of color or of different ethnicity or sexuality. In this respect, feminist critics and theorists are no doubt right to deride the claims of some men that they (or, indeed, all men) are as disadvantaged as women by the patriarchal order. Nevertheless, it remains the case that, within such an order, men are not seen as all created equal, except in one respect: as *males*, they have traditionally possessed to some degree an advantage over females, in relation to authority over others, prospects of employment, and so on.

The patriarchal order: hierarchy and rivalry

If we imagine the patriarchal order as a hierarchical pyramid, we can understand the distribution of power, in the first place, as stratified horizontally. Accordingly, therefore, those with a good deal of power are situated towards the apex, whereas those (including most women) with less are positioned at different levels, all the way to the base. This structure may be understood as chiefly benefiting men (at all levels of the pyramid), who as a result tend, as a group, to wield power. The sociologist R.W. Connell[1] refers to this as the "patriarchal dividend," a phrase that neatly encapsulates, in a metaphor drawn from the stock exchange, the ideas both of investment and the return on that investment (see, for example, R.W. Connell, 2000: 25). That dividend includes:

> men's control of governments, corporations, media; men's better jobs, incomes and command of wealth; men's control of the means of vio-lence; and the entrenched ideologies that pushed women into the home and dismissed their claims for equality.
>
> (R.W. Connell, 1995: 41)

However, the patriarchal dividend also implies the exercise of power by some men over others at the same level or in the same category; for example, within an organizational structure, peers or colleagues, within the category of physical type, physically imposing, "macho" males in relation to other men of a slighter physical build or "feminine" appearance, and so on. The uneven distribution of power means that the benefits and advantages of accessing power encourage individual subjects to wield as much of it as possible, whether to maintain their current position in the pyramid, to reach a higher one, or even only to fend off the more aggressive applications of power by other men.

In the second place, we may think of the patriarchal pyramid as marked by vertical as well as horizontal axes. That is, men may contest one another for power in terms of positioning not only along and within the various levels of power available in the horizontal stratification, but also across levels in the vertical formation of the hierarchy. For example, in a corporate structure a man higher up in the scale of power allocated by formal rankings in the organization (the gamut of positions, from the president and/or CEO of a company down to the office "boy" employed to run errands as well as sort and deliver the company's mail) is likely to be driven both by an ambition for promotion upward not only in the organizational structure of the company but also in the hierarchy of power, and the equal or perhaps even greater desire to hamper and frustrate any efforts of his peers to compete with, discredit, and/or displace him. At the same time, of course, he will be keeping an eye on subordinates who might nurse ambitions regarding his own position in the organization and in the structure of power.

Activity 4.4

- Consider other structures and situations with which you may be familiar in which you perceive the horizontal and vertical workings of a patriarchal order. For example, these might include the dynamics of the classroom and/or the playground; behaviors and attitudes that characterize a sports team or game; the organization of clubs, fraternities or other similar societies; etc.

  ○ Analyse the specific nature of the power dynamic, and how it is put in play.
  ○ How does that dynamic affect the behavior of the males involved?
  ○ Does that dynamic affect women too, and if so, in what way or ways?
  ○ Do questions of race or ethnicity, age, physical ability or configuration, sexuality, etc., influence the dynamic in any way?

These horizontal and vertical flows of power within the patriarchal economy necessarily imply, in turn, a state of constant struggle among males to acquire or seize power, and to retain it against all other rivals. In short, it pits the individual man against most, if not, indeed, all other men. However, we should not think of this struggle as limited to environments such as the corporation: it functions in all dimensions of an individual male's life. For example, in sporting events such as football, basketball, or baseball, the ostensible unity and homogeneity of the idea of the team, as a kind of organism, is contradicted by the singling out of the individual player as "most valuable player" or "man of the match (or game)," or by behaviors calculated to foreground individual players in various ways against their team members (for instance, through their endorsement of products in advertising).

Even close friends often find themselves competing with one another. For instance, how many times have you witnessed (or even participated in) drinking matches whose goal has been to demonstrate one man's superior capacity to hold his liquor over that of another or others? Knowledge and/or skill in certain fields may also lend themselves to rivalry, whether overt or covert. For example, one often hears men instructing others about repair, politics, social observations and truths, and the like. Sexual matters, too, may occasion more or less friendly rivalry amongst men: in terms of who engages first in sexual intercourse (a common competition amongst adolescent males, as is also the contest to see who can ejaculate the greatest volume of semen, or who can ejaculate the farthest), who is successful in bedding a woman desired by several men, and so on. Penis size also becomes something over which men compete, from childhood and adolescence onward, whether by explicit comparison or by more or less covert "sneak peeks" in communal showers, changing rooms, and public toilets. (We return to the issue of penis size later in this chapter.)

Activity 4.5

- Can you think of any other situations or contexts in which males may be understood as competing with one another?

  - Is the situation or context one in which the boys or men are conscious of the competition?
  - What are the terms of the competition: for example, physical prowess and strength, intellectual agility, technical ability, etc.?
  - What is the "prize" gained by the "winner"? For example, in an athletic meet, there may be an explicit prize: a trophy, prize money, or the like. However, in less obvious contests the prize might be something less tangible (respect or adulation, for example) or something more tangible but less official than a trophy (for instance, invitations to social events, or even the offer of sex).
  - What is the consequence for the "loser"?

We noted above that Connell's formulation "the patriarchal dividend" is a metaphor drawn from the stock market. If that dividend confers power, authority, and control on men in general, and on particular men in specific situations, as the return on an "investment," we might wonder what that investment could be, and what its cost might be to the individual male. The answer to both questions is: the submission of that male to the dynamic of the patriarchal hierarchy, in what I have elsewhere called the "Masculinity Stakes, a race or competition in which only winners count" (Buchbinder, 1994: 35).

However, this is not a contest from which an individual male can choose to withdraw fully. The patriarchal order preexists our individual births; and to be born is to be required to negotiate that order so as to find our place in it. That some men might later in their lives opt bravely to refuse its dynamic and demands nevertheless requires them first to have understood its workings by participating in them. Moreover, any such refusal will no doubt be judged as a repudiation in some degree of their own manhood and, hence, masculinity. The consequences, therefore, of an individual man's disengagement from the patriarchal dynamic is likely to be severe, and felt by that man, despite his courage in resisting the pressure of the patriarchal order.

The phallus and phallic power

In order to create the divisions and consequent categories through which power flows in different measures to individuals, recognizable signs of difference need to be established. The primary sign, of course, is that of sexual difference. Within a patriarchal order, the group designated "male," by which is meant "possessing a penis," constitutes the principal beneficiary of those flows of power. For many, this is sufficient to define what they understand as "patriarchy." However, there are certain problems inherent in so stark an understanding of the nature of the patriarchal order. For example, as we saw in chapter 2, there are individuals in possession of a penis who nonetheless either regard themselves or are regarded by others as not-male. Clearly, a more subtle understanding is required about who benefits from patriarchal power.

Moreover, if the simple possession of a penis were sufficient to authorize men to share equally in the privileges and power of patriarchy, how are we to explain the clearly observable fact that not all men share equally in those privileges and that power? Such factors as sexuality, age, race or ethnicity, and social class or level of wealth play a critical part in the nature of an individual man's access to power, and in the attribution of power to that man by others in the social structure. And what of female-to-male transsexuals: to what degree does such a subject's possession of a penis, artificially produced and implanted in the body, enable him to share in that privilege and power? Instead of considering the penis as an absolute guarantee of masculine power, therefore, let us think of the actual, fleshly penis as a kind of promissory note to its possessor, or like the lottery ticket that admits the possessor of a penis to the chance of winning millions of dollars, but does not *guarantee* that success. The possession of a penis is simply *a necessary precondition* to the accrual of power under a patriarchal order. Power itself is actually vested elsewhere, in a symbol called *the phallus*.

A Greco-Roman word signifying the penis,[2] the phallus should be thought of as *the abstract representation of male power*, focused and figured as a penis, because this is how, culturally, we identify the male, as against the female. Imagined culturally as gigantic and as permanently erect, unlike the actual penis, the phallus is that to which all penises refer, and for which every fleshly penis is, in some sense, a metaphor or a sign. However, no physical penis, no matter how large, can ever rival the imagined grandeur and splendor of the phallus, which we may think of as engorged, not with blood (as a real, erect penis would be), but with power. By representing the sum of potential masculine power, the phallus becomes also an object of desire, because (notionally anyway) the individual who attained it would wield all the power that it both possesses and represents.

However, such an ambition is necessarily doomed in advance, not merely because the phallus is symbolic only, but also because it would bring to an end the very dynamic (masculine rivalry through hierarchical positioning) that motivates and sustains patriarchy itself. The phallus, then, may be thought of as always *to be attained*, but as ultimately *unattainable*. It is this essential contradiction that motivates the desire for power within the patriarchal economy: there is always the hope that the promissory note represented by the possession of a penis will be honored; that the number on the lottery ticket will, in the end, prove to be the winning one.

For a man to gain phallic power, it is not required that he demonstrate explicitly that his penis approaches the size of the symbolic phallus, or even that it is bigger than those of other men. Such power may be signified, first, by a series of symbols that indicate power, such as actual power within an organization ranging from the family to the multinational corporation and the government; or that signal power through such possessions as wealth, large houses, cars and other vehicles, expensive clothing, or such attributes as the company of attractive, well-dressed women, and so on.

Second, these symbolic signifiers and displacements of phallic power tend to form chains of equivalences, so that, in a kind of patriarchal algebra, the final term turns out always to be the phallus. For example, a wealthy man who owns an expensive and powerful car or motorbike clearly wields economic power, and hence has access to the symbolic phallus. We may render this sequence thus: powerful vehicle = wealth = power = the phallus. A different sequence might focus on a man's sexuality. For instance, a bevy of attractive women who are themselves drawn to a particular male would signify not only his sex appeal but would also imply something about his genital power, whether this was simply penis size or, less obviously, his sexual technique. Here the equivalence in relationship between actual penis and symbolic phallus is much closer, and we may express this sequence thus: desirable women = the capacity to be sexually attractive (for whatever reasons) = desirable penis = power = the phallus. One might multiply such equations infinitely, not only by finding different configurations of power and its manifestations, but also through combinations. For instance, a wealthy man with a lot of "stuff" that signals his wealth (a mansion, perhaps, a holiday home, expensive vehicles, financial generosity, and so on) might attract women, for a number of reasons: the seductive effect of wealth and its companion, power; financial security; social status, and so on. We would then perceive a sequence expressed as follows: the ownership and possible flaunting of expensive goods = attraction of women = the attribution of a generous genital endowment and/or formidable sexual technique = power = the phallus.

Activity 4.6

- Consider the cultural mythology of penis size attributed to difference of race: for example, the black man's "super-penis" or the Asian male's "micro-penis":

   - How do such popular myths construct the masculinity of the "raced" subject concerned, and what other attributes (for example, overt sexuality, the acquisition of such goods as jewellery, clothing or automobiles, the display of wealth, ambition to succeed socially and economically, etc.) might such a male seek in order to confirm those myths or subvert them?
   - In what ways do these myths affect the construction of domi-nant white masculinity, and what strategies might be invoked to support or counter that construction?

- Think about males of your acquaintance who, in your view, either wield obvious phallic power or, conversely, seem to wield little or no such power:

   - To what can you attribute this presence or absence of masculine power?
   - How is it manifested: that is, through which possessions, behav-iours, or actions is the presence or otherwise of power made clear?
   - What do you perceive to be the "payoff" for the possession of such power, in terms of how it positions the individual male in relation to other males, and in relation to females?

However, phallic power, as we have seen in the earlier examples in this chapter of Queen Elizabeth I and Margaret Thatcher, is not limited strictly to biological males only. Women who achieve status and power in various kinds of organiza-tions may be considered also to wield phallic power, not because they possess a penis, but because the organization itself runs, as it were, on the fuel of phallic power. Thus, the resentment often felt and expressed by both women and men towards a woman in a position of power may be traced to a sense of disorientation created by the apparent contradiction of a nonpossessor of a penis occupying a position traditionally evolved for and held by those who do possess one, within the context of an organization motivated by phallic power. Such a woman is likely, as a consequence, to be represented as "mannish," and caricatured accordingly – sometimes even with the implication that she might be a lesbian, and all that this implies in the cultural imagination about lesbians and their lack of femininity.

Moreover, women in positions of power often tend to dress in ways that downplay their femininity; for example, in suits that are often described as "power dressing," a telling term. By contrast, we may think of such a costume as a form of protective mimicry, to enable such a woman to "fit in" within a context of masculine, that is, phallic, power. Veronica Palmer, the character played by Portia de Rossi in the TV series *Better Off Ted*, is clearly intended as a caricature of such a woman. Largely humorless, severe in her hairstyle and way of dressing, often quite incapable of understanding emotion or of empathizing or sympathizing with others (unlike a "real" woman, presumably), Veronica, the executive responsible for Research and Development at Veridian Dynamics, is terrifying to many of her underlings, not least because she seems so masculine both in appearance and in the way she wields power (*Better Off Ted*, 2009–10). (Incidentally, this is not to say that we would find a man with similar characteristics – humorlessness, severity of demeanor, and coldness of behavior – any more palatable; however, we are more likely to accept such traits in a man.)

Jeff Lindsay's *Dexter* novels provide a further couple of examples. Deb Morgan, Dexter's sister, is represented as aggressive and ambitious, both traits usually assigned to men. *Darkly Dreaming Dexter*, for instance, she resents being made to wear what she calls a "sex suit" (Lindsay, 2004: 19) in order to work undercover as a prostitute:

> A good-looking young woman working vice on the Tamiami Trail usually ends up as bait on a sting, standing outside almost naked to catch men who wanted to pay for sex. Deborah hated that. Couldn't get worked up about prostitution, except as a sociological issue. Didn't think bagging johns was real crime fighting. And, known only to me, she hated anything that overemphasized her femininity and her lush figure. She wants to be a cop; it was not her fault she looked more like a centerfold. …
> … I had never seen a beautiful woman dressed in such a revealing costume who looked less sexually appealing than Deb did.
> (Lindsay, 2004: 16–17)

She is capable of physical violence, as, for example, when, in frustration, she "kicked out savagely and put a small dent in my metal desk" (Lindsay, 2004: 45), or when she punches Dexter in the ribs and shoves him because she believes he failed to notify her when he came up with a lead on the killer that the Miami police are hunting (Lindsay, 2004: 97–99). Driven by her desire to become a "real" cop and thus to emulate her beloved father Harry (Dexter's foster father), Deb tends to deny both her body and her femininity, and so masculinizes herself by desiring the phallic power embodied in and by the figure of the "real" cop.

In Detective Migdia LaGuerta, both Deb's and Dexter's superior, we are offered a different instance, this time of a woman who wields that phallic power, albeit ambiguously:

> There was a rumor going around a few years back that Detective Migdia LaGuerta got into the Homicide Bureau by sleeping with somebody. To look at her once you might buy into that. She has all the necessary parts in the right places to be physically attractive in a sullen, aristocratic way. A true artist with her makeup and very well dressed, Bloomingdale's chic. But the rumor can't be true. To begin with, although she seems outwardly very feminine, I've never met a woman who was more masculine inside. She was hard, ambitious in the most self-serving way, and her only weakness seemed to be for model-handsome men a few years younger than she was. So I am quite sure she didn't get into Homicide using sex. She got into Homicide because she's Cuban, plays politics, and knows how to kiss ass. That combination is far better than sex in Miami.
>
> (Lindsay, 2004: 26)

Unlike Deb, LaGuerta knows how to work the system to her own advantage; and, again unlike Deb (at least in this novel), she is sexual: indeed, predatory. For example, Dexter, drawn by a combination of dream and intuition, pursues a refrigerator truck late at night, only to be driven off the road by the driver of the truck, who hurls a woman's severed head at his car. He subsequently finds himself the object of LaGuerta's sexual attentions:

> At a little after 8 AM LaGuerta came over to where I was sitting on the trunk of my car. She leaned her tailored haunch onto the car and slid over until our thighs were touching. I waited for her to say something, but she didn't seem to have any words for the occasion. Neither did I. So I sat there for several minutes looking back at the bridge, feeling the heat of her leg against mine and wondering where my shy friend had gone with his truck. But I was yanked out of my quiet daydream by a pressure on my thigh.
>
> I looked down at my pants leg. LaGuerta was kneading my thigh as if it were a lump of dough.
>
> (Lindsay, 2004: 88)

It becomes apparent, as the narrative unfolds, that LaGuerta seems to believe that she has a sort of *droit du seigneur* over Dexter, in much the same way as a male boss might think that a female employee is part of his private sexual domain (a situation explored and implicitly criticized in the TV series *Mad Men*, set in the 1950s, and hence in the era before Women's Liberation and second-wave feminism [*Mad Men*, 2007–]). Put otherwise, LaGuerta's interior masculinity finds its expression, in part, in exterior, predatory sexual behavior. Dexter "manages" both Deb and LaGuerta, although in different ways; but the masculine behavior of each is implicitly criticized (Deb's for making her less than feminine, and LaGuerta's for using her femininity as a mask for her masculine ambitions).

Conferring masculinity: patriarchy as panopticon

In the end, however, no matter how "power-dressed" a woman might be, she is unable to confer masculinity upon men. Only other men can do that, although women may *confirm* a man's masculinity, whether through verbal praise, attitudinal behavior, emotional demonstrativeness toward the man, or making herself sexually available to him. Because, within the patriarchal order, an individual man must take his place (indeed, must carve out a place for himself) alongside other men, it follows that his attempt to do so is both monitored and evaluated by other men, which in turn affords them considerable power over him.

This necessarily puts the individual male in a difficult and inevitably anxiety-producing position. His status as masculine depends on the judgment of those against whom the patriarchal order pits him as a competitor for phallic power. Their assessment of him as masculine or not-masculine will then be conditional on whether other men judge him as like themselves, superior to themselves, or different from/inferior to themselves. In this way, *the criteria for being judged masculine function to reproduce the current notion in the culture of what constitutes masculinity.*

To understand how this works, let us turn to Foucault's deployment, in *Discipline and Punish: the birth of the prison* (Foucault, 1977), of the idea of the panopticon, a design for a disciplinary or correctional facility developed in 1785 by the British Utilitarian philosopher and social reformer Jeremy Bentham:

> at the periphery, an annular [ring-shaped] building; at the centre, a tower; this tower is pierced with wide windows that open onto the inner side of the ring; the peripheric building is divided into cells, each of which extends the whole width of the building; they have two windows, one on the inside, corresponding to the windows of the tower; the other, on the outside, allows the light to cross the cell from one end to the other. All that is needed, then, is to place a supervisor in a central tower and to shut up in each cell a madman, a patient, a condemned man, a worker or a schoolboy. By the effect of backlighting, one can observe from the tower, standing out precisely against the light, the small captive shadows in the cells of the periphery. They are like so many cages, so many small theatres, in which each actor is alone, perfectly individualized and constantly visible. The panoptic mechanism arranges spatial unities that make it possible to see constantly and to recognize immediately. ... Full lighting and the eye of a supervisor capture better than darkness ... Visibility is a trap.
>
> (Foucault, 1977: 200)

If we think of the patriarchal order as functioning in a manner comparable with the panopticon, Foucault's remark about the isolation and theatricalization of each "actor" becomes peculiarly apt, especially if we take into consideration Judith Butler's notion of the performativity of gender. That is, *each individual male is required to perform his masculinity before an observer of some kind*; an observer, moreover, who judges each man's rendition of masculinity.

Foucault goes on to add that each individual in the cells of the panopticon can be viewed by the supervisor but not by the inmates of neighboring cells, so that there can be no communication among those in the cells. The individual "is seen, but he does not see; he is the object of information, never a subject in communication" (Foucault, 1977: 200). Foucault remarks further:

> Hence the major effect of the Panopticon: to induce in the inmate a state of conscious and permanent visibility that ensures the automatic functioning of power. So to arrange things that the surveillance is permanent in its effects, even if it is discontinuous in its action; that the perfection of power should tend to render its actual exercise unnecessary; that this architectural apparatus should be a machine for creating and sustaining a power relation independent of the person who exercises it; in short, that the inmates should be caught up in a power situation of which they are themselves the bearers.
>
> (Foucault, 1977: 201)

Foucault here is working his way to explaining that the device of *the panopticon is both the product and the agent of power*. Its chief function is to cause the cell inmates individually to monitor their own behavior, so that the surveillance from the central tower, which represents the source of power, need not be constant (indeed, need not even take place) *because the inmates will carry out that surveillance upon themselves, by themselves*. In the panoptic structure, power, says Foucault,

> should be visible and unverifiable. Visible: the inmate will constantly have before his eyes the tall outline of the central tower from which he is spied upon. Unverifiable: the inmate must never know whether he is being looked at at any one moment; but he must be sure that he may always be so. In order to make the presence or absence of the Inspector unverifiable, so that the prisoners, in their cells, cannot even see a shadow, Bentham envisaged not only venetian blinds on the windows of the central observation hall, but, on the inside, partitions that intersected the hall at right angles and, in order to pass from one quarter to the other, not doors but zig-zag openings; for the slightest noise, a gleam of light, a brightness in a half-opened door would betray the presence of the guardian. The Panopticon is a machine for dissociating the see/being seen dyad: in the peripheric ring, one is totally seen, without ever seeing; in the central tower, one sees everything without ever being seen.
>
> (Foucault, 1977: 201–2)

The analogy between the panopticon and patriarchy is not exact. For example, in the culture men are not kept physically separate from one another; yet there has never been a mass revolt of men against the regulations and the imperatives of patriarchy. The reasons for this are severalfold. In the first place, of course, there is the issue of masculine power: because the patriarchal order makes power and status available to those males who conform to its requirements and prohibitions, it is in men's vested interests to preserve that order. However, there are other reasons that emerge in the light of Foucault's use of Bentham's imagined panopticon. Because *both* the inmates of the cells *and* the concealed observer consist of the collectivity of men, the panoptic effect of the patriarchal order is carried out on individual men by all other men. In other words, each man must perform his masculinity to the satisfaction of other men, and, in turn, must function, with other men, as the observer and judge of the gender performance of other males.

This means that there must necessarily exist a distance between one male and others, because each seeks the approval of those others with regard to his performance of the masculine, and, at the same time, assesses the equivalent performance of the others. In this, at least, although there is no physical barrier separating one man from his peers, as in the actual panopticon, there are self-imposed boundaries that mark men off from each other. It is useful, therefore, to think of the patriarchal order as a kind of panopticon, keeping all males under observation in order to control their behavior to ensure that the criteria of masculinity are observed and maintained. (At the same time, of course, a complementary panoptic patriarchal surveillance of women seeks to reproduce the criteria of femininity.) In practical terms, this means that men are simultaneously panoptic subjects (the agents of the patriarchal panopticon) and panoptic objects (the focus of the surveillance of the patriarchal panopticon). They both observe, and are observed by, one another, as a way of keeping male behavior in line with the current norms of masculinity and acceptable gender standards. Any failure in this regard by an individual male inevitably and often instantaneously incurs some form of disciplinary action, ranging from comparatively harmless censure, teasing or ridiculing, through to more serious forms of response, such as ostracism, physical punishment, even the infliction of death.

Each man, therefore, is always-already the potential victim of a band of gender "policemen" whose task it is to patrol the boundaries of gender and to ensure that all members of the culture respect these and act accordingly. All too often, such a patrol can turn into a form of vigilantism, overt and usually self-appointed, as when, for example, gay men are badly beaten, tortured, or even killed by other men who perceive male homosexuality as a threat, whether to their own masculinity or to the criteria established by the patriarchal order as determining what constitutes the masculine. An instance of this is the case in Wyoming, in 1998, of Matthew Shepard, who, at the age of 22, was beaten and killed because he was gay, a news story that made international headlines. Such is the power of the kind of covert panoptic surveillance encouraged by the patriarchal order that, *even in private, men tend to behave according to the norms of masculinity as if they were under actual and continuous observation.*

Activity 4.7

- Reflect on your own observations or experiences of the patrolling and controlling functions of the patriarchal panopticon:
    - What were the circumstances of such incidents?
    - Who were the instigators, overt or covert, of the pressure or action?
    - Was the event intended to punish, to act as a warning to others, or both?
    - What was your own reaction?

Male homosociality and male homosocial desire

Nevertheless, we should not imagine, under the patriarchal order, a state of affairs in which every man's hand is set permanently and immutably against his fellow man. The desire for "male bonding" is promoted strenuously in various quarters. These include discussions about father–son relationships, the schooling of boys, especially in same-sex educational institutions, and the encouragement, by Robert Bly and others in the mythopoetic men's movement, to men to spend time with one another rediscovering their masculinity. This suggests that although men may function in an agonistic or combative relationship with one another in a patriarchal economy, they also *require* the companionship of other males. Such bonding may occur in a variety of contexts, for example, common hobbies or pursuits (such as fishing, auto repair and maintenance, or carpentry) or the establishment of a buddy or group of buddies (with whom one drinks, watches television, attends football matches and the like, or just "hangs out").

Even so, despite extreme closeness and camaraderie among male friends, there remains a certain distance, and the maintenance of certain boundaries. Too close a friendship or bond, and the men concerned risk the perception that they are sexually as well as socially involved. Moreover, some element of the dynamic of competitiveness encouraged within the patriarchal order often characterizes the behavior of even the closest of male friends, disguised as such rivalry might be in the form of joking at one another's expense, egging one another on to undertake various exploits, or trying to outdo one another as the more sexually active friend.

This ambivalence in male–male relationships is explored by Eve Kosofsky Sedgwick in her important study *Between Men: English literature and male homosocial desire* (Sedgwick, 1985). She defines "homosocial" as

> a word occasionally used in history and the social sciences, where it describes social bonds between persons of the same-sex; it is a neologism, obviously formed by analogy with "homosexual," and just as obviously meant to be

distinguished from "homosexual." In fact, it is applied to such activities as "male bonding" which may, as in our society, be characterized by intense homophobia, fear and hatred of homosexuality.

(Sedgwick, 1985: 1)

Sedgwick is interested in the relationship between homosociality and desire:

> To draw the "homosocial" back into the orbit of "desire," of the potentially erotic, then, is to hypothesize the potential unbrokenness of the continuum between homosocial and homosexual – a continuum whose visibility, for men, in our society, is radically disrupted.

(Sedgwick, 1985: 1–2)

She compares the ruptures in that continuum to what she sees as the much more consistent sets of relations among women:

> At this particular historical moment, an intelligible continuum of aims, emotions, and valuations links lesbianism with other forms of women's attention to women: the bond of mother and daughter, for instance, the bond of sister and sister, women's friendship, "networking," and the active struggles of feminism. The continuum is crisscrossed with deep discontinuities – with much homophobia, with conflicts of race and class – but its intelligibility seems now a matter of simple common sense. However agonistic the politics, however conflicted the feelings, it seems at this moment to make an obvious kind of sense to say that women in our society who love women, women who teach, study, nurture, suckle, write about, march for, vote for, give jobs to, or otherwise promote the interests of other women, are pursuing congruent and closely related activities. Thus the adjective "homosocial" as applied to women's bonds … need not be pointedly dichotomized as against "homo-sexual"; it can intelligibly denominate the entire continuum.

(Sedgwick, 1985: 2–3)

The "particular historical moment" to which Sedgwick alludes encompasses feminism and the women's movements of the 1960s and 1970s (her book was published in 1985), when the notion of the "sisterhood" of women had a greater currency than it perhaps possesses today. Nonetheless, it no doubt remains true that the continuity between "woman" and "feminine," on the one hand, and, on the other, "lesbian," whatever the ambivalence that some may feel about it, is less troubled and fragmented than that between "man/masculine" and "homosexual male," because for many men the latter term is definitively excluded by the former terms.

Sedgwick is careful to explain that, by "male homosocial desire," she does not mean to imply "genital homosexual desire as 'at the root of' other forms of male homosociality." Rather, she uses the term "desire" "to name a structure," that is, "the affective or social force, the glue, *even when its manifestation is hostility or hatred or something less emotively charged*, that shapes an important relationship" (Sedgwick, 1985: 2; emphasis added). She goes on to propose that such important relationships may be structured according to a "triangle of desire," an idea that she borrows and adapts from René Girard's study *Deceit, Desire, and the Novel: self and other in literary structure* (Girard, 1972). Girard argues that, in a number of European novels, an inexperienced and often younger male takes another, more worldly and often older male as a model for attaining a certain goal: social status, an advantageous marriage, wealth, romantic love or, more simply, the satisfaction of sexual desire. Often these apparently discrete aims may be reconciled and combined in the one character. Thus, for example, a female object of desire may offer social status and wealth through advantageous marriage, as well as romantic love and the satisfaction of sexual desire.

Girard perceives the protagonist's desire for that goal as being rerouted through the other, more experienced male, who functions not only as model but also as rival. In discussing this "calculus of power ... structured by the relation of rivalry between the two active members of an erotic triangle," Sedgwick observes:

> What is most interesting for our purposes in his study is its insistence that, in any erotic rivalry, the bond that links the two rivals is as intense and potent as the bond that links either of the rivals to the beloved: that the bonds of "rivalry" and "love," differently as they are experienced, are equally powerful and in many cases equivalent. For instance, Girard finds many examples in which the choice of the beloved is determined in the first place, not by the qualities of the beloved, but by the beloved's already being the choice of the person who has been chosen as a rival. In fact, Girard seems to see the bond between rivals in an erotic triangle as being even stronger, more heavily determinant of actions and choices, than anything in the bond between either of the lovers and the beloved.
>
> (Sedgwick, 1985: 21)

Sedgwick reworks this triangular structure by particularizing the goal as a woman or, often more specifically, a woman's body, and by rerouting the flow of desire to demonstrate the functioning of homosocial desire within the texts she examines. In this reconceptualization of the triangle of desire, desire flows initially from the first male character towards the second. However, because that desire has been traditionally proscribed among men, it is redirected so that the woman becomes both its pretext and the alibi. In effect, then, the woman becomes the site on which the men can meet and develop their homosocial bond under the sign and protection of a "natural" heterosexuality. However, it is important to note that the homosocial bond does not necessarily imply homosexual activity or even overt sexual desire. Rather, it is often in an effort to *avoid* any such implication *for the participants in the bond themselves as well as any observers* that woman's presence is required.

The presence and power of the homosocial bond is exemplified in the TV series *How I Met Your Mother* (*How I Met Your Mother*, 2005–). Ted Mosby (played by Josh Radnor) pursues an on-again/off-again relationship with Robin Scherbatsky (Cobie Smulders), whereas the relationship between Marshall Eriksen (Jason Segel) and Lily Aldrin (Alyson Hannigan) similarly approaches and then withdraws from, only to return to, the possibility of marriage. Their friend Barney Stinson (Neil Patrick Harris), self-confident to the point of arrogance, is a womanizer who is cynical about these relationships, and frequently meddles in them.

However, across the series it becomes clear that the important connections are those among the men, who counsel and console one another, and whose friendships, although they have their ups and downs, generally remain stable: they are "bros," or brothers. The female characters, important as they are to the plots of the various episodes, tend to function as the sign of the male characters' masculinity. Were the female characters to be removed, the series would be left with plots dealing with male–male relationships the closeness and intimacy of which might invite the assumption or suspicion of homosexual desire on the part of the male characters. Indeed, it is the very presence of the female characters that inspires many of the plots, which, however, focus as much on the interaction among the men in relation to the women as on the interaction among the men and women themselves. In terms of the erotic triangle of which Girard and Sedgwick write, the women in this series tend to function as relays by means of which the men may safely interact with one another, and express their feelings for one another.

The Bro Code is a print spin-off from the series ostensibly written by the fictional Barney Stinson but more probably by Matt Kuhn, who takes a self-effacing secondary authorship (the title page informs us that the book was written by Barney Stinson "with Matt Kuhn"). The book articulates Barney's selfish and sexist ideology in such a way as to postulate that heterosexual men are always locked in a struggle with women for superiority and power. Indeed, the very first "article" is titled "Bros before ho's," [sic] which suggests that battlelines are always-already drawn between men and women. The use of the slang term for women, "ho's," signifying "whores," is both morally judgmental and socially demeaning, labeling women as an entire class ("Barney Stinson" and Kuhn, 2008: 11). In Sedgwick's terms, this misogyny (usually defined fairly strongly as "a hatred of women," but which perhaps more accurately might be construed as a rejection, exclusion, or dismissal of women) has the effect not only of uniting men as a class of "bros," but also of using women (the apparent object of desire) as a means by which to effect that male solidarity. Stinson's "bro code," like Barney himself in the TV series, thus operates simultaneously to promote sexual rivalry, whether actual or potential, and to provide a model for both male–male and male–female behavior.

Jason Segel stars also in *I Love You, Man*, a movie often characterized as a "bromance," a variation of the genre of romantic comedy, or "rom-com." The term "bromance" signifies a close emotional, but not necessarily sexual, relationship between two men; and movies so designated explore this idea (*I Love You, Man*, 2009). The frame of reference of *I Love You, Man* is that of a fairly typical rom-com, a narrative about a (heterosexual) couple who undergo various situations before eventually being wedded, the ceremony providing the narrative closure for both the romance and the bromance. However, the movie focuses not on the female lead, but rather on the male within this frame of reference. Peter Klaven (Paul Rudd), a realtor, offers marriage at the beginning of the movie to Zooey Rice (Rashida Jones), and all seems set to progress according to schedule. However, because he has no close male friends, Peter must confront the problem of whom he will choose to be his best man. Moreover, he overhears Zooey's friends express surprise and some reservation about the fact that he has no male friends. Concerned and rendered anxious both by this lack and the implication that somehow he is incomplete as a man because of it (Zooey comments to her friends that Peter's best friend seems to be his mother, an observation that might incline the viewer to assume that Peter is fundamentally gay), Peter sets out to find himself a best friend.

Taking advice from his gay younger brother Robbie (Andy Samberg), Peter goes on a number of "man-dates" via introductions by Robbie and their mother, or Internet dating sites. These "meets" turn out to be disasters: one man has an annoying voice and personality, another is a lonely elderly person looking for some form of companionship, and yet another is gay and assumes that Peter is, too. At an open house that he holds for the Hollywood star Lou Ferrigno's property, for which he is the real estate agent, Peter encounters Sydney Fife (Jason Segel), an apparently free spirit who visits open houses in order to eat the food often set out for the potential customers. A friendship develops between Peter and Sydney, who encourages the rather staid, straitlaced realtor to open up and take various risks. Peter asks Sydney to be his best man at the wedding, but later withdraws his offer because, he decides, Sydney is immature, and has stirred up difficulties between Peter and Zooey. Moreover, he discovers that Sydney, who borrowed $8000 from him, has used the funds to put up various billboards advertising Peter's skill as a realtor, in order to improve Peter's property listings and numbers of customers. But Peter is embarrassed by these advertisements – although the strategy turns out to be extremely successful, and Peter is overwhelmed by clients seeking to place their properties with him, or to purchase the Ferrigno house, which he has been experiencing problems in selling.

The difficulties between Peter and Zooey resolved, the wedding proceeds as planned, but Peter mopes, clearly missing Sydney's company and friendship. Several scenes indicate that Sydney, too, misses Peter. On the day of the wedding ceremony, Peter's groomsmen turn out to be a motley crew made up of the men from the various man-dates he went on, and Lou Ferrigno. However, Zooey, noticing Peter's lack of *joie de vivre*, calls Sydney and invites him to the ceremony. Although it turns out that he always planned to attend, invited or not, Zooey's invitation legitimates his presence there. Despite its being relatively restrained, the reunion of the two men is emotional: clearly, they are both overjoyed to be friends once again. Zooey thus provides both the motivation for the friendship and homosocial bond between Peter and Sydney, and the reconciliation between them when it looks like both friendship and bond have been seriously fractured. Again, she (and her group of female friends) function as a relay by means of which the two men are enabled to develop and cement their bond. In this way, the plot contrives to offer Peter a new, more "complete" way of enacting his masculinity, and engages Zooey in a relationship not only with the newly masculinized Peter but also with Sydney. Thus, the narrative avoids the implication of an exclusively homosocial bond between Peter and Sydney.

The triangle of desire discerned by Sedgwick as central to homosocial relationships is to be found also in the novel *Fight Club*, where it is made explicit:

> We have a sort of triangle thing going here. I want Tyler. Tyler wants Marla. Marla wants me.
>
> I don't want Marla, and Tyler doesn't want me around, not anymore. This isn't about *love* as in *caring*. This is about *property* as in *ownership*.
>
> Without Marla, Tyler would have nothing.
>
> (Palahniuk, 1996: 4; original emphasis)

Although the triangle is complicated by the fact that Tyler Durden is a projection of the narrator's mind, the former functions for most of the narrative as an independent character. In setting up the all-male Project Mayhem, Tyler establishes a rigid hierarchical structure. To become a member of this project (a "space monkey"), a candidate must undergo a period of trial (Palahniuk, 1996: 127–30), and is assigned to a group that operates in the same way as a spy cell. The candidate must obey Tyler's directives without question and to the letter – although, given Tyler's charisma, this requirement prompts little resistance among the men admitted into this "club." Project Mayhem becomes in effect an extreme and fairly overt form of patriarchal order, with Tyler as its absolutist head. The fact that the narrator experiences more and more reservations about Tyler's attitudes and behaviors leads to his marginalization from both Tyler (his own alter ego) and the space monkeys. This produces the psychopathology that leads to the struggle with Tyler atop the Parker-Morris Building, which concludes with the narrator shooting himself through the cheek.

In both the novel and the movie, homosocial bonds are created through the fight club itself. The men who attend form strong attachments through the violence meted out by one of them to another, and through the physical damage that they all share:

> A lot of best friends meet for the first time at fight club. Now I go to meetings or conferences and see faces at conference tables, accountants and junior executives or attorneys with broken noses spreading out like an eggplant under the edges of bandages or they have a couple of stitches under an eye or a jaw wired shut. These are the quiet young men who listen until it's time to decide.
>
> We nod to each other.
>
> (Palahniuk, 1996: 54)

Like members of a secret society, those who engage in fight club recognize and acknowledge one another; and Palahniuk's narrative is framed by its opening statement: "A lot of best friends meet for the first time at fight club." The secrecy of fight club and the tacit recognition by its members of one another thus merge into the homosocial bonding implied by "best friends."

The homosocial bond between the narrator and Tyler, developed through the fight club established by the latter, is intensified further through Marla's presence. The more Tyler evinces sexual desire for her, the greater the narrator's sense of isolation and marginalization from Tyler. In this we may perceive a dysfunctional version of the erotic triangle. Yet, at the same time, Tyler's sexual involvement with Marla, whom the narrator despises, creates in the narrator a powerful desire for Tyler, one that is not necessarily homosexual but is certainly erotic. This is strongly suggested in the movie by such elements as the shots of Tyler's (Brad Pitt's) body, or the conversation between Jack (as the narrator [played by Edward Norton] is called in the movie) and Tyler while the latter is naked in the bath. A key symbol of the homoeroticism implicit in the Tyler–narrator relationship is to be found in the kiss Tyler bestows on the narrator. Having licked his lips so that the kiss will leave an imprint of saliva on the back of the narrator's hand, Tyler pours lye on it (Palahniuk, 1996: 72–73):

> Combined with water, lye heats to over two hundred degrees, and as it heats it burns into the back of my hand, and Tyler places his fingers of one hand over my fingers, our hands spread on the lap of my bloodstained pants, and Tyler says to pay attention because this is the greatest moment of my life.
>
> (Palahniuk, 1996: 74)

The elements in this passage (the kiss, together with its indelible scar, on the back of the narrator's hand; the two men maintaining physical contact through their hands, on the narrator's lap) combine to create an image that strongly suggests the erotic. And it is this presence of the erotic underlying the homosocial bond that, in Sedgwick's theorization of homosocial desire, both characterizes, yet troubles such a bond. It becomes both pleasurable *and* risky, because it threatens always to become open homosexual desire.[3]

Activity 4.8

- Reflect on movies or TV shows you have seen that have centered on men or boys, and their relationships with one another.

  ○ Can you perceive in these movies or shows the workings of homosocial desire and bonding?
  ○ Do these dynamics require the presence of a female character? If so, how is she represented?

- ○ How is homosocial bonding made to relate to the patriarchal economy represented?
- ○ Does it make a difference whether the movie or show is a comedy or a serious drama? That is, do the representations of homo-sociality, of woman's place in this dynamic, and of the centrality or otherwise of homosocial bonding to patriarchal power differ, according to difference of narrative genre?

Hegemonic masculinity and the repertoire of the masculine

If asked to define or describe what constitutes a man or masculinity, most people would respond with a list of traits that are likely to include such features as physical size, muscularity, strength, bravery and resourcefulness, fairness, competitiveness, stoicism in the face of adversity and pain, calm composure, and intelligence (but not to excess – the "brainiac," "nerd", or "geek" is not usually thought of in terms of an ideal masculinity). In addition, the "typical" man is expected to be physically active, fond of sports and the outdoors life, attractive and virile, (hetero)sexually active, and competent with mechanical objects. Of course, there are also less positive, even ugly characteristics, such as aggres-siveness, violence, and ruthlessness (and we might include here the prejudicial tendency, in a white-dominated culture, to regard race as a determining factor of what constitutes the masculine). However, these are generally constructed in the cultural imagination as distortions or violations of (indeed, deviations from) the more positive aspects of the masculine.

It is significant that it is the conventional, hegemonic model of masculinity that operates in J.K. Rowling's extremely popular series of Harry Potter novels and the movies based on these, because these are aimed primarily at young readers and therefore are likely to confirm that model for them. If we strip away the glamor of magical abilities, we can see that Harry himself and his friend Ron Weasley are represented as two foolhardy adolescent boys, enthusiastically devoted to Gryffindor, their house at Hogwarts School, and desperate to compete successfully against the other houses, especially Slytherin. They rush to adven-ture and into danger, suffering the consequences, yet go back for more. On the other hand, Hermione Granger, who is largely backgrounded in all this adventure-seeking, functions as the "brains" and cautious adult member of the team. Yet it is she who is competent in researching histories and spells, and who warns Harry and Ron of the dangers into which they insist on thrusting themselves (Rowling, 1997, 1998, 1999, 2000, 2003, 2005, 2007; *Harry Potter and the Philosopher's Stone*, 2001; *Harry Potter and the Chamber of Secrets*, 2002; *Harry Potter and the Prisoner of Azkaban*, 2004; *Harry Potter and the Goblet of Fire*, 2005; *Harry Potter and the Order of the Phoenix*, 2007; *Harry Potter and the Half-Blood Prince*, 2009; *Harry Potter and the Deathly Hallows, Part 1*, 2010; *Harry Potter and the Deathly Hallows, Part 2*, 2011).[4] However, in recent decades, it has become customary to expect the "typical" man also to register emotion, feelings, and sensitivity, although his counterpart of the later nineteenth century and most of the twentieth demonstrated his masculinity through an emotional impassivity that went hand in hand with, and was often identified with, stoicism.

Activity 4.9

- Revisit your answers for the first activity in chapter 1.

    ○ What traits of masculinity did you note down that have been included in the present discussion?

    ○ Did you draw those characteristics from your actual knowledge and experience of men and masculinity, or rather from cultural texts such as movies, TV and literature, and/or popular cultural myths about men and masculinity?

    ○ Did you include any traits that have not been discussed in the present chapter? Are these, in your view, conventional ones, or are they characteristics of behavior and gesture that have only recently been added to the cultural notion of what constitutes the masculine?

The reality is that most men do not exhibit all of these positive characteristics; indeed, an individual male who did so might be thought ideally masculine, but also a kind of cartoon version of masculinity. Rather, we may say that the ensemble of these traits constitute a hypothetically ideal masculinity that men in the culture are enjoined to take as their model. But what of those men who manifest only a few of these traits, or even none at all? Such individuals might, in the popular cultural imagination, include gay men, effeminate heterosexual men, countercultural men (such as hippies, New Age men, and so on), or men from ethnicities and/or cultures in which such characteristics may not be valued, or may be ascribed to women as well as men. We may add to this group such types as sedentary men, overweight or obese men, pacific (that is, nonaggressive) males, men who appear to be conventionally heterosexual and masculine but whose interests extend to such things as needlecraft or cookery; and so on.

From this we may infer that "the masculine" is capable of embracing an extremely wide range of ways of being a man. However, the culture and, especially, the patriarchal order sanction only a limited number of these, albeit still a very broad variety of possibilities. It is to this constrained repertoire that Connell refers in his notion of *hegemonic masculinity*, an idea developed early in Connell's writing, for example, in *Which Way Is Up? Essays on sex, class and culture*, published in 1983 (R.W. Connell, 1983), but "systematized" (R.W. Connell and Messerschmidt, 2005: 830) in "Toward a new sociology of masculinity," coauthored with Tim Carrigan and John Lee (Carrigan et al., 1985). So influential did this journal article prove that 20 years later Connell, together with James W. Messerschmidt, thought it timely to review the way the notion of hegemonic masculinity had been used by others, and to rethink the idea itself (R.W. Connell and Messerschmidt, 2005).

The concept of hegemony derives from the work of the Italian Marxist Antonio Gramsci in the 1930s, and is related to the notion of ideology:

> it refers principally to the ability in certain historical periods of the dominant classes to exercise social and cultural leadership, and by these means – rather than by direct coercion of subordinate classes – to maintain their power over the economic, political and cultural direction of the nation. The crucial aspect of the notion of hegemony is not that it operates by forcing people against their conscious will or better judgement to concede power to the already-powerful, but that it describes a situation whereby our consent is actively sought for those ways of making sense of the world which "happened" to fit in with the interests of the hegemonic alliance of classes, or *power bloc*. Hence our active participation in understanding ourselves, our social relations and the world at large results in our complicity in our own subordination.
>
> (Hartley, 1994a: 133; original emphasis)

John Hartley observes further that

> hegemony naturalizes what is historically a class ideology, and renders it into a form of common sense. The upshot is that power can be exercised not as force but as "authority"; and "cultural" aspects of life are de-politicized. ... Alternative strategies – based on oppositional politics or counter-hegemonic consciousness – not only appear as "unofficial" in this context, but also are likely to be represented as literally non-sense; impossible to imagine, incapable of being represented.
>
> (Hartley, 1994a: 134–35)

He adds:

> However, the continuing conflicts of interest between classes, which forms of ownership and industrial organization of production cannot help but continuously reproduce, ensure that hegemony can never be total. There are always emergent forms of consciousness and representation which may be mobilized in opposition to the hegemonic order. This means that a lot of work, called *ideological labour*, goes into the struggle between hegemonic and counter-hegemonic forms. And what's at stake in the long term in this struggle can be political and economic power itself.
>
> (Hartley, 1994a: 135; original emphasis)

To sum up: hegemony is the means by which a dominant class or group of classes (a power bloc) imposes upon the rest of a society its belief system and the social and cultural practices that go with this, while at the same time encouraging in the subordinate classes the understanding that this is the way things "should be." The resulting effect is the complicity of those classes in their own subordination. However, that subordination can never be total or complete because of what Hartley calls "the continuing conflicts of interest between classes."

In Connell's idea of hegemonic masculinity, therefore, are embedded the notions, first, that the dominance of masculinity ensures the dominance also of the patriarchal order, which shapes the masculine in particular ways at any given historical moment of a society. Second, that dominance is naturalized in such a way as to seem only right and reasonable, so that people in the society accept it and so become complicit with it. However, as Hartley notes, this cannot be a once-and-for-all imposition. Because marginalized or disenfranchised groups and individuals are likely to chafe against their subordination and possible oppression (as happened in the case of the women's, civil, and gay rights movements), the hegemonic group is obliged to continue to find strategies by means of which its authority and power may be sustained.

A helpful overview of Connell's notion of hegemonic masculinity is provided by Donald P. Levy in his entry on the topic in the *International Encyclopedia of Men and Masculinities*:

> Hegemonic masculinity describes: (1) a position in the system of gender relations; (2) the system itself; and (3) the current ideology that serves to reproduce masculine domination. ...
>
> Connell seeks to explain: (1) how some men succeeded in making it appear normal, natural, and necessary for them to enjoy power over other men and most women; (2) why it is that so many men and women participate willingly in their own oppression; and (3) how resistance to hegemonic masculinity can promote gender justice.
>
> (Levy, 2007: 253)

Connell stresses that gender is constructed within, and takes its meaning from, a historical context. It is thus subject to change as that context changes. Moreover, gender is *relational*: masculinity and femininity are not absolute, discrete, and independent categories, but rather derive from one another their meaning and significance. Importantly, Connell also underlines the fact that masculinity is not monolithic, and that the different masculinities functioning in a society at a given time are also relational. Levy identifies the four types isolated by Connell

> more as positions in relation to one another than as personality types: hegemonic, complicit, subordinated and marginalised. The hegemonic position is the currently accepted male ideal within a particular culture at a particular time. As such, the hegemonic male is an ideal-type. ... Connell notes that this image changes over time and place as well as being subject to contestation within a particular culture.
>
> (Levy, 2007: 253–54)

Hegemonic masculinity, then, functions more as an ideal or fantasy of the masculine than as a reality that actual men may embody.

"Most men," continues Levy, "fall within the second category, complicit":

> These men accept and participate in the system of hegemonic masculinity so as to (1) enjoy the material, physical and symbolic benefits of the subordination of women, (2) through fantasy experience a sense of hegemony and learn to take pleasure in it, and (3) avoid subordination.

He adds:

> The relations among the four positions are hierarchical. A man in the subordinated position suffers that fate [of being subordinated] despite appearing to possess the physical attributes necessary to aspire to hegemony. Men run the risk of subordination when they do not practise gender consistent with the hegemonic system and ideology. Marginalised men are those who cannot even aspire to hegemony, most often men of color and men with disabilities.
>
> (Levy, 2007: 254)

Thus, Connell establishes a spectrum of ways of being masculine which is dominated by a more or less unattainable model of masculinity. Accordingly, those men who seek to approximate the current hegemonic position both desire the approval of other men (here we might recall our earlier discussion in this chapter of our application of Foucault's idea of the panopticon to the way in which patriarchy surveils men's behavior) and reinforce the dominance and power of that position. By contrast, those men positioned in the categories of subordinate and marginalized masculinities are the most likely to contest the hegemonic, because it disadvantages them. It is also likely that resistance to the hegemonic position and any consequent shifts in how that position is constructed come from those men in the latter categories, because they have more to gain thereby, whereas those positioned as complicit with the hegemonic model have more to lose by any change in that model.

However, it should be emphasized that Connell's notion of complicit, subordinated, and marginalized masculinities should not be taken to indicate a severely restricted set of possibilities for men's actual daily practice or social behavior. Many kinds of masculinities are distributed across these three positions. Moreover, it is possible (notionally, anyway) for an individual man to migrate from one position to another, as, for example, in the case of a gay man who decides to "go straight" (although such a decision no doubt remains contentious, in the light of arguments for and against homosexuality as a genetic inheritance, the result of conditioning within a particular type of family, or a "lifestyle choice").

In a critical assessment of Connell's notion of hegemonic masculinity, Demetrakis Z. Demetriou distinguishes between external hegemony (hegemony over women) and internal hegemony (hegemony over men) (Demetriou, 2001: 341), and asks: "But what is the relationship between these two forms of domination? Are they one and the same thing; are they complementary to each other; or, is the one the result of the other?" (Demetriou, 2001: 343). He seeks to answer these queries by reference to Gramsci, who himself distinguished between "leading" and "dominating" classes, the former referring to classes allied to the leading class, and the latter to those opposed to it, and therefore to be dominated. Leadership in turn creates a "historic bloc" that "unites all the allied groups under the umbrella of the group seeking hegemony by making their conception of the world homogeneous and consistent with the project of domination, a process that inevitably involves subordinating some of the interests of the groups that are led" (Demetriou, 2001: 344–45). Demetriou thus draws an analogy between led groups and internal hegemony, and dominated groups and external hegemony.

He is careful to distinguish between what he calls "hegemony in the arena of gender relations" and class hegemony, but points out that "there are some striking structural similarities in the two processes that cannot be ignored" (Demetriou, 2001: 345). In thus invoking Gramsci, Demetriou critiques Connell for offering a less nuanced notion of hegemonic masculinity. His argument proposes instead that the notion of a "historic bloc" can be mapped onto the idea of hegemonic masculinity, to suggest a historical specificity that emerges from the negotiations between the dominant model of masculinity and those that are subordinated by or marginalized from it.

Hegemonic masculinity, then, constitutes a conventional or ideal(ized) masculinity. *It is that notion of the masculine to which men subscribe, whether or not they themselves embody it.* In the second place, it is important to realize that *masculinity itself is made up of a repertoire of possible ways of being a man (of performing "manliness"), out of which is constellated a set of particular traits, attitudes, and behaviors that become understood as hegemonic masculinity.* It follows, therefore, that hegemonic masculinity is both historically and culturally contingent: it means something different both to different cultures, and to a single culture at different moments in its history. To *hypostasize* that masculinity (that is, to assume its concrete reality, despite its being an abstract concept) and so to *reify* it (to make it into a tangible thing) is to attempt to fix it and render it stable *despite* historical circumstance and cultural context.

We need, therefore, as Frank Mort puts it, to "grasp masculinity as *process* rather than as static and unchanging" (Mort, 1988: 196; emphasis added). Mort discusses the shifting and varied masculinities of the young men of Britain in the 1980s, and their use of fashion as a way of articulating a particular kind of masculinity, however bound to a specific context, social group, or individual purpose it might be at a particular moment, both in the culture and in the male wearer's own life history. Nonetheless, as we saw in our consideration in chapter 3 of Judith Butler's notion that gender is performative, masculinity in a broader sense than in Mort's discussion may also be thought of as process. It is always-already a work in progress, undertaken and performed by individual males within a particular life, social, cultural, and historical context. What counts as the masculine is therefore liable to be adjusted and "tweaked" according to circumstantial need.

The very notion of a hegemonic masculinity implies, of course, that there are subordinate masculinities, which may be marginalized to a greater or lesser extent. However, we should not therefore assume that the hegemonic or dominant exists in a permanent, static relationship to the subordinate, any more than the hegemonic form itself is permanently fixed and stable. As Demetriou suggests, aspects of nonhegemonic masculinities may be coopted and/or adapted as a way of "leading," in Gramsci's terms, an internal hegemony; and those aspects vary from historical moment to moment, and from culture to culture. The two principal effects of this are, first, the fortification and maintenance of patriarchy, both as order and economy; and, second, the naturalization of both patriarchy and hegemonic masculinity as "common sense," simply the way things *are*. However, it is possible for subordinated forms of masculinity to move from the margin to the center, as the hegemonic masculine comes under pressure because of historical, social, or other changes in the culture, such as occurred during the 1960s. Indeed, the hegemonic masculinity current at a given historical moment may even become the object of interrogation, such that its authority and very hegemony are challenged, enabling the possibility for a new constellation of traits, attitudes, and behaviors to form.

Activity 4.10

- Select a movie or TV show you have recently watched, or a novel you have recently read.

    o Can you perceive indicators of hegemonic and subordinate masculinities among the male characters?
    o On what basis is that hegemony/subordination constituted?
    o Can you imagine a constellation of traits, behaviours, and attitudes that might make up a different kind of hegemonic masculinity? Of what might that constellation consist?

- How is the relation between hegemonic and subordinate masculinities, and the possible tension between them, played out in your own experience?

Suggested further reading

Adams, R. and Savran, D. (eds.) (2002) *The Masculinity Studies Reader*, Maldon, MA and Oxford: Blackwell.

Edwards, J. (2009) *Eve Kosofsky Sedgwick*, London and New York: Routledge.

Harper, P.B. (1996) *Are We Not Men? Masculine anxiety and the problem of African-American identity*, New York and Oxford: Oxford University Press.

Kimmel, M.S. and Ferber, A.L. (eds.) (2010) *Privilege: a reader*, Philadelphia: Westview Press.

Majors, R. and Billson, J.M. (1992) *Cool Pose: the dilemmas of black manhood in America*, New York: Touchstone.

Mosse, G.L. (1996) *The Image of Man: the creation of modern masculinity*, New York and Oxford: Oxford University Press.

Whitehead, S.M. and Barrett, F.J. (eds.) (2001) *The Masculinities Reader*, Cambridge, UK: Polity Press.

5 Troubling patriarchy

In the preceding chapter, we explored the nature and dynamics of patriarchy. However, questions that necessarily arise in relation to such a topic might include the following: can one escape the gravitational pull, as it were, of the patriarchal order and economy? Can patriarchy be dismantled? To answer the last question first, we might reflect that the patriarchal order and economy suffuse and shape the culture we inhabit, together with its definition of the relationships among sex, gender, and sexuality. Thus, patriarchy directs not only what we see but also how we see it. Accordingly, it would be irrational to expect an overnight revolution that did away with both the patriarchal order and the patriarchal economy, and put something in their place that functioned properly from the very start. So it would seem that we may be stuck with patriarchy for some time to come.

However, we should recall from chapter 2 Foucault's idea that power is *productive*. That is, it would be erroneous to assume that the power of patriarchy is purely repressive (or, from the feminist perspective, oppressive): it *generates* structures, dynamics, identities, possibilities. And one of the possibilities inherent in the very fact of power, as Foucault is careful to point out, is resistance to the power of patriarchy. We should recall that, for him, power *requires* resistance for its own self-definition and efficacy *as* power. Accordingly, we might consider that already built into patriarchy is the possibility of its resistance.

However, resistance does not necessarily imply successful overthrow. Rather, for Foucault, resistance occurs at multiple points in the discursive formations that both characterize and give a particular identity and shape to a culture. In that multiplicity of sites of resistance lies the potential to bring about shifts and changes in both the patriarchal order and, as a consequence, the patriarchal economy also. However, we should not imagine that such a strategy of resistance is likely to run direct and unchallenged. Power structures and systems are adept at blocking and neutralizing resistive counterstrategies. They are also able to coopt and assimilate both the motives of resistance and those who resist, taming them in such a way as to *appear* to change while at the same time strengthening the hold upon power and people.

Take, for example, the way certain clothing fashions and tastes in music have emerged in or have been popularized by gay subculture, only to be taken up by the culture at large. "De-gayed" and so rendered "safe" for the heterosexual majority, those clothing fashions and musical tastes then become a sign of the general social acceptance of gays and their subculture, despite an actual social blindness to the expression of antigay sentiments and even an active encourage-ment of homophobia. Thus, we may be confronted by the ironic paradox of someone who hates and perhaps persecutes gays, but who wears fashions pioneered by gay men, and listens to music that first became popular in gay nightclubs.

Given the capacity of dominant, powerful discourses to coopt acts that question and contest their power, and to resignify them to their own advantage, resistance in Foucauldian theory (as well as in theories of ideology), as a general strategy, *needs to be maintained*: a single moment of resistance does not consti-tute a victory for the resisters. It needs in addition to be supple, agile, moving from discursive site to discursive site, as conditions change. It is perhaps thus that patriarchy may be challenged and made to develop gradually a different order and economy, if it is not to be replaced entirely with some other discursive system, together with its own attendant social and conceptual organization.

The present chapter, then, is concerned with ways of understanding both patriarchy and masculinity in order to see the points at which resistance might be possible. The title of the chapter is intended, with a nod to Judith Butler's important book *Gender Trouble* (Butler, 1990), to suggest, in the first place, a discussion of the contradictions and paradoxes implicit in the term "patriarchy," and, in the second, an exploration of three ways in which the idea and apparently incontestable power of patriarchy might be challenged and disrupted: hence, "troubled."

Abjection, misogyny, and homophobia

As the discussion in chapter 4 about homosocial desire indicated, and as Sedgwick makes clear early in her book (Sedgwick, 1985: 1–5), the issues of homosexual desire and behavior play a central part in the social and cultural construction of masculinity. Indeed, we may postulate that masculinity has traditionally depended upon and required a double definition by negation: *masculinity is not appropriate to women* (a definition by gender); and *masculinity is not to be attributed to homosexual men* (a definition by sexuality).

There are a number of implications consequent upon such a relational construc-tion of the masculine. Significantly, it means that there is no stable definition of masculinity *in and of itself*. As we saw in chapter 2, we cannot argue that mascu-linity proceeds naturally from physiological maleness alone. Moreover, as we saw in chapter 3 in Judith Butler's notion of gender performativity, the associa-tion of masculinity with the male body is neither natural nor inevitable. Simply, it is required discursively in order to keep the existing gender system in place. It follows, therefore, that if the masculine depends on its relation to two other terms, *any shift in the nature or meaning of these latter terms must necessarily produce a shift in the cultural definition of masculinity*.

This goes some way to explaining why the rise of feminist and gay rights movements in the 1960s precipitated both a sense of crisis and an anxiety around gender for many people. As women claimed rights such as social and legal equality, the recognition of the autonomy of female sexual desire, and the power to decide what to do with their own bodies with regard to abortion, and as homosexual men and women (and, later, other nonheteronormative subjectivities, such as transsexuals) gained greater social visibility and claimed rights of their own, many men began to feel that masculinity itself was under siege. It is to this that Sally Robinson refers, both in the title of her book, *Marked Men: white masculinity in crisis*, and in her argument. Men felt "marked," in the sense of being singled out for retribution, but also because, in sociological terms, to be "marked" is to be made visible within a discourse the power of which depends on at least one of its terms remaining unnoticed (Robinson, 2000).

Another way of conceiving the definition of the masculine by double negation is to understand that conventional masculinity sustains itself by *abjecting* both the feminine and the homosexual from within itself. "Abjection," in the sense in which it is being used here, derives from the Latin *jacere*, "to throw," together with the prefix *ab-*, "away," and refers to the rejection and/or refusal of certain objects, events, or ideas. Embedded in the notion of abjection are the informing elements, first, of disgust, nausea, or horror; and, second, of the need to expel, discard, or exile objects that prompt such strong reactions. In *Powers of Horror: an essay on abjection*, the French theorist Julia Kristeva suggests that subjectivity itself is, at least in part, constituted through abjection: "The abject is not an ob-ject [sic] facing me, which I name or imagine. ...The abject has only one quality of the object – that of being opposed to *I*" (Kristeva, 1982: 1). That is, the abject is that which lies outside the sense of self, *but which helps the self to define its very subjectivity*.

However, because "what is *abject*, ... the jettisoned object, is radically excluded," it "draws me toward the place where meaning collapses" (Kristeva, 1982: 2; original emphasis). The abject is concerned with that which is unclean and which, consequently, defiles: vomit, pus, urine, menstrual blood, semen, the facts and the odors of excrement, perspiration, decaying flesh, etc. Such bodily facts disturb our sense of a clear boundary between ourselves, as defined by our bodies, and what exists outside us; and between our understandings of what life means and what death signifies. Therefore Kristeva observes: "It is thus not lack of cleanliness or health that causes abjection but what disturbs identity, system, order. What does not respect borders, positions, rules. The in-between, the ambiguous, the composite" (Kristeva, 1982: 4).

The opposition between cleanliness and defilement, between purity and impurity, is central to the notion of abjection. Kristeva points out that

Anthropologists ... have noted that secular "filth," which has become sacred "defilement," is the *excluded* on the basis of which religious prohibition is made up. In a number of primitive societies religious rites are purification rites whose function is to separate this or that social, sexual, or age group from one another, by means of prohibiting a filthy, defining element. It is as if dividing lines were built up between society and a certain nature, as well as within the social aggregate, on the basis of the simple logic of *excluding filth*, which, promoted to the ritual level of *defilement*, founded the "self and clean" [the two meanings of the French *propre*] of each social group if not of each subject.

(Kristeva, 1982: 65; original emphasis)

However, Kristeva draws our attention to the fact that "filth is not a quality in itself, but it applies only to what relates to a *boundary* and, more particularly, represents the object jettisoned out of that boundary, its other side, a margin" (Kristeva, 1982: 69; original emphasis). That is, an object, person or event becomes defiling only when a boundary has been transgressed, and a margin that defines the polluted from the pure, the improper from the proper, is established at the edge of that boundary. Yet, at the same time, that which is polluting blurs the boundary between the proper (in both senses as "appropriate to" or "characteristic of," and "clean and pure") and the improper. It suggests that the boundary is permeable, maybe even only temporary.

Abjection thus sets up the possibility that the boundaries that establish the meanings of "filthy" and "clean" are, at the same time, undermined and rendered ineffectual. It is for this reason that Kristeva observes, "what is *abject*, ... the jettisoned object, ... draws me toward the place where meaning collapses" (Kristeva, 1982: 2; original emphasis):

A wound with blood and pus, or the sickly, acrid smell of sweat, of decay, does not *signify* death. In the presence of signified death – a flat encephalograph, for instance – I would understand, react, or accept. No, as in true theater, without makeup or masks, refuse and corpses *show me* what I permanently thrust aside in order to live. These bodily fluids, this defilement, this shit are what life withstands, hardly and with difficulty, on the part of death. Today, I am at the border of my condition as a living being. My body extricates itself, as being alive, from that border. Such wastes drop so that I might live, until, from loss to loss, nothing remains in me and my entire body falls beyond the limit – *cadere* [Latin for "to fall"], cadaver. If dung signifies the other side of the border, the place where I am not and which permits me to be, the corpse, the most sickening of wastes, is a border that has encroached upon everything. It is no longer I who expel, "I" is expelled.

(Kristeva, 1982: 3–4; original emphasis)

"Meaning," in Kristeva's terms, thus includes not merely semantic understanding. It embraces also such key social and cultural elements as structure and hierarchy, rank and precedence, investments of power, permissible and impermissible relationships. If we take, for example, the question of incest, we can see that the taboo sexual relationship between a parent and child, or between a pair of siblings (setting aside such issues as genetic inbreeding) confuses structure and hierarchy, and therefore also rank and precedence, and the power that accrues to these. How, for instance, is a woman to respond socially to a sexual partner who is also her biological father? The former role might imply equality, whereas the latter role might require subordination on the part of the woman. Moreover, what of any child born of such a pairing? Would she or he be considered a child or grandchild of the father? How would this affect such issues as the transfer of title or property, or the logic of inheritance as set out in the father's last will and testament? It becomes clear, when we ask such questions, that incest is abjected and inspires disgust as a practice at least partly because it dangerously collapses many of the structures and required behaviors (the meanings) by which society functions. As a result, such practices and those who engage in them become defined as both defiled and defiling.

If we return now to the issue of masculinity, bearing in mind Judith Butler's idea of the performativity of gender, we can begin to understand how misogyny (the rejection of women) and homophobia (the [irrational] fear of homosexuality and of homosexuals) in effect constitute the boundaries of masculinity itself, and so help to construct the masculine. That is, in order for the masculine to define itself as proper to only the heterosexual male and his body, any possibility or trace of the feminine or the homosexual must be abjected, expelled to produce *other* subjects, and *other* kinds of body. Indeed, *the masculine is constituted by the simultaneous abjection of the feminine and the male-homosexual,*[1] and the accompanying crystallization of both misogyny and homophobia as ways to manage these abjected constituents. Beyond this, *the patriarchal order itself can be seen to depend on the process of abjection*, together with the strategies of management of that which has been abjected. Put otherwise, *both* masculinity *and* the patriarchal order require, and come into existence simultaneously with, the abjection of the feminine and the male-homosexual.

Activity 5.1

- Reflect on instances of abjection in your own experience.
- Did these have to do with bodily functions only? (For example, you might consider the way in which the homeless may represent a particular form of abjection.)

    o What elements or facts are being abjected?
    o How do these help to constitute the socially or culturally "proper" through the process of abjection?

- You might, in addition, consider other possible forms of abjection: for example, racial or ethnic difference, physical disability, aging, etc.
- How is the fact of death treated, both in reality and in cultural representations in movies, TV or literature?

Indeed, the homosexual male represents for masculinity perhaps the extreme condition of abjection. In form he resembles the "clean" or undefiled heterosexual ("proper") man, yet in sexual practice he is generally represented as feminine or feminized, because it is culturally assumed that he permits his body, like the female body, to be penetrated by another male. In this way, the gay male can be constructed as *both* a failed man *and* a failed woman. Small wonder, therefore, that the very idea of male homosexuality can often arouse feelings of repugnance, outrage, and horror amongst heterosexuals, especially men; or that those feelings in turn can produce reactions of rejection of and/or violence toward gay men. These can then be justified by recourse to various rationalizations, such as the argument from nature: the idea that homosexual behavior is "unnatural," although we saw in chapter 2 that this assumption is open to question. Another "rationalization" is to be found in biblical proscriptions, although such appeals to the Bible are usually highly selective. For example, the injunction in Deuteronomy 22:11 against wearing clothing made of a blend of linen and wool is rarely invoked.[2] We may conclude that these arguments are retrospective projections to explain and justify to the culture the maintenance of both the patriarchal order and the masculine through the abjection of the male-homosexual.

The case of the feminine is not much better. Women's bodies are perceived as "leaky," or at any rate as leakier than men's, because they menstruate and lactate, functions that blur the boundaries between the interior and exterior of the body. Moreover, those bodies are understood as more or less permanently open to the exterior world, because they permit the ingress of the male body in the form of the penis in sexual intercourse, and the egress of the infant's body in childbirth. Accordingly, therefore, like the male homosexual's body, woman's body comes to be thought of as impure, unclean, defiled, and defiling. However, unlike the body of the male homosexual, the female body is necessary to procreation, and must therefore be preserved as the appropriate object of erotic desire. The inferiorization through abjection of the feminine accordingly draws on a rationale that resembles that applied to the male-homosexual, but inflects it differently.

For example, the argument from nature postulates, on the basis of observation of (some) animal behaviors, that women constitute "the weaker sex," and must be protected and managed. The appeal to the Bible as the authority on gender politics both appears to support this argument from nature, and strengthens it by means of religious authority. It begins with the story of the Fall, in the Garden of Eden. Eve, we may recall, was created, not directly from raw material, as Adam was, but rather from already "processed" material, namely, Adam's rib (Genesis 2:21–3), making her a sort of second-hand, recycled goods. She not only succumbed to the temptations of the serpent, and ate of the divinely forbidden fruit of the Tree of Knowledge of Good and Evil but successfully tempted Adam to do the same (Genesis 3:1–6). Woman's moral weakness and intellectual inferiority, together with the menace that she represents as a sexual temptress, are thus inscribed early in the foundational text of Judeo-Christian culture. Reinforced both by similar representations of women in the Bible (for example, the seductress Delilah, in Judges 16) and, over the centuries, by secular depictions of woman, Eve has provided a long-standing model for a misogynistic attitude towards women in general. Again, we may detect here a retrospective justification for the abjection of women and of the female body, as a way of constructing the masculine.

Even science can be marshaled in support of this cause. For example, *Idols of Perversity: fantasies of feminine evil in fin-de-siècle culture* is a study of negative representations of women and of the female body in the late nineteenth century, particularly after the emergence of the theories of evolution and development of anthropology as a legitimate discipline. In it, Bram Dijkstra observes: "But when we consider what 'improvements' evolutionists such as [Charles] Darwin and [Carl] Vogt made in our conceptions of the role of woman in society, we discover that where woman was concerned the theory of evolution represented a baroquely inscribed license to denigrate and destroy" (Dijkstra, 1986: 163). Evolution theory was deployed as a way of theorizing racial differences, and of inferiorizing peoples who were not Caucasian. Vogt, for example, thought that the "Negro" was considerably more "simious" (apelike) than Caucasian peoples (Dijkstra notes that Vogt's "standard of measurement" was the "German male"), and that in non-Caucasian peoples, whom he thought closer to the animal than Caucasian ones, the female tended to be the more animal-like. "From this conclusion," comments Dijkstra, "it was but a short step to the decision that everything in the revolutionary process pointed to the fact that the development of woman in general tended to parallel that of the 'inferior' races rather than the evolving white male" (Dijkstra, 1986: 167).

In a more benign inflection of this kind of theory, which saw the evolutionarily undeveloped races, and, in the white one, woman, less as animals than as under-developed children,

> it became a foregone conclusion that a link was to be discovered between woman's 'stunted' evolution and her reproductive responsibility. ... [W]oman was mentally a child because she needed all her "vital energy" to have children. Brain work required much vital energy – and hence brain work was properly the realm of the male. To think was to "spend" vital energy just as much as it took to give birth to a child. Hence men created in the intellectual realm, while women needed to conserve energy to create in the physical realm.
>
> (Dijkstra, 1986: 169)

The notion emerged that woman was, according to the terms of evolution theory, at least potentially, if not actually, "degenerate." This was a term commonly used in the nineteenth century to describe people and behaviors that indicated either a failure to evolve or a sliding back down the evolutionary ladder. It was used also of effeminate or homosexual males, as Christopher E. Forth notes:

> Degeneration could effectively transform men into "women" or "savages," and women would become more mannish and dominant than their weakened

male counterparts. It threatened Western society with a reversal of hierarchies of race, gender and class.

(Forth, 2008: 145)

By constructing woman as under-evolved, by comparison with man, such theories succeeded in abjecting women and the female body more emphatically and apparently without possible contradiction, because it was done in the name of science. However, it becomes clear that this was part of a long tradition of distancing the feminine, together with the male-homosexual, in order to *produce* the masculine.

However, ironically (and paradoxically), in order for that which is disgusting, nauseating, or otherwise unacceptable to be abjected, *it first has to be imagined as integral to that entity or agency that does the abjecting.* So, for the masculine to regard itself as clean and purified by the expulsion of the abject to somewhere "out there," outside and beyond the masculine and the male body, it first has to perceive itself as containing the abject "in here," inside and part of the masculine and the male body. The fear that what has been expelled "out there" may return "in here" renders unstable not only the masculine, but also the patriarchal order itself, together with the gender system by which these sustain themselves.

Activity 5.2

- Think about movies or TV shows you have viewed recently (for example, those featuring superheroes), and reflect on the ways that secondary characters of a particular movie or show might be understood as made up of elements abjected from the hero or heroes.

  ○ What cues or clues are given in the movie or show to suggest this?

  ○ Are there any elements of gender and, specifically, of masculinity, that you perceive as having been abjected from the body or character of the hero to those of the secondary character?

  ○ In a number of movies, including those centered on a superhero, macho, aggressive masculinity may be abjected, and displaced to become a component of the villain character or other secondary characters. What does this suggest about current ideas of the masculine, and of what must be abjected in order that it be reconstituted and characterized in a particular way?

Ex-nomination

At this point, we would be entitled to ask how, if both masculinity and the patriarchal order are so frail and so tenuously maintained, they have come to dominate the gender system and, with it, the social order itself. One answer to this question is offered by an analysis of social history, which in turn suggests that historically the patriarchal order has been subject to change, and has adapted to new social conditions. For example, in *The Secret History of Domesticity*, Michael McKeon proposes that

> Patriarchalism [a political theory advanced by the seventeenth-century English Royalist Sir Robert Filmer] entailed an analogy between the state and the family that legitimated each institution by associating it with the "naturalness" of the other. As a theory of political obligation, patriarchalism enjoined upon subjects a subordination to the magistrate [who represented royal authority] analogous to that of family members to the male head of the household.
>
> (McKeon, 2005: 11)

McKeon adds that this "patriarchalist analogy is not simply a metaphor linking two separate entities; it defines the continuity between, the interpenetration of, things that are distinct but inseparable from each other." In other words, the monarch is to the state as the father is to the family and household. And, just as the state's people are subject to the monarch's authority and owe the king (or queen) allegiance and obedience, so members of the family and household are subject to the father's authority and likewise owe him allegiance and obedience. McKeon notes that, "In a dynastic monarchy, moreover, the analogy between the state and the family is reinforced by their metonymic relationship: political sovereignty is a function of familial inheritance" (McKeon, 2005: 11). That is, the fact of dynastic monarchy (a new king's inheritance of rule from his father) strengthened the imagined correlation between royal authority in the state and paternal authority in the family.

However, argues McKeon, articulating such theory explicitly, as in Sir Robert Filmer's work, exposes it to criticism. He cites the poet John Milton: "[B]y calling kings fathers of their country, you think this metaphor has forced me to apply right off to kings whatever I might admit to fathers. Fathers and kings are very different things ..." (McKeon, 2005: 11). McKeon comments, "The very substance of patriarchalism ... was countermanded by the manner of its articulation" (McKeon, 2005: 13); that is, in articulating the social theory of patriarchalism, Filmer and others rendered it vulnerable to criticism. The ensuing separation of royal authority over the state from paternal authority over the family and household thus marks a new phase in the history of the patriarchal order, one that establishes the order both as natural and as authoritative.

The patriarchal order and economy, then, do not always take the same shape, employ the same strategies, or (besides ensuring the ascendancy of men over women) serve the same functions. By adapting to changing historical and social conditions, patriarchy seeks to guarantee its own survival. This is very different from the dominance of males in nature, a "fact" often cited in support of male dominance in human society. This is by no means a consistent law in nature: consider, for instance, the dominance of the female of the species among bees or ants. Moreover, dogs or lions or eagles do not have to adjust to changing *social* conditions, although they may well have to adapt to changing environmental ones. The adaptive longevity of patriarchy lends it the illusion of an immutable fact of human nature, if not also of the animal world.

Another and rather different answer to the question of how the patriarchal order has sustained its authority is suggested indirectly by the French semiotician Roland Barthes in his collection of essays titled *Mythologies*. In a passage in "Myth today," he discusses a particular phenomenon in French history and society. Since the French Revolution in 1789, political and social power has been exercized by a middle class, or bourgeoisie, of varying kinds, but for whom "the same status – a certain regime of ownership, a certain order, a certain ideology – remains at a deeper level" (Barthes, 2009: 163). However, although the notion of a bourgeoisie "as an economic fact … is *named* without any difficulty: capitalism is openly professed[,] … [a]s a political fact, the bourgeoisie has some difficulty in acknowledging itself: there are no 'bourgeois' parties in the Chamber" (Barthes, 2009: 163–64). Barthes goes on to note that, "As an ideological fact, it [the bourgeoisie] completely disappears: the bourgeoisie has obliterated its name in passing from reality to representation, from economic man to mental man" (Barthes, 2009: 164).

He concludes that this social class "makes its status undergo a real *ex-nominating* operation: the bourgeoisie is defined as *the social class which does not want to be named"* (Barthes, 2009: 164; original emphasis). The question remains: how is this ex-nomination of the bourgeoisie brought about? Barthes proposes that, "Politically, the haemorrhage of the name 'bourgeois' is effected through the idea of *nation*. This was once a progressive idea, which has served to get rid of the aristocracy; today, the bourgeoisie merges into the nation, even if it has, in order to do so, to exclude from it the elements which it decides are allogenous [different in kind] …" (Barthes, 2009: 164; original emphasis). That is, by identifying itself with "the nation," with which of course every citizen identifies her- or himself, an entire class (the bourgeoisie) disappears. It is not simply that it identifies itself *with* "the nation," but rather that it identifies itself *as* "the nation."

It follows, therefore, that the citizens of the *state* who like to think of themselves as members of a *nation* are induced to characterize that membership as essentially bourgeois in nature. When "everyone," despite actual individual social class, race, ethnicity, or profession, starts to think of her- or himself as effectively bourgeois because a member of a "bourgeois nation" (*is transformed*, as it were, *into* bourgeois), the bourgeoisie itself becomes so normalized that it disappears. We no longer notice it, any more than we notice the air we breathe. This is why Barthes observes that "Bourgeois ideology can therefore spread over everything and in so doing lose its name without risk: no one here will throw this name of bourgeois back at it" (Barthes, 2009: 165).

Activity 5.3

- Consider how, in your own experience, the appeal to "nation" and patriotism might ex-nominate any class, race, cultural, or economic differences between the dominant group and subordinate ones.

    ○ For example, how does the familiar and resounding phrase, "My fellow Americans" erase material difference in order to create what Benedict Anderson calls an "imagined community" (Anderson, 2006)?

We may draw a productive parallel between Barthes's analysis of the fashion by which a particular social class has come to dominate the entire social structure and the way that the patriarchal order has succeeded in establishing the masculine as the gender norm, and hence as able to dominate the gender system and, through this, the social order itself. For as long as patriarchy remained tacit as a key principle of experiencing gender difference and hence a dominant discourse in the organization of society, it was difficult to contest its power. For example, in the nineteenth century individual women who defied its regulation of their lives could be censured. They could even be confined to prison or a mental institution, whether because they protested against the socially accepted treatment of women, for instance, or by asserting the autonomous nature of female sexuality and sexual desire, thereby flying in the face of pronouncements of men like William Acton (1813–75), a doctor and surgeon of whom Steven Marcus remarks, "Though his name has long since been forgotten, Acton was something of a figure in his own time" (Marcus, 1969: 2):

> I should say that the majority of women (happily for them) are not very much troubled with sexual feeling of any kind. What men are habitually, women are only exceptionally. It is too true, I admit, as the divorce courts show, that there are some few women who have sexual desire so strong that they surpass those of men. ... I admit, of course, the existence of sexual excitement terminating even in nymphomania, a form of insanity which those accustomed to visit lunatic asylums must be fully conversant with; but, with these sad exceptions, there can be no doubt that sexual feeling in the female is in the majority of cases in abeyance ... and even if roused (which in many instances it never can be) is very moderate compared with that of the male. ... The best mothers, wives, and managers of households, know little or nothing of sexual indulgences. Love of home, children, and domestic duties, are the only passions they feel.
>
> As a general rule, a modest woman seldom desires any sexual gratification for herself. She submits to her husband, but only to please him; and, but for

the desire of maternity, would far rather be relieved from his attentions. No nervous or feeble young man need, therefore, be deterred from marriage by any exaggerated notion of the duties required from him. The married woman has no wish to be treated on the footing of a mistress.

(cited in Marcus, 1969: 31–32)

Of interest in this passage is the assertion of a difference between men and women that is grounded not only in sex but also in sexuality. "Proper" women (that is, women who are sober and clean, and behave appropriately, according to the social and marital roles laid out for them; in other words, marriageable women) are distinguished on the basis of sex drive from nymphomaniacs (rightly confined to "lunatic asylums") and mistresses, whom Acton clearly considers to be only one step up from the common prostitute. Such a "proper" woman is thus unlikely to make inordinate sexual demands on her husband, however "nervous or feeble" he might be.

It is important to note, moreover, that for Acton female sexuality is closely linked to male desire, and to "the desire of maternity." In other words, sexual desire on the part of a woman cannot be autonomous, but depends rather on pleasing her husband and fulfilling his desire, and/or her wish to conceive and bear children. To admit an independent *female* sexuality and sexual desire would challenge male authority over woman, her body, and her desire. It would also undermine the definition of the masculine through the abjection of the feminine, including female sexuality, which could then no longer be classified as in some way repellent, to be dominated and controlled rather than allowed its free play.

The point to grasp here is that *women came to see themselves in the same terms.* "Nice" women were those who accepted their roles as subordinates to men, whether as wives, secretaries, "salesgirls," social acquaintances, and the like, and as relatively asexual maternal figures, whether as actual mothers or surrogates like teachers or nurses. "Nasty" women were those who did not know or accept their "place." These were insubordinate women who defied male authority, asserted their own sexuality, or who refused to acknowledge their dependence on men not only in economic and social terms but also in terms of the construction of their own subjectivity.

There were, and still are, both social and personal consequences attendant upon the masculine perception of a woman as "nice" or "nasty." Thus, when Sandra Harding proclaims, "Women have always resisted male domination" (Harding, 1988: 5), we must understand this to mean "individual women," rather than "women as a class." Indeed, Harding later remarks that "there have always been women willing and able to produce sexist and misogynistic thought" (Harding, 1988: 11). From this we may gather, first, that not *all* women have resisted male domination. Second, for many women complicity with and obedience to the patriarchal imperative that subordinates women and affirms their inferiority to men are not necessarily experienced as treachery to their own sex. Quite the contrary: such women are often likely to see their rebellious, refractory sisters as traitors to their femininity and ordained roles. And, of course, there are also women who may well resist or, at any rate, resent male domination, but are so situated that compliance becomes simply a survival strategy.

Historically, one can find many earlier illustrations of the ways that the patriarchal order has exerted often silent, yet irresistible pressures that in turn have determined the flows of power. Even how the two sexes have been theorized can indicate the presence of those patriarchal pressures. For example, as Thomas Laqueur observes in *Making Sex: body and gender from the Greeks to Freud*, from the ancient world through to Europe in the early nineteenth century, the assumption was that "at least two genders correspond to but one sex" (Laqueur, 1990: 25). He quotes as an epigraph to his second chapter the following statement by Galen of Pergamum (c. 130–200 CE): "Turn outward the woman's, turn inward, so to speak, and fold double the man's [genital organs], and you will find the same in both in every respect" (Laqueur, 1990: 25). Laqueur remarks, "Instead of being divided by their reproductive anatomies, the sexes are linked by a common one. Women, in other words, are inverted, and hence less perfect, men. They have exactly the same organs but in exactly the wrong places" (Laqueur, 1990: 26).

The assumption clearly was that men and male anatomy constituted the norm, while women and female anatomy represented an inferior variation of it. Of course, as Laqueur notes parenthetically, "The arrow of perfection *could* go either or both ways," and he quotes a remark made by the character Mlle de l'Espinasse in Denis Diderot's *D'Alembert's Dream*, a series of philosophical dialogues written in 1769 and published in 1830: "Perhaps men are nothing but a freakish variety of women, or women only a freakish variety of men" (Laqueur, 1990: 26; original emphasis). However, historically, "the arrow of perfection" pointed chiefly to the masculine and the male anatomy.

The normalization of the masculine and man's body can be seen everywhere. From Leonardo da Vinci's famous *Vitruvian Man* (c. 1485), in which a man's body is placed simultaneously within a circle and a square, as an exercise in ideal proportion, to the traditional, although now largely discontinued, use of the masculine as a generic noun (or pronoun) (for example, "the history of Man on earth"), the feminine is understood as included, but backgrounded, silenced, rendered invisible, and hence, in effect, absent. "Man" thus becomes the universal category. "Woman" functions either as a minor subcategory, or vanishes altogether. The feminine pronouns "she" and "her" have in the past often been used to signify certain inanimate objects or abstract collectives. Thus, a ship or an automobile could be referred to as "she"; for instance, "She left port last Sunday" or "Now that she's been repaired, her engine is running smoothly." So, indeed, could an entire nation state; with reference, for example, to France, Britain, or America, one could speak of the country as "she" and of the people as "her citizens." Such phraseology implied that there existed a continuity or parallel between woman and objects, especially mechanical ones, or abstract ideas, with further implications about the ways each might be thought of and treated.

Activity 5.4

- Can you find examples, from your own experience in talking to others, reading or watching TV or movies, of the ex-nomination of "man" so that this term becomes a catch-all term that erases sex/gender difference, or even differences of class or of race/ethnicity?

  ○ Where such differences may be highlighted, what is the effect of that highlighting? (For example, this might be the isolation and inferiorization of a group or individual, or their marginalization.)
  ○ What might be its purpose (for instance, to foreground the implicit positive virtues of the ex-nominated group, etc.)?

Moreover, the "female ailments" or "women's disorders" mentioned in everyday conversations, often with a sense that these somehow constituted a topic tabooed for men and better spoken of (secretively) amongst women, have separated the female body discursively from the male one. This latter has been assumed implicitly to be healthy; it is only comparatively recently that we have begun to hear about "men's health issues." Even pregnancy could be viewed as a female malady that was "cured" by childbirth, with the implication that not only were men lucky to escape this particular affliction, but the fact that they have done so is a further indication of their physiological superiority. Small wonder, then, that one of the early campaigns of feminism in the 1960s (and it continues) was to secure both the grammatical and semantic inclusion of women in the language of institutions, the media, and daily speech.

Thus, although women, as a subordinate group, may have chafed against male dominance and so also against the authority of the patriarchal order, many individual women historically have naturalized their position as subordinate and inferior to men simply as women's lot in life or women's role. By contrast, men, particularly those whose subjectivity conforms to and so matches the socially dominant and hence privileged group (for instance, in our own culture, the white, heterosexual, middle-class male), generally have not questioned their apparently natural role as dominant and superior. Nor, of course, have they interrogated the patriarchal system that enabled such dominance and superiority. To use Barthes's term, the patriarchal order was ex-nominated, and so rendered natural and universal; at least, that is, until the 1960s and the years following, when the word "patriarchy" entered common usage, thanks to the work of the women's movements and feminist critique of the social order and its dynamics. Renomination, then, provides a strategy by which to render patriarchy visible and, like Filmer's patriarchalist theory, vulnerable not only to criticism, but also to change. In Sally Robinson's terms, it is not only the dominant form of masculinity that becomes marked, that is, both visible and accountable, but so too does patriarchy itself (Robinson, 2000).

Queer theory and social critique

A further radical challenge to the supremacy and power of patriarchy emerged in the 1990s in the form of queer theory. Proponents of "queer" as a descriptor and of queer theory were uncomfortable with the minority and identity politics that characterized Gay Liberation in the 1960s. They therefore sought to rethink the notion of sexual "otherness" and difference so that nonheteronormative people (lesbians, gays, the transgendered, transsexuals, and so on) could be included as part of the wider community, rather than being corralled (by the general public as well as by doctors, psychologists, politicians and others) as "abnormal."

Such a definition constructed in the heteronormative as inherently "other" to that general public, and as seeking assimilation into the larger community through tolerance, whether by educating the public or demanding equality via the principle of civil rights or the repeal of laws that criminalized homosexuality. The descriptor "queer" is thus a reclaiming and refunctioning of a term used earlier as a term of abuse and humiliation, much as "nigger" has been reclaimed and refunctioned by African Americans as a positive and powerful descriptor intended to challenge a history of slavery, insult, and marginalization. However, whereas "nigger" remains a sensitive term that non-African Americans tend to avoid, "queer" is consciously deployed to embrace more than only "gay," "lesbian," or "homosexual."

Michael Warner remarks of the minority politics adopted by activists and theorists that "'sexual orientation' has often been used as though it were parallel to 'race' or 'sex,'" observing that the attempt to use this to define nonheteronormative subjects as belonging to a "'nation,' 'community,' even 'ethnicity'" has produced results that "have been partly unhappy, for the same reasons" (Warner, 1993: xxv). He continues:

> Among these alternatives the dominant concept has been that of a "gay and lesbian community," a notion generated in the tactics of Anglo-American identity politics and its liberal-national environment, where the buried model is racial and ethnic politics. Although it has had importance in organizational efforts (where in circular fashion it receives concretization), the notion of a community has remained problematic if only because nearly every lesbian or gay remembers being such before entering a collectively identified space, because much of lesbian and gay history has to do with noncommunity, and because dispersal rather than localization continues to be definitive of queer self-understanding ("We Are Everywhere"). Community also falsely suggests an ideological and nostalgic contrast with the atomization of modern capitalist society. And in the liberal-pluralist frame it predisposes that political demands will be treated as demands for the toleration and representation of the minority constituency.
>
> (Warner, 1993: xxv–xxvi)

Warner suggests that the notion of a gay and lesbian community is an artificial construct. It is not an "organic" community that preexists the individual gay or lesbian in the same way that an ethnic or racial community does for its members. Moreover, what members of this artificial community have in common is their sexual orientation, and perhaps similar experiences in recognizing and coming to terms with that orientation, as well as having to confront the issue of homophobia, and whether or not to "come out of the closet." Although these are of course powerful factors in creating a sense of common experience, other common experiences, such as belonging to an ethnic or racial group, sharing a socioeconomic background, and inheriting a long and significant history *as* a community, are much more varied and diffuse.

Steven Seidman points out, indeed, that

> Modern Western homophobic and gay-affirmative theory has assumed a homosexual subject. Dispute revolved around its origin (natural or social), changing social forms and roles, its moral meaning, and political strategies of repression and resistance. There has been little serious disagreement regarding the assumption that homosexual theory and politics has as its object "the homosexual" as a stable, unified, and identifiable human type.
>
> (Seidman, 1996: 11)

The notion of "queer," argues Seidman, critiques that notion of the homosexual as "a stable, unified, and identifiable human type":

> Drawing from the critique of unitary identity politics by people of color and sex rebels, and from the poststructural critique of "representational" models of language, Queer theorists argue that identities are always multiple or at best composites with literally an infinite number of ways in which "identity-components" (e.g., sexual orientation, race, class, nationality, gender, age, able-ness) can intersect or combine. Any specific identity construction, moreover, is arbitrary, unstable, and exclusionary. Identity constructions necessarily entail the silencing or exclusion of some experiences or forms of life. For example, asserting a black, middle-class, American lesbian identity silences differences that relate to religion, regional location, subcultural identification, relation to feminism, age, or education. Identity constructs are necessarily stable since they elicit opposition or resistance by people whose experiences or interests are submerged by a particular assertion of identity. Finally, rather than viewing the affirmation of identity as necessarily liberating, Queer theorists view them as, in part, disciplinary and regulatory structures. Identity constructions function as templates defining selves and behaviors and therefore excluding a range of possible ways to frame the self, body, desires, actions, and social relations.
>
> (Seidman, 1996: 11–12)

Queer theory thus problematizes the notion of identity as integral, stable, and self-sufficient, seeing it rather as the product of a range of exclusions and suppressions, and itself permitting only a selective and therefore limited range of behaviors, attitudes, and practices. Implicitly, therefore, "identity" is always-already at least partially complicit with dominant discourses. In arguing instead for subjectivity that allows free play to the many and various constituent elements that make up "the (nonheteronormative) person," queer theory aligns itself with other poststructuralist and postmodern theories that also seek to undo and interrogate the "taken-for-granted" assumptions that underlie our culture and our social structure and dynamics.

The notion of a gay and lesbian community (as Warner suggests) creates a nostalgic sense of belonging, especially in the context of an "atomized" society. However, it does not address the larger issue of the continuing separateness of such a community from the greater society, on whose grace and favor that community nevertheless depends. Its localization, especially in larger cities, is often physical, in the form of a gay and lesbian "ghetto," which in turn makes it vulnerable to actual attack by homophobic members of the larger society. Furthermore, whereas the notion of a gay and lesbian community may have been imagined at the outset as global, reaching out to nonheteronormative people everywhere, in practice its politics may tend towards the insular, its political and social concerns influenced by its immediate social, historical, and cultural context.

The emphasis in queer politics and theory on, in Warner's terms, "dispersal rather than localization" therefore seeks to broaden and redefine the scope of what constitutes "normal":

> The preference for "queer" [as opposed to "gay"] represents, among other things, an aggressive impulse of generalization; it rejects a minoritizing[3] logic of toleration or simple political interest-representation in favor of a more thorough resistance to regimes of the normal. …"[Q]ueer" gets a critical edge by defining itself against the normal rather than the heterosexual. … The universalizing utopianism of queer theory does not entirely replace small minority-based versions of lesbian and gay theory – nor could it, since normal sexuality and the machinery of enforcing it do not bear down equally on everyone, as we are constantly reminded by pervasive forms of terror [aimed at homosexuals both as individuals and as a group], coercion, violence, and devastation. The insistence on "queer" – a term initially generated in the context of terror – has the effect of pointing out a wide field of normalization, rather than simple intolerance, as the site of violence.
>
> (Warner, 1993: xxvi)

Violence, then, is generated, not merely through the intolerance of individuals or groups, but rather through a discourse of normalization which defines the nonheteronormative as abnormal (in turn permitting the latter to be classified in categories ranging from "sick" through "sickening" to "menacing") and so, in effect, licenses intolerance and any consequent acts of violence. The task of "queer" as descriptor and as theory is, therefore, to interrogate both the grounds and bounds of "the normal." "'Queer,'" observes Warner, "is also a way of cutting against mandatory gender divisions, though gender continues to be a dividing line":

> Its brilliance as a naming strategy lies in combining resistance on that broad social terrain with more specific resistance on the terrains of phobia and queer-bashing, on one hand, or of pleasure, on the other. "Queer" therefore also suggests the difficulty in defining the population whose interests are at stake in queer politics.
>
> (Warner, 1993: xxvi)

That population ought not be conceived as restricted only to the nonheteronormative. Rather, the project of "queer" has been to expand and thereby make more spacious ideas about sex, gender, and sexuality. It posits, for example, that sexual orientation is more fluid than the conventional notion that there are heterosexuals and there are homosexuals, with bisexuals occupying an uneasy space between these two categories.

Indeed, this had already been suggested in Alfred C. Kinsey's important 1948 study *Sexual Behavior in the Human Male*. The so-called "Kinsey Scale," developed in conjunction with Wardell Pomeroy and Clyde Martin, locates male sexuality across seven categories, ranging from 0 (exclusively heterosexual) to 6 (exclusively homosexual). The Kinsey team discovered that, although most men reported that they were exclusively heterosexual, and a small number that they were exclusively homosexual, "many individuals disclosed behaviors or thoughts somewhere in between." Kinsey observed that "Males do not represent two discrete populations, heterosexual and homosexual. The world is not to be divided into sheep and goats … The living world is a continuum in each and every one of its aspects" ("Kinsey's Heterosexual-Homosocial Rating Scale," 1996–2011).

In *The Male Body: a new look at men in public and in private*, Susan Bordo points out that

> A person's genetic inheritance may be a fact of nature. But that inheritance will set him up for a struggle with the social and sexual identities assigned to him only if those categories are too rigid to accommodate his experience. Some cultures have greater diversity among gender categories than we do. …
>
> … If the available categories of social identity are flexible, fewer people will feel themselves – whatever their biological dispositions – in conflict with them. Part of what seems to be going on nowadays is that some people are trying to reconstruct the categories as well as their bodies. More profoundly, as people alter, expand, and experiment with – surgically and otherwise – the bodily forms that constitute our repertoire of sexual possibilities (or, for that

matter, racial possibilities), the categories *inevitably* will become inadequate. Spend some time loitering around the halls of the middle-class high school, watching young people walk by. It's no longer as easy as it once was to figure out who is "gay" and who is "straight," who is "black" and who is "white." I put these categories in quotes to emphasize how socially mutable they are and the fact that people's realities were *never* as simple as we imagine them to be from certain bodily signs. Nowadays, the codes are getting even less reliable than they once were, as young people "mix it up" – genetically, sexually, stylistically. ...

This mixing-it-up is what contemporary theorists are talking about when they use the term "queer" to cover a whole range of sexual styles replacing the old dualistic categories of sexual orientation and gender "identity" which forced us to declare ourselves gay or straight, masculine or feminine, male or female.

(Bordo, 1999: 40–2; original emphasis)

"Queer," therefore, both acknowledges and insists that sexuality is not a case of either/or, but rather a spectrum along which different kinds of sexuality are distributed. Moreover, the term also suggests fluidity or mobility, such that the individual subject may find her- or himself occupying different positions along the spectrum at different times, under different circumstances.

So, for example, a man who in his sexual practice is entirely heterosexual may nonetheless find himself thinking in nonheterosexual ways: discovering something erotic in a representation of a nude male body, for instance, or developing a "crush" on another male, whether because of the latter's beauty of face or physique, or his role or performance as an athlete or a movie star. Such an individual's entertaining (however indistinctly or fleetingly) of the notion of an erotic involvement with another man although not necessarily acting upon it does not make him gay, or even a closeted gay. But it may well define him as queer. Likewise, a homosexual subject who may consider (again, however indistinctly or fleetingly) the erotic possibilities of the female form or of an actual woman, may also think of himself as queer. In other words, it is possible to be straight and queer, *and* gay and queer. Thus, Seidman remarks:

Queer theory has accrued multiple meanings, from a merely useful shorthand way to speak of all gay, lesbian, bisexual, and transgendered experiences to a theoretical sensibility that pivots on transgression or permanent rebellion. I take as central to Queer theory its challenge to what has been the dominant foundational concept of both homophobic and affirmative homosexual theory: the assumption of a unified homosexual identity. I interpret Queer theory as contesting this foundation and therefore the very telos [goal or target] of Western homosexual politics.

(Seidman, 1996: 10)

Activity 5.5

- How do you define yourself, in terms of sex, gender, race, class, sexuality?

  ○ Are there any aspects of that self that seem to you the most important ones, and why? How would foregrounding other aspects change your perception of your own identity, or other people's perception of you?
  ○ What aspects might be excluded (for instance, regional origin, subcultural identification, political affiliation, religious affinity, position in family, and so on) and which might produce a different understanding of your identity?
  ○ What might be the reasons for your self-definition, in the light of such different understandings?

Queer reading

Indeed, it is perhaps therefore more useful to think of "queer" as functioning as a verb rather than a noun or an adjective. That is, while one may *be* (a) straight or (a) gay, one *does* queer, or one queers, by interrogating assumptions about sexual identity, challenging the requirements of patriarchy regarding sex, gender, or sexuality. One can also read the culture and its artifacts (social behaviors, literary texts, movies and TV, and so on) against the grain by questioning the meaning preferred by dominant discourse, and/or juxtaposing to it another response or understanding that does not cancel the preferred meaning but rather runs parallel to it while at the same time contesting it. To read the culture queerly is thus to "que(e)ry" it, not by substituting such a reading for a more conventional one, but rather by supplementing the latter with the former. Put more simply, a queer reading is not *instead of* but rather *as well as* the conventional one.

Alexander Doty explains how he deploys the term "queer" in his *Making Things Perfectly Queer: interpreting mass culture*:

> "Queer" texts/textual elements, then, are those discussed with reference to a range or a network of non-straight ideas. The queerness in these cases might combine the lesbian, the gay, and the bisexual, or it might be a textual queerness not accurately described even by a combination of these labels ... "[Q]ueer" is used to describe the non-straight work, positions, pleasures, and readings of people who either don't share the same "sexual orientation" as that articulated in the texts they are producing or responding to (the gay man who takes queer pleasure in a lesbian sitcom narrative, for example), or who don't define themselves as lesbian, gay, bisexual (or straight, for that matter). Finally, "queer" is occasionally used as an umbrella term, à la "homosexual,"

when I want to make a collective point about lesbians, and/or gays, and/or bisexuals, and/or queers (whether self-identified queers or queer-positioned non-queers).

(Doty, 1993: xviii)

He elaborates further the inclusiveness of the term "queer," saying that he needed

a term with some ambiguity, a term that would describe a wide range of impulses and cultural expressions, including space for describing and expressing bisexual, transsexual, and straight queerness. While we acknowledge that homosexuals as well as heterosexuals can operate or mediate from within straight cultural spaces and positions – after all, most of us grew up learning the rules of straight culture – we have paid less attention to the proposition that basically heterocentrist texts can contain queer elements, and basically heterosexual, straight-identifying people can experience queer moments. And these people should be encouraged to examine and express these moments *as* queer, not as moments of "homosexual panic," or temporary confusion, or as unfortunate, shameful, or sinful lapses in judgment or taste to be ignored, repressed, condemned, or somehow explained away within and by straight cultural politics – or even within and by gay or lesbian discourses.

(Doty, 1993: 2–3)

He goes on to read queerly a number of movies and TV programs, among these the series *Laverne and Shirley*, which ran from 1976 to 1983. Set in Milwaukee in the late 1950s, this show centered on two young women in search of love and marriage. Doty argues that this series offers, despite its avowedly heterosexual narrative, another, more shadowy story about the relationship between these two women. For him, *Laverne and Shirley* represents only one of a group of TV shows in which there is a "crucial investment in constructing narratives that connect an audience's pleasure to the activities and relationships of women – which results in situating most male characters as potential threats to the spectator's narrative pleasure":

It is this kind of narrative construction I am calling "lesbian." The spectator positions and pleasures audiences take in relation to these lesbian sitcoms I called either "lesbian" (for self-identified lesbians) or "queer" (for anybody else).

(Doty, 1993: 41)

That is, because a lesbian viewer is likely to see (or to want to see) the relationship between two women in such a show as at least potentially lesbian, her reading is not queer. However, for any other viewer, including a gay man, such a reading *is* queer, and queers the series. Importantly, a straight-identified viewer who might occasionally perceive the surfacing of such a reading in her or his consumption of the series experiences, in Doty's terms, a "queer moment."

Even so, it might be argued that a self-identified lesbian viewer who understands a program like *Laverne and Shirley* as offering, however covertly, an alternative lesbian narrative or subtext nonetheless queers the primary narrative and representation of social and sexual relations. As Doty himself observes, "after all, most of us grew up learning the rules of straight culture," and these include the ways in which texts are to be decoded and understood, especially from the perspective of the dominant. A lesbian reading of *Laverne and Shirley*, therefore, demonstrates the ultimate inability of the dominant to control meaning in absolute terms, and thereby also to control people's behaviors and inclinations. In this respect, such a reading must surely count as queer and as queering the text.

Queer reading draws on the approach of deconstruction (also called "poststructuralism"), strongly identified with the work of the French philosopher Jacques Derrida:

> In a series of astute readings of major philosophical and literary texts, Derrida showed that, by taking the unspoken or unformulated propositions of a text literally, by showing the gaps and *supplements*, the subtle internal self-contradictions, the text can be shown to be saying something quite other than what it appears to be saying. In fact, in a certain sense, the text can be shown not to be "saying something" at all but many different things, some of which subtly subvert the conscious intentions of the writer. By throwing into relief the self-betrayal of the text, the effects of the supplement and of *différance*, of *trace* and of *dissemination*, Derrida shows that the text is telling its own story, quite a different story from what the writer imagines he is creating. A new text thus gradually begins to emerge, but this text too is subtly at variance with itself, and the deconstruction continues in what could be an infinite regress of dialectical readings.
>
> (Po[ole], 1999: 202–3; original emphasis)

The text and hence also the author thus say more than they know or are consciously aware of. Queer reading accordingly seeks to quarry from the text meanings that open it up to understandings that contest, although without necessarily canceling, ideologically preferred interpretations of the text:

> The main effect of Derrida's deconstructive teaching has been to destroy the naïve assumption that the text has "a" MEANING, which industry, application and attentive good faith will eventually winnow out ... Meaning is not encased or contained in language, but is co-extensive with the play of language itself. ...
>
> (Po[ole], 1999: 203 [word in upper case cross-refers to another entry in this volume])

Accordingly, therefore,

> there is no one guaranteeing "meaning" which inhabits the text and which constitutes its "presence." The link between text and meaning is cut. Authorial intention dissolves in the play of signifiers; the text is seen to subvert its own apparent meaning; and there is no reference from the language of the text to some mystical interior of the text, in which some non-linguistic essence ("meaning") would or could ultimately be found.
>
> (Po[ole], 1999: 203)

If it is the case that there is no guarantee of the singular, unified meaning of the text, however complex or multilayered that meaning might be, then potentially all texts become available to queer readings.

As an example of how a reader or viewer may employ a queer reading and hence experience a queer moment, let us turn to a text that would, at least on the surface, appear to be completely conventional: Gerald Moore's *Am I Too Loud? Memoirs of an accompanist*. Published in the 1960s, this autobiography predates the inception of "queer" as signifying a challenge to the dominant and its ortho-doxies. To all intents and purposes, the book is a straightforward account of Moore's life story and his role as the accompanist to many classical musical stars, such as the violinists Jascha Heifetz and Yehudi Menuhin, or the sopranos Elisabeth Schwarzkopf and Victoria de los Angeles. Although he mentions that he was married twice, Moore is discreet about his private life, simply expressing in a number of passages throughout the book his warm love for his wife Enid; nor, perhaps, would one expect someone born in England in 1899 to offer a scan-dalous tell-all narrative about his life. Nevertheless, one may experience a queer moment or two in the course of reading *Am I Too Loud?*

Moore includes in his memoir a chapter on the German baritone Dietrich Fischer-Dieskau, whom he describes as a "young giant … He is big in every way: physically, intellectually and musically …" He goes on to observe that Fischer-Dieskau "had only to sing one phrase before I knew I was in the presence of a master." The reverence (which some might characterize as near-adulation) for the singer that these remarks imply is both intensified and modulated by the disclo-sure that

> Age makes no difference and if anybody can open the door and shed a new light on things I gratefully accept the fresh air and the illumination. I found this with the boy violinist, Josef Hassid, and I find it now with Fischer-Dieskau.
>
> (Moore, 1966: 161).

The phrase "age makes no difference," here applied to how musicians, of what-ever age, may learn from one another, has also been used in the context of emotional and sexual relationships, and some readers may find that such a statement begins to color Moore's remarks about Fischer-Dieskau, both retrospectively and prospectively. The fact that the pianist Moore was significantly older than the baritone when they first met in 1951 might also influence the way in which one reads the phrase "I found this with the boy violinist ...", suggesting a cross-generational emotional and perhaps sexual attachment, although in fact Moore met Hassid many years earlier, when Moore himself was a younger man. Moore goes on to observe that

> Concerts with him [Fisher-Dieskau] are inspiring experiences, but to me the supreme thrill is rehearsing with him. At rehearsal he is as nervous and transported as an archaeologist bringing along hidden treasure to light. ... He greets me with his cherubic countenance wreathed in smiles, for despite the fierce effort our work requires, mentally and physically, it is anticipated by both of us with keenest pleasure.
> This man, Fischer-Dieskau, has taken me deeper into the hearts of Schubert, Schumann, Wolf, Brahms than I have ever been before.
>
> (Moore, 1966: 162)

The motifs of being thrilled to be in the other's presence, the smiling greeting, the anticipated "keenest pleasure": these all can be understood not only to qualify Moore's rehearsals with Fischer-Dieskau but to suggest a certain erotic quality to their meetings. This is underscored by the final sentence in the passage quoted above. Although overtly and consciously about music, the phrasing suggests something erotic, even sexual: if one replaces "the hearts of Schubert, Schumann, Wolf, Brahms" with something like "the heart of ecstasy" (reminiscent as that phrase may be of the fevers of romance fiction), one sees the erotic potential in that statement.

The point of this exercise has not been to "prove" that Gerald Moore was gay; there is no evidence in the memoir itself of any such sexual orientation. Moreover, in all probability he was unaware of the implications of what he was writing. This is not an example of the *transcoding* of an otherwise heteronormative text so that a gay or lesbian audience might derive pleasure from understanding that text in a subversive way, as Vito Russo demonstrates about film in *The Celluloid Closet: homosexuality in the movies* (Russo, 1987). Rather, the intent has been to show how a queer moment may emerge in the reading of what appears to be otherwise a conventional and unexceptionable text – and to indicate the possible pleasure that one may derive from a reading that opens up the text to a multiplicity of understandings.

More recently, the producers of many texts have often sought to "prequeer" those texts, whether because of a philosophical or personal commitment to the notion of queer, or the desire to be as inclusive as possible in order to attract a wider audience or readership. To take only two brief examples, the TV series *Two and a Half Men* and *The Big Bang Theory* both incorporate queer elements (*Two and a Half Men*, 2003–; *The Big Bang Theory*, 2007–). In each of these, the avowed sexuality of the principal male characters is heterosexual. However, in several episodes of each, one or another of the characters is temporarily recoded as gay.

Thus, for instance, in "Most chicks won't eat veal," the first episode of the first series of *Two and a Half Men*, the brothers Charlie and Alan Harper (played, respectively, by Charlie Sheen and Jon Cryer), who are shopping in a supermarket with Alan's 10-year-old son Jake (Angus T. Jones), are mistaken for a gay couple by another shopper, an attractive young woman. This is deeply ironic, since Charlie's womanizing tendencies have already been established for us earlier in the episode.

Likewise, in episode two of the second series of *The Big Bang Theory*, titled "The codpiece topology," we learn that, at Comic-Con (a large convention held in San Diego for comic-book enthusiasts), the Indian astrophysicist Raj Koothrappalli (Kunal Nayyar) mistook someone dressed as an Orion slave girl to be a real woman, only to discover, after buying "her" dinner, that "she" was in fact, as Howard Wolowitz (Simon Helberg) puts it, "Richard the slave girl."

Such moments of course open up the possibility of queering the characters involved, despite their representation as undeniably heterosexual. However, a more subtle process of queering the characters may be found in the nature of the relationships established among them. Thus, for example, in *Two and a Half Men*, the household set up by the two brothers and Jake mimics and parodies the conventional family households with which we are familiar. The hard-drinking, hard-womanizing Charlie is presented as the "husband" and "father" figure, because it is his house in which the trio live, and his money that supports them. The fussy, weak-willed, economizing (that is, cheap or mean) Alan, who is an actual father, plays the role of the "wife" and "mother." In *The Big Bang Theory*, the household shared by Sheldon Cooper (Jim Parsons) and Leonard Hofstadter (Johnny Galecki) reveals a similar dynamic, in that it is the compliant Leonard

---

Activity 5.6

- Reflect on any novels, TV series or movies with which you are acquainted and which, in your view, may be queered, or which may offer queer moments:

    ○ In what does that queering consist? For example, are there characters and/or situations that are represented in ways that challenge or undermine an assumed heteronormativity?

    ○ What pleasure or pleasures might such a reading or understanding offer the reader or viewer?

    ○ How does such a reading or understanding offer a challenge to the normativization of the masculine and of patriarchy itself?

who must mediate the social norms and protocols around the arrogant and self-regarding Sheldon. This is a role that has traditionally been assigned to women.

Queer theory and queer reading challenge and subvert the authority and control of patriarchy and patriarchal masculinity, querying and undermining both the patriarchal order and the patriarchal economy, which mandate a two-sex, two-gender/two-sexualities-only system, together with the subordination (and oppression, if not also actual suppression) of one term to the other in each category. Although the disruptions to the traditional hierarchy and flows of power offered by queer theory and queer reading may be only provisional (after all, outside such texts patriarchal power continues to function), they weaken patriarchal authority by exposing its vulnerabilities and the fact that its authority and its power are *constructed*, and therefore neither natural nor God-given. To those who may be marginalized or who may feel oppressed by the patriarchal order and its distribution of power, such exposure may bring pleasures above and beyond those offered by a conventional reading of the culture's texts.

The various theories with which this chapter has been concerned can thus be applied to understandings of the patriarchal order and its power that critique that order. By demonstrating that that order's strength is founded on misdirections (the abjecting of elements so as to constitute an out there/in here that in turn produces the "us" of dominant discourse and the "other" excluded from or marginalized by that discourse), silences (including those created by patriarchy's ex-nomination), and the rereading of male homosociality and the culture at large so as to queer them, it becomes possible to challenge the patriarchal order and, to some degree, to undermine it: perhaps even to change it.

Suggested further reading

Hall, D.E. (2003) *Queer Theories*, Houndmills, Basingstoke and New York: Palgrave Macmillan.

Jagose, A. (1986) *Queer Theory*, Carlton South, Victoria (Australia): Melbourne University Press.

Thomas, C. (ed.) (2000) *Straight with a Twist: queer theory and the subject of hetero-sexuality*, Urbana and Chicago: University of Illinois Press.

6   (Em)Bodying masculinity

The simple fact that a body is sexed male is not sufficient for it to be characterized as *masculine*. Such factors as posture, manner of walking, gesture, and voice are interpreted by others as signaling levels or intensities of masculinity, or their lack. Take, for example, the stereotype of the gay man. He is frequently imagined as standing with one hip thrust out, "sashaying" rather than walking as a "proper man" should, gesticulating with limp wrists, and speaking in a high voice that lisps or emphasizes sibilants. Of course, some gay men behave in this way, but so do some straight men; many other gay men do not, and are indistinguishable from straight men in this regard. The point to grasp here is that such stereotyping indicates that we read the bodies of others for information, which we then assemble into a more or less whole meaning, to which we can then respond. In this chapter we explore some of the ways that the body, and in particular the male body, has yielded meaning through its "embodiment" of masculinity.

Traditionally, women have been constructed as coextensive with their bodies (they *are* bodies), whereas men are deemed to *use* their bodies. This latter principle is observed, for example, in the gymnasium, where the motto "No gain without pain" makes explicit the secondary and subordinate nature of the body. Even where the aim is the enhancement, whether merely physical or also visual, of the body itself, the body must be subjected to a rigorous discipline in the cause of achieving an idealized goal outside and beyond it.[1] That is, where women have been identified with emotion and sensation, conceived of as located purely in the body, men have been defined as oriented towards reason and the will. This distinction between the genders underlies the assumption that woman's proper environment is the private sphere, where emotion and sensation can be allowed relatively free rein, whereas men are better suited to the public sphere, the realm of reason and argument. Moreover, lack of self-control has tended to be identified with the private sphere, whereas a greater or lesser strict self-discipline, particularly in relation to the body, has characterized the public sphere.

Nature and nurture

This dichotomization, which constructs woman as body and desire, and man as mind and will, has a long history. In *The Body and Society*, Brian S. Turner reminds us that "Greek philosophy established a distinction which we still recognize, namely between human behaviour that is determined either by instinct (nature) or by virtue (nurture)" (Turner, 2008: 5). For the Greeks, behavior defined by virtue[2] was paramount in a civil society in which people had to get on with one another and protect the city-state, together with its ideals and achievements. The philosopher Plato argued that the body, being material and subject to constant change (that is, it is part of nature), is of less value than the soul, understood to be changeless, or the intellect, the task of which is to seek permanent, stable truth (the soul and the intellect are both aspects of and contribute to nurture).

Yet, at the same time, the fifth century BCE saw the flowering, in Athens at least, of a multitude of representations in sculpture and vase-painting of the *body*, especially the athletic and usually youthful male body, as an aesthetic object to be admired and imitated. At least one tradition of thought in Greek philosophy sought to resolve this ambivalence about the body by assuming a correlation between beauty of the body and beauty of the soul/mind, so that the development of the latter was reflected in the development of the former. The youthful athletic male body in Greek culture came to be seen, in Kenneth R. Dutton's view, as the ideal made flesh. The representation "depicted man, not as he actually was, but as he could or should be" (Dutton, 1995: 24). The constant reappearance and re-representation of this body from classical Greek times through to the twentieth century have been accompanied by cultural reworkings and resignifications.

Dutton proposes that modern eroticized notions of the perfect(ible) male body may be traced back to two Renaissance models, both on the subject of the Biblical King David: the statues by Donatello and Michelangelo (Dutton, 1995: 65–69). Dutton suggests that Donatello's *David* (1420?–1460?) fails to become the key model because it presents too adolescent (and hence dangerously feminine) a male figure, whereas Michelangelo's *David* (1501–4) represents its subject as heroic of stature and body. It is male flesh made ideal. We can see these two models played out in the difference between the idealized, athletic, and muscular body favored by many advertisers, on the one hand, and, on the other, the more attenuated, almost weightless form of the "waif" figure that occasionally competes with the other model. The waif's slim body, which can be read as an interrogation of the dominant representation of the male body, reflects the extreme youthfulness and incomplete physical maturity, and hence unfinished masculinity, of the Donatello model, whereas the athletic male body asserts itself, like Michelangelo's *David*, as fully masculine through its size, muscularity, and hard definition. Such representations of the male body not only *preserve* traditional traits of masculine dominance but may be said to *reclaim* them in defiance of recent historical developments in the culture.

We can discern this opposition at work in a number of popular-cultural texts. The movie *Fight Club* (1999) provides a particularly salient instance. Brad Pitt's hard, muscular body articulates the Michelangelo model, whereas Edward Norton's rather more ordinary body represents, compared with Pitt's, the Donatello model. Unsurprisingly, the film also foregrounds Pitt's greater attractiveness and aesthetic appeal over Norton's rather average looks. Unlike the body of the waif model, the athletic male body appears to dominate and organize the space around it. As the charismatic Tyler Durden, Pitt's body is often positioned at a distance from other characters' bodies, and lit in such a way as to distinguish it from the other male bodies in the same scene. His athletic and muscular flesh is often exposed titillatingly to the viewer of the movie in glimpses of his body revealed in the gap between shirt and pants. Indeed, in one scene, when he comes to the door in order to question Jack as to why he has been peeking into Tyler's bedroom (where Tyler has been engaged in sex with Marla), Pitt's body is to all intents and purposes completely nude, revealing his impressive musculature.

A third type overlooked by Dutton and generally ignored in popular-cultural representations, except for contrastive and/or comic purposes, is the overweight, even obese male body, usually but not always associated with the aging man. We may call this figure the Silenus type, after the older, obese satyr in Greek myth who accompanied the god Dionysus in his revels, and who is often represented as eating various foods and drinking wine. If the waif figure is too flimsy and insubstantial a representation of masculinity, the Silenus type is too weighty, too material. Although he may also dominate the space in which he is represented, it is through sheer mass rather than through a subtle and alluring play of clearly defined lines, planes, and volumes. Yet we should recall that this figure in other cultures and in the fairly recent past of our own can also signify wealth and well-being and, through these, power. Such a figure may be understood to have acquired its very materiality through the ability to profit from the physical labor of others, and through the capacity to assimilate nutrition in both quantity and quality.

Today, the idealized athletic male body, whatever it owes to genetic inheritance, also usually owes a great deal to specialized diet and, particularly, to many hours per week spent in exercise. Ironically, the muscular male body, which until comparatively recently signified the working-class body, used to be the *byproduct* of physical labor. It is now the *goal* of physical effort performed in gymnasia, on home exercise machines, and so on. All of these imply as well as require leisure time in which to accomplish the exercise, together with the financial resources necessary to purchase gym memberships or exercise equipment. The athleticism and muscularity of this body consequently now tend to signify a subject who is no longer working-class.

Activity 6.1

- Thinking about movies or TV shows with which you are familiar, can you identify characters who are represented as Donatello, Michelangelo, or Silenus types?

    ○ How do these types function in the narrative? For example, do they have access to power, and if so, in what does that power consist?

> ○   With which kinds of roles are these types associated (for instance, drama, comedy, satire; principal or supporting roles, etc.)?
> ○   Does identifying the physical types of male bodies in relation to movie or TV narratives affect the way in which you make meaning from them?

The classical Greek practice of aestheticizing the body in sculpture and vase-painting appears to emphasize the body at the expense of the soul/mind, which suggests that too neat a separation of body and mind, however intellectually desirable and workable, is not practicable in an individual's daily experience. Nor should that ambiguity of the body as the vessel of, yet separable from, the mind or soul be understood as localized to Greek culture only. It underlies the Christian tradition also. Early Christian culture adopted the principle of the separation of body and soul, seeing the former not only as impermanent but as morally as well as physically corruptible, and hence capable of corrupting others. A powerful and long-lived tradition emerged in which the body was constructed as requiring strict surveillance and discipline in order to minimize the damage it could inflict upon the soul of the Christian believer, and the ensuing effect on the status and well-being of the soul in the afterlife. Put otherwise, the body as nature had to be controlled through nurture; or, in Turner's terms, instinct needed to be disciplined by virtue.

The body has thus historically been defined as dangerous. Subject to sensation and emotion, it was understood to be at the mercy not only of its own appetites, but also of the circumstances and conditions obtaining in the external world. By contrast, the mind came to be seen as separable from all that. It was thus capable of surmounting the senses, including sensations such as pleasure and pain, as well as the constant flux and change in the world around it. Regimens of self-discipline and asceticism were adopted in order to free the mind from the demands of the body.

The dichotomy between body and intellect became gendered. Woman and the feminine were assigned to the body, man and the masculine to the mind. The Platonic notion that the senses were not to be trusted and that intellectual activity alone could properly engage with the world and assess its truth was challenged during the Enlightenment (for instance, by John Locke's assertion that we can apprehend the material world only through our senses). However, the dichotomy continued to hold sway. The inferiorization of women in the nineteenth century, as we saw in chapter 5, was premised to a great extent on the idea that they, more than men, were susceptible to and hence victims of their own bodies. It was men's task, by contrast, to dominate and control their own bodies, not only by adopting methods of discipline, but also by *instrumentalizing* the body; that is, by seeing the body as a means to a greater end outside and beyond itself.

We tend commonly to regard the body as a natural given and assume a one-to-one correlation between the sex of the body and its gender. However, as we noted in chapter 2, that correspondence may be thought of as a culturally and socially determined fiction necessary to our ability to function as members of a social structure that requires us to behave in particular ways. The body may be conceived, then, as a surface on which are inscribed a multiplicity and complexity of meanings. Among these we may count the tension suggested by Turner between the body understood as the product of nature and the body understood as the product of nurture. In broad terms, the female body became associated with nature through its identification with the sensuous and the emotional, and conceived as susceptible to indulgence and excess, whereas the male body was associated with culture, through its alignment with discipline and reason.

The "savage" and the "civilized" body

The nature/nurture distinction, mapped onto the male body, in Greek culture took on the dichotomy between savagery and civilization. The "natural" body, therefore, was in some measure bestial and unaesthetic in appearance ("savage"), whereas the "nurtured" body was one that had been worked over and rendered beautiful ("civilized"), that is, socially acceptable, if not always aesthetically so. This is evident, for example, in the disparity between sculptures of *kouroi* or athletic youths, and those of satyrs (mythical male creatures that were half-human, half-goat). The youths are posed gracefully, both body and posture suggesting self-discipline and control, even (and perhaps particularly) when the body is represented as caught in mid-action (for example, the famous *Discobolus* of Myron, from the fifth century BCE), whereas the satyrs are often represented as prancing in wild, and therefore uncontrolled, revelry. Especially revealing is the representation of the penis in each type of statue. Conventionally, the *kouros* or youth has small genitals neatly tucked against the body, whereas the satyr is frequently shown sporting an enormous and rampant erection.[3] From this, we might understand that the self-control, or lack of it, suggested by such sculpture extended also (perhaps especially) to sexuality, and the individual male's ability to control himself also in that respect.

The savage/civilized dualism came later in Western cultures to be applied also to the bodies of those defined as "other" to the dominant, understood as white, Christian, male, and noble or at least upper middle class. Those "others" constituted a range that included, as we saw in chapter 5, women, children, members of other ethnicity or race, and, of course, the peoples of the colonized world in the Americas, Africa, Asia, South-East Asia and the South Pacific. However, attitudes shifted and varied with regard to the inhabitants of the colonies.

For example, the sixteenth-century French writer Michel de Montaigne, in his essay "Of cannibals," makes comparisons between cannibal ("savage") cultures and the "civilized" world, to the discredit of the latter (Montaigne, 1971),[4] and in the seventeenth century, a perception arose that primitive peoples were "noble savages," a phrase that first appears in John Dryden's play *The Conquest of Granada* (1672).[5] Yet both contemporaneous and other accounts by explorers and seamen alternate between disgust and admiration in their descriptions and illustrations of people indigenous to non-European locations, whereas many Western writers have tended to inferiorize other races.

For example, Paul Hoch notes that Africans were thought to be, in the words of Edward Topsell's *A Historie of Foure-Footed Beasts* (1607), "Libidinous as Apes" and "so venerous [lustful] they will ravish their Women." Hoch comments:

> Just as ape males were thought especially likely to rape negro women, negro males were held to be especially prone to rape females of the race next above it on what was conceived of as A Great Chain of Being stretching from the beasts below to the angels above.
>
> (Hoch, 1979: 51)

The black body, and particularly the body of the black male, thus came to be inscribed discursively in a number of ways. At once noble savage and, in Hoch's phrase, black beast, the black man was attributed with contradictory traits. Even his penis, imagined as always-already larger and more imposing than that of the white man, became an ambiguous symbol. At one level, it signified his superior claim to the benefits of masculinity. At a second level, it indicated his closeness to the animal and the natural, rather than the human and the civilized (this included a supposed hypersexuality). At a third level, the assumed greater size of the black man's penis became a sign of the sexual danger that he represented to white women, as well as to the phallic power of the white man. This ambiguity is remarked by Hoch, who quotes the historian Thomas F. Gossett, writing in 1973: "One still hears the idea expressed by white men in the Deep South … that they wish they could be negroes, at least on Saturday nights" (Hoch, 1979: 55). That is, those white men wish to assume, for a prescribed and therefore limited period, the powerful sexuality and lust attributed to blacks, a fantasy that indicates clearly a combination of envy and admiration, disgust and desire, attraction and repulsion.

Classical and grotesque bodies

David Morgan discusses the nature/nurture or instinct/virtue dichotomy in the context of Mikhail Bakhtin's "distinction between the grotesque body and the classical body":

> Generally speaking and with some simplification, classical bodies are controlled, in conformity with dominant (in this case European, Western?) aesthetic standards, and are constructed as being much closer to culture or to the civilized. In contrast, the grotesque body is uncontrolled, unappealing according to dominant aesthetic standards, and constructed as being much closer to nature. There are clear, historically located, class connotations to this distinction, the classical body being much closer to models prevailing

amongst the aristocracy or the Court society, while the grotesque body is more likely to be represented as a member of the peasant or the lower classes. Such bodies were also identified with particular special sites. In eighteenth century England, classical bodies were more associated with the coffee houses, the grotesque bodies with taverns ...

(Morgan, 1993: 81–82)

Morgan notes that the classical/grotesque distinction "was developed and probably applies best in relation to pre-industrial European society," and that therefore "In a more industrial society, the boundaries become less clear and it may be suggested that the contrasts between the classical and the grotesque are of reduced significance." However,

their variations as models of masculinity still persist and still have their significance. In the face of the disciplines of capitalism and bureaucracy, the classical body becomes the rational body but the grotesque body still, at least symbolically, tends to be associated with the working or the lower classes. Yet today, as in former times, the grotesque body is by no means wholly stigmatized. Beer-bellied, prone to fits of violence or uncontrollable mirth and lacking any of the conventional signs of self-discipline, the grotesque body can serve as a warning to society as a whole. ... Yet, at the same time, the grotesque body's symbolic closeness to natural instincts, its apparent rejection of the conventional limitations of a proper time or place may be a source of admiration, an ironic comment on the "unnaturalness" of respectable or civilized society.

(Morgan, 1993: 82–83)

Morgan points out that "all the variations of masculine bodies in modern times" cannot be assigned in a simple manner to one or the other category of the classical/grotesque binary; nor can the latter "be simply mapped on to class distinctions":

Indeed, it is likely that both working- and middle-classes have their variations on the classical/grotesque theme. Thus working-class cultures may include variations on the classical body theme in the case of the "hard man" who knows how to take care of himself in a clear and disciplined manner, or the "sharp dresser," taken up as a feature of many, largely working-class, youth cultures. Similarly, various manifestations of respectability should be seen not simply as desires to imitate middle-class class, but as attempts to develop an authentic variation on working-class experience.

Middle-class or bourgeois culture also, it may be suggested, has its own variations on the grotesque body theme. There is, of course, the familiar, if often stereotypical, figure of the bohemian or the artist who is accorded some licence by the largely middle-class society in which he moves and from which, to a large extent, he derives his livelihood. ... Another variation may be the well-rounded belly of the successful man, the apparent excess here being an obvious manifestation of conspicuous consumption, even where control and discipline might well be exercised in other areas of his life.

(Morgan, 1993: 83)

One might add that the same body can be categorized, according to circumstance and context, as either classical or grotesque. For example, a man might, when he is at work, maintain a classical posture: composed, rational, and controlled. He may, moreover, spend several hours a week at a gym, disciplining his body. But, when enjoying a night out with the boys, he might drink heavily and behave in ways that suggest self-indulgence, sensuality, and *lack* of self-control, thereby inviting a perception of his body as signifying the excess associated with the grotesque body.[6]

Brisure and the male body

The penis, that critical marker of maleness, is perhaps the clearest signifier of the classical/grotesque distinction. If we draw up a table of characteristics of the nature/culture (or nurture), instinct/virtue, and grotesque/classical dualisms, as we have so far discussed them, we find that the characteristics under the category of the grotesque seem to apply to the penis, considered separately from the social, reasoning body of the male subject:

CLASSICAL	GROTESQUE
cultural	natural
social	individual
self-controlled	lacking control
disciplined	undisciplined
obedient/compliant	disobedient/noncompliant
virtuous/pious	vicious/sinful
rational	irrational
intellectual	corporeal
oriented to other	oriented to self
etc.	etc.

Interestingly and significantly, the column on the right includes some traits often associated, rightly or wrongly, with the feminine, which in turn, as we have noted, is associated with nature rather than reason. Because the table thus suggests that the penis represents a site of nature/instinct on the male body, in effect the penis ironically and contradictorily seems to be also a site of the feminine on the male body. We may characterize the penis in terms of Bakhtin's notion of the grotesque, which he sees as akin to the monstrous: "the aesthetics of the grotesque are to a certain extent the aesthetics of the monstrous" (Bakhtin, 1984: 43). The monstrous/grotesque thus emerges out of an instability of categories and a consequent blurring of boundaries, so that one form or representation is seen as passing into another or giving birth to it (Bakhtin, 1984: 32). The satyr provides here an excellent example: part human, part goat, he is monstrous not only in the confusion of species, but also in the blurring of boundaries between speech/nonspeech, reason/instinct, and so on.

The penis, then, may be understood as unruly, not subject to will or reason. Indeed, it appears to have a mind of its own, often producing moments of embarrassment for the male individual. It is liable, for instance, to become erect, especially in adolescence, without any obvious or necessary provocation to do so. It can also fail to achieve erection, often at the most inopportune moment. Involuntary nocturnal emissions (wet dreams) may provide their own moments of shame or embarrassment, as can episodes of premature ejaculation. Such unruliness can be transformed from a sometimes embarrassing necessity into a virtue, so that a man's inability to control his penis and his sexuality comes to be seen as the marker of a greater masculinity. The undisciplined and undisciplinable penis has thus been used by men to justify various kinds of behavior, ranging from lecherous talk and gestures (think, for example, of construction workers' commentary and wolf whistles upon seeing an attractive woman walk by) to actual sexual violence. However, in earlier moments in Western, Judeo-Christian culture a man's masculinity was frequently invested *in his ability to control sexual desire* through celibacy and chastity, whether out of philosophical and ethical principles or a submission to the teachings of Christian morality. In other words, his phallic power resided in his denial of, rather than his acceding to, sexual desire. Yet, as we saw in chapter 4, despite the individual man's inability finally to control it, the penis in its guise as the phallus is a central symbol in the patriarchal order and especially in the economy of masculine power.

It is in this confusion and contradiction that the grotesqueness of the penis resides, and not just in classical Greek or medieval Christian cultures. It becomes clear also in contemporary attitudes toward the penis. The British theorist Richard Dyer, for instance, remarks:

> One of the striking characteristics about penis symbols is the discrepancy between the symbols and what penises are actually like. Male genitals are fragile, squashy, delicate things; even when erect, the penis is spongy, seldom straight, and rounded at the tip, while the testicles are imperfect spheres, always vulnerable, never still. There are very exceptional cases where something of the exquisiteness and softness of the male genitals is symbolized. ... Such imagery ... suggests that male genitals can be thought of as beautiful, and there are instances of male nude painting and photo-graphy which do treat the genitals as if they are something lovely to look at ... Yet such examples are marginal. Far more commonly the soft, vulner-able charm of male genitals is evoked as hard, tough, and dangerous. It is not flowers that most commonly symbolize male genitals but swords, knives, fists, guns. ...
>
> (Dyer, 1985: 30)

In other words, both to protect its vulnerability and to maintain the idea of phallic power, the penis becomes culturally represented as weapon-like. Culture, or nurture, overwrites nature.

Tellingly, Dyer goes on to say:

> Yet penises are only little things (even big ones) without much staying power, pretty if you can learn to see them like that, but not magical or mysterious or powerful in themselves, that is, not objectively full of real power.
>
> (Dyer, 1985: 31)

"Pretty if you can learn to see them like that": this statement is packed full of meaning. In the first place, "pretty" is not a descriptor frequently applied to men and masculinity, unless one is looking to express some derogation: "a pretty boy" is generally sneering code for "a (presumed) gay man." Nor is "pretty" a term often used of the male body, for it implies a body that is passive and subject to the gaze of another, something more usually associated with the female body and the feminine. To apply a term that signifies not only the aesthetic but also a complex of gender relations and politics (activity/passivity, subject/object of the gaze, and so on) to the penis is, once again, to overwrite nature with culture.

More importantly, in the second place, Dyer's phrasing suggests that most people are unlikely to see the penis as pretty – that this is a learned or acquired perception. Perhaps men, and heterosexual men in particular, are unlikely to see the penis in this way, despite possessing one themselves. The penis is never just a fleshly organ. It is imbued with cultural and gender-political meaning, constituting it an object of desire that is both sexual and part of the phallic dynamic of the patriarchal economy. Therefore, for a man to look at or even think of another man's penis is to invoke the ambiguity of erotic desire coupled with phallic ambition. It is also, of course, to invoke specifically *homo*erotic desire, in turn raising the specter of the homosexual that the masculine is so concerned to abject and render, if not invisible or nonexistent, then at least marginal and inferior.

In the reluctance implied in Dyer's wording we may discern a *separation* of nature from nurture or culture: a reluctance, indeed, to recover for culture something of nature that is regarded as intrinsically unaesthetic and intractable to the needs and dictates of culture. In this connection, we might regard the practice of circumcision as just such an attempt to recuperate into culture the penis as both an object and bodily symbol of nature. If we exclude the process of circumcision as the alleviation of a medical condition such as phimosis (the uncomfortable or painful constriction of the glans, or head, of the penis by a too-tight foreskin), the reasons usually advanced for the practice of circumcision (religious requirement, genital hygiene, maintenance of a family tradition, and the like) suggest the colonization of nature, in the form of the penis, by culture. Other, more subjective reasons suggest still more strongly that colonization, for example, reducing odor associated with the uncircumcised penis, making the penis look more "honest" because the glans is no longer concealed by a foreskin (and so perhaps made to look larger than it is in fact), or simply because, to some eyes, the circumcised penis is simply more aesthetically pleasing.

Even the idea that men "possess" a penis rather than that this organ *is part of them,* suggests that the penis is not generally conceived as an integral part of the male body. The American writer John Updike articulates this clearly. Speaking about erection and ejaculation, he remarks,

> Men's bodies, at this juncture, feel only partly theirs; a demon of sorts has been attached to their lower torsos, whose performance is erratic and whose errands seem, at times, ridiculous. It is like having a (much) smaller brother toward whom you feel both fond and impatient; if he is you, it is you in curiously simplified and ignoble form. This sense, of the male body being two of them, is acknowledged in verbal love play and erotic writing, where the penis is playfully given its own name, an individuation not even the rarest rapture grants a vagina.
>
> (Updike, 1994: 10)

The idea of the male body as doubled (on the one hand, the body proper and, on the other, the penis as a separate entity, with its own agenda) again reflects the nature/nurture or instinct/virtue dichotomy inherent in our understanding of our own bodies. This disassociation of penis from body is explored in more detail by the Australian Peter McMillan in his self-revealing *Men, Sex and Other Secrets,* in a chapter tellingly titled "A boy and his dick" which echoes also some of Dyer's comments:

> I am extremely fond of my dick. In the thirty-five years that it has been here, I have never become blasé about having a penis. This most extraordinary part of my body still fascinates me daily. It has powers and abilities far beyond those of the rest of my body. It is remarkably variable in size and shape. When I am cold is almost disappears, at other times it is long and fleshy. It can be very entertaining when it is long and fleshy. I can play tricks with it. If I rotate my hips quickly, then it whips from side to side, and if I bounce up and down on the balls of my feet, then it whizzes around in circles like a propeller. When it gets hard it becomes the most obtrusive and prominent part of my body.
>
> I am always fascinated by it when it gets hard – not when it is hard, although it is interesting then too – but when it is getting hard. It undergoes the most sudden and dramatic metamorphosis; from being limp and lifeless, all of a sudden it becomes thicker and fleshier, and then, amazingly, it starts to stand up of its own accord!
>
> (McMillan, 1992: 11)

McMillan then goes on to remark:

> Perhaps because of its appended nature, my penis is that part of me which seems to be least a part of me. It often seems to have a life and a mind of its

own, its mood and demeanour changing independently of any physical or psychological process of which I am aware or can control.

(McMillan, 1992: 11–12)

The notion that the penis is "appended" and therefore "least a part of me" reflects the doubling of which Updike speaks, exemplified by the account of McMillan's fascination with his penis. His admission that "It often seems to have a life and a mind of its own" invites us to see the penis (and not just his) as located in nature, not nurture.

The male body is thus ambiguous. When controlled and disciplined, it suggests virtue and civilization (nurture), but when allowed to follow its inclinations and appetites, it signifies primitiveness and savagery (nature). A useful term in this connection is the French word *brisure*, to which the philosopher Jacques Derrida draws attention in his *Of Grammatology*. He quotes from a letter by Roger Laporte:

> *You have, I suppose, dreamt of finding a single word for designating difference and articulation. I have perhaps located it by chance in Robert['s Dictionary] if I play on the word, or rather indicate its double meaning. This word is* brisure *[joint, break] "–broken, cracked part. Cf. breach, fracture, fault, split, fragment … – Hinged articulation of two parts of wood- or metalwork. The hinge, the* brisure *[folding-joint] of a shutter. …"*

(Derrida, 1976: 65; original italics and brackets)

Ambiguously, therefore, *brisure* signifies *both* a break or split *and* a hinge or joint. We can apply this term to the body, for the latter can be thought of as a site on which nurture is *split away* from nature, but at the same time it is also a site on which nurture and nature *meet, or hinge together*. In a sense, then, the body is always-already conceptually divided, yet (organically at least) unified.

Activity 6.2

- Think about the male bodies typically represented in movies, TV, and advertising:
  - Which would you define as leaning more towards the classical, and which towards the grotesque, and why?
  - Are there any representations of the male body that you would define as leaning more towards the civilized or towards the savage? Why?
  - How does this change or sharpen the meanings that you derive from such representations?

- From your own social experience, can you think of any instances when male bodies were defined, or defined themselves, as either classical or grotesque, or as civilized or savage?

  - What were your own responses to these instances – for example, admiration, envy, rejection, indulgence, amusement?
  - Consider the possible reasons why you might have reacted in the way you did.

Disciplining the body

A history of the disciplining of the male body and the regimens imposed upon it is set out in Christopher E. Forth's *Masculinity in the Modern West: gender, civilization and the body* (Forth, 2008). He draws on a number of kinds of documents, including conduct books intended for men, and material in which the precepts for male behaviors acceptable to a particular culture at a particular historical moment are implicit only, rather than set out as a series of instructions. Inevitably, such documents, at least those of early modernity, address a literate dominant class, whether noble or middle class. However, the criteria that defined and constituted what a man should be, how he should behave, and even how he should present himself to others were no doubt applied also to some extent to men of lower social degree. Because those criteria were part of a discourse of masculinity that shaped the self-view of the ruling classes, a working-class man's failure to meet some or all of them helped to constitute him as more animal and less civilized than the middle- or upper-class man.

As Forth points out, these precepts promoted characteristics and behaviors that seem remarkably familiar today, such as the need for a man to be courageous, socially skilled, adept with weapons, stoic in the face of adversity, and so on. They also often addressed such issues as the care and maintenance of the body through certain types of physical activity (horse-riding, fencing, hunting, and the like, as well as, by the beginning of the twentieth century, regimes of callisthenics and similar kinds of exercise) and the adoption of a suitable diet. Many of these recommendations, of course, were beyond the scope of the working-class male, whether because of accessibility and/or cost, or because, by definition, he worked (often long hours) and had no leisure time to devote to such activities.

The disciplining of the individual body through regimens of diet and exercise could be (and was often) aligned with the idea of nation and national vigor. For example, Forth devotes a section of his book to the growing concern in the late nineteenth and early twentieth centuries in Europe and America over what was perceived to be the softening and feminization of the male body because men were succumbing to the comforts and pleasures of civilization. This in turn raised fears of a cultural decadence, leading, it was thought, to a deterioration of the nation as a whole. Not only would it produce a weakened gene pool (an anxiety that led to the development of eugenics as a way of breeding for a superior population) but it would have deleterious effects on the ability of nations to defend their borders or go to war. Likewise, it would affect the capacity of colonial nations to govern their colonies, and capitalist commerce as the backbone of Western wealth (Forth, 2008: 141–68). The state of the male body in the general population thus came to be identified as an index of the state of the nation, in terms of its health, capacity, and vitality.

The tradition of the conduct book for men continues. However, it is inflected rather differently, given contemporary anxieties around masculinity and men in a period after, but including, the women's movements and feminism, together with the increased visibility of nonheteronormative male sexualities and subjectivities after Gay Liberation. For example, the cover of the Australian Sam de Brito's *Building a Better Bloke* bears the invitation "Become a man women want" (de Brito, 2008). The chapter titles are indicative: chapter 2, for instance, is "What is attractive to women?"; chapter 3, "On being a man"; chapter 4, "Hygiene and Grooming"; chapter 5, "Fashion"; chapter 6, "Diet"; chapter 7, "Fitness." By contrast, the American Steve Santagati's *The Manual* (the first syllable of "manual" is emphasized) is ostensibly addressed to women. Its subtitle reads "a true Bad Boy explains how men think, date and mate – and what women can do to come out on top" (Santagati and Cohen, 2007). Nonetheless, the book may be reverse-engineered, as it were, and read as a conduct book for men who might wish to become "bad boys" themselves, with all that this implies about sexual success with women, the flouting of social convention, and the admiration, however concealed or grudging, by other males. The emphasis on the heteronormativity, not only of the respective authors, but also of the assumed readership, is telling: after all, gay men too might wish to build themselves into "better blokes" or to date (or even be) bad boys. Of note in such manuals for men, by contrast with similar kinds of documents from the early twentieth century, is the foregrounding of the individual rather than the national, and the attendant narrowing of reasons from concern about the fate of the nation to the attainment of such goals as looking good and attracting women.

Activity 6.3

- Find some books and articles that express anxiety about the future of men and masculinity (as discussed in chapter 1) and compare these with articles in men's magazines about self-improvement.

  - Is there a match between these two groups of documents, in terms of an emphasis on the national or the individual?
  - How do the articles in the men's magazines position their readers with regard to emphasis on the body, the intellect, social behaviors, sexuality, etc.?

Re-presenting and reading the body

As we noted at the outset of this chapter, we read social meanings off the body, for signs not only of sex and hence gender, but also of other categories, such as race, sexuality, age, and social class or group. "The body" here should be taken to include not just skin, flesh, and musculature, but also the clothing in which the body is presented to the world, as well as its decoration, whether items of jewelry, tattooing, or scarification (the deliberate, and often ritual, incising of the flesh in order to create scars). Rather than being innocent or blank, therefore, our bodies offer to those around us a "text" to be deciphered and read, and to be responded to (consumed) in terms of that reading. How we dress and move, the nature of our gestures, and whether we are physically fit, for instance, relay meaning to others. Consequently, most of us are inclined to try to control those meanings by controlling the signs by which others construct such meaning. Thus, we not only *present* ourselves to others, we *represent* ourselves in particular ways.

Morgan argues for a greater embodiment of masculinity, pointing out the sheer fact that the male body has often been masked in order to foreground masculine rationality rather than its physicality, and its association with public rather than private space:

> Often men in public space are, officially or unofficially, uniformed as soldiers, policemen, clergy or stockbrokers. The nature of uniform is, among other things, to divert attention away from the particularities and idiosyncracies [sic] of specific bodies and to focus on generalized public roles and statuses. The disciplining of a body of men is at the expense of individual bodies. ... However, the ways in which men occupy public space and the degree to which such presences are licensed or circumscribed vary considerably.
>
> (Morgan, 1993: 72)

Yet the body does not exist in a spatial vacuum. It is always perceived in a physical, localized context of some kind, and that context often conditions and directs the way a specific body is to be seen or offered for consumption, read, and understood.

Indeed, the very way a body occupies space itself has meaning. Conventionally, the female body is expected to take up as little spatial volume as possible. Women have often been instructed, for instance, to sit with their knees together, in a compact posture (eating disorders frequently suffered by women, such as anorexia nervosa or bulimia, may thus be understood in part as a compulsion to reduce body volume in relation to physical context). Men, by contrast, are encouraged to occupy as much spatial volume as possible, not only in terms of the size of the male body relative to the female one, but also in terms of *the colonization and territorialization of space*. Men's gestures, accordingly, tend to be larger and more physical than women's (for instance, a pantomimed punch).

Men are inclined to sprawl their limbs across furniture; even their voices tend to be louder and more emphatic, and so occupy space symbolically. Such a colonization of space of course signals a claim to power, not only in relation to women and their occupation often of the same space, but also in relation to other men and the often unstated, but nonetheless active, negotiations of power-positionings that take place in male groups.

Activity 6.4

- Looking at images of men, consider how the male body is arranged spatially in a selection of those images.

  ○ For example, does the body sprawl, and so take up more space?
  ○ Is the male body elevated in some way above any other bodies in the image, say, by being represented as standing, whereas others are seated, or by camera angle? And so on.
  ○ What possible meanings emerge for you from those images, aside from the obvious one, namely, that the male body may occupy more space and therefore may be more dominant? For example, is there a sense of control? Of menace? Of indifference on the part of the model toward the viewer?
  ○ Are there any shifts of meaning occasioned by the nature of the body represented – for instance, through the representations of race, age, class, and so on?
  ○ Imagine those male bodies with other characteristics (different clothing, a different posture, a different race or age, etc.). How would those changes alter the meaning or meanings you make of the image in question?

- Perform the same exercises in a social situation, for instance, in a bar or restaurant, in someone's house at a gathering of some kind.

  ○ Do you discern the same or different results?

However, it is not sufficient for the male body simply to take up space. Imagine, for instance, boarding a bus or a train, and finding that the only available seat is next to a particularly obese man. Now imagine the same situation, but this time the only available seat is next to a man with a strongly muscular body, say, a bodybuilder. Both men might, objectively speaking, occupy the same volume of space. However, the obese gentleman is more likely to be regarded as a nuisance, because we tend to think of such a person as taking up space *illegitimately*; that is, he takes up some of the space available to *us*. On the other hand, the man with the muscular body appears to colonize and possess the space he occupies. We might find that impressive, or even intimidating; but we would be less inclined to respond with a sense of irritation, even although he might, like the obese person, take up some of the space that *we* would like to share and occupy. Put more starkly, we would be more likely to think, at least, of the obese man that he ought to lose weight. We would be less likely (whatever our feelings about bodybuilders in general) to consider that the bodybuilder ought to lose some of his musculature. The obese or merely overweight male body is seen as an index of self-indulgence, lack of self-control, and of excess. These "nonmasculine" traits are perceived to be yoked to a body that is all curves and softness, rather than the more masculine hard lines and planes. Accordingly, the obese or overweight male body is seen as a feminized body, lacking discipline and self-control. By contrast, the body of the muscular male is seen as the result precisely of discipline and control, no matter how large a volume of space the body might occupy.

In terms of Connell's notion of hegemonic masculinity, the ideal (as opposed to the *idealized*) male body is one that is taut, hard, and shapely, not overweight, soft, and spilling over into space that others might want to take up. Such an ideal body, with its distinct (and distinctive) hard outline serves to create and emphasize a difference between itself and its physical context. More: it also functions as *a barrier against that context*, firmly asserting its independence and self-sufficiency, as Antony Easthope observes:

> the body can be used to draw a defensive line between inside and outside. So long as there is very little fat, tensed muscle and tight sinew can give a hard, clear outline to the body. Flesh and bone can pass itself off as a kind of armour. The skin surface can take part in the masculine fascination with armour from ancient breastplate and greaves down to the modern American footballer, whose body subtly merges into strapping, pads and plastic plating.[7] A hard body will ensure that there are no leakages across the edges of the inner and outer worlds. Nature, it seems, has betrayed the perimeter of the male body. It has opened up there a number of gaps and orifices, though mercifully fewer than for the female body. What holes remain must be firmly shut, for as Norman Mailer makes clear in his war book, *The Naked and the Dead*, the first worry for men in combat is "keeping a tight arsehole [sic]." Tensed, the whole frontier can be kept on red alert.
>
> (Easthope, 1986: 51–52)

In *Men, Sex and Other Secrets*, Peter McMillan provides an interesting personal gloss on both the male body's occupation of space and its self-containment:

> I am unable to perceive in my body any qualities which are not in some way related to strength and ability. I cannot see any simple, natural beauty in my body.
>
> So what would my body have to look like for me to be proud of it? The first desirable quality of a man's body is size. I must be able to occupy space, to have a big presence. Big men are admired and respected, because

they are big. Short men are pitied and ridiculed, because they are small. If a big man is unassuming and quiet, he is regarded as a gentle giant, the strong, silent type. He has chosen temporarily to waive his right to be loud, attention-seeking and demanding, a right he possesses by virtue of his size. If a short man is unassuming and quiet, he is ignored. If a short man insists on being noticed, if he is assertive and demanding, then he is assumed to be compensating for his lack of height: he is suffering from a short man's complex, and is therefore ridiculous.

But it is not sufficient just to occupy space. The space must be defended. In the jungle of the school playground, the fat boys were ridiculed even more than the short ones, as though they were begrudged the space they occupied, because they did not manage to occupy it decisively enough, and the borders were not clearly enough defined. The other desirable quality of the male body, therefore, is muscle hardness and definition. These qualities suggest a man who is certain of himself, of who he is and where he stands. His separateness from the rest of the world is clearly marked by the hard edges of his body. His hardness suggests no vulnerability, his muscularity suggests the ability to be self-contained and self-controlled, as well as to act on the world outside of himself. For the male body to be impressive, it must reflect not just substance, but competency. It must reflect a man's right to say "I am" through his ability to do, to take on the world and win.

(McMillan, 1992: 9)

There is, therefore, a tension between the apparently self-sufficient, sealed male body and the sense of vulnerability to the outside world that the male subject may feel, whether that vulnerability is abstract (the sense of an individual male's placement in the material world) or concrete (the sense of a man's agency in that world, and his capacity to engage with it physically, for example, through fighting).

The extreme form of the exterior world's incursion into the male body is the physical penetration of the latter by that world. Such penetration is often regarded not only as a sign of weakness but also of feminization. This is especially true, of course, of the sexual penetration of the male body, but it holds also for invasions of the male body by such things as bullets, parts of machinery, and so on. It is no doubt for this reason that men will often articulate a kind of heroic masculine stoicism when wounded, often quite severely ("It's nothing – just a scratch!"). It is better, it seems, to suffer extreme pain in comparative silence than to scream in agony; although even this is permissible, provided the man in question has acted courageously, borne his pain in silence for a while, or otherwise demonstrated his credentials as masculine subject.

The body, then, needs to be considered not only as an object in itself, but also as an object within a context. That context may serve simply as background, for example, in an advertisement; or it may impinge upon the body in some way, for example, in a football match, in which the context includes other male bodies. McMillan again provides an illuminating example from his own life:

In my street there are a number of teenage boys, seventeen to eighteen years old, who play games of soccer on the road. In their conversation, in their physical presence, there is a very affected masculinity. In a group they are quite convincing. There is a kind of studied, low-key arrogance about them, and a posture that says, "I am cool, but dangerous. Don't fuck with me." I am sure they pose no real threat at all; they peruse passers-by more with curiosity than malevolence. But because they are male and I am male, whenever I have to walk past them to go to the shop, I assume an air of studied maleness myself. I walk with a deliberate and muscular stride, set my jaw and look purposefully ahead. I want them to think I am so completely self-contained and sure of myself that I do not need to notice anybody else's existence, but if somebody did intrude into my well-defended space, the consequences would be sudden and terrible.

(McMillan, 1992: 10)

Here again we may note the combination of self-containment of the male body together with its occupation (its territorialization) of social space.

Activity 6.5

- Select from a variety of images of the male body; for instance, these may represent the body at rest, in motion, engaging with other bodies, and so on.

  - What is the relationship of the body in each image to its context?
  - How does this affect the way you make meaning of the image?
  - Would a change of context change your reading of the body in the image?

- Choose one or two scenes from a movie, a TV series, or a documentary.

  - How do you "read" the male body or bodies in such a text in relation to their context?
  - How does the movement of the body or bodies through different contexts (setting, grouping of characters or figures, etc.) change your understanding of the body's meaning?
  - Perform the same exercises in a social situation, for instance, in a bar or restaurant, in someone's house at a gathering of some kind.
  - Do you discern the same or different results?
  - Would those results be different if one or more of the males present were of a different race, class, or age?

- Would they be different in the presence of one or more women? Would the race, class, or age of the woman or women produce still other results?

Representations of the male body are to be found everywhere: in print, advertising, movies and on TV, and of course the visual arts. These are not merely aestheticizations. They relay and circulate meanings. They are what Connell calls the "public face of hegemonic masculinity," which, he points out, "is not necessarily what powerful men are, but what sustains their power and what large numbers of men are motivated to support. The notion of 'hegemony' generally implies a large measure of consent. Few men are Bogarts or Stallones, many collaborate in sustaining those images" (Connell, 1987: 185). Today, in addition to the types of men and male bodies available through movies and TV for boys and men to admire and emulate, advertising bombards us daily with images of the masculinities constructed through the bodies of male models advertising everything, from men's fragrances to vacations overseas.

The past few decades have seen a flourishing in Western popular culture of public representations of the male body, especially in a naked or near-naked state, unprecedented since the days of the High Renaissance. A parade of young men, more or less clothed, smile coquettishly, stare with indifference, scowl sullenly or pout at us, the readers or viewers (or even ignore us altogether) from billboards, the pages of magazines and newspapers, and the screens of our televisions and cinemas. Their bodies have become not only the objects of spectacle, but, in the most common representations, spectacular objects, seemingly defining for our culture the ideal male body and, by implication, masculinity itself.

Indeed, if the proliferation of advertisements and commercials for "off-road" (four-wheel drive, SUV) vehicles is any gauge, the male body is fast becoming a rival to the female body as a metaphor for the landscape. Rugged and rough terrains engage in a symbolic relationship with the ridged abdominal muscles and defined biceps of the idealized male body. Unlike the landscape-as-female-body, which traditionally has been represented as there for men to conquer and penetrate through exploration and exploitation, these "masculine" landscapes suggest rather a desirable and untouchable wildness. The off-road vehicle and the landscape/male body are therefore often shown to be complementary and appropriate to one another, even when no actual male body is present or visible in the advertisement.

For a man to look at the bodies of other men, as we have noted, is fraught with dangers and difficulties. As Mark Simpson observes in *Male Impersonators: men performing masculinity*, the escalation in the depiction of the male body (perhaps especially in its naked or near-naked state) has occasioned amongst men "[t]he fear of the trivialization of masculinity and the revelation that it might, after all, have no substance, no core and no dignity. ..." He goes on to remark that men moreover

> have good reason to be concerned. Everywhere they look they see naked male flesh served up to the public on billboards, magazine covers and television screens. Men's bodies are on display everywhere; but the grounds of men's anxiety is not just that they are being exposed and commodified but

that their bodies are placed in such a way as to passively invite a gaze that is *undifferentiated*: it might be female *or* male, hetero *or* homo. Traditional male heterosexuality, which insists that it is always active, sadistic and desiring, is now inundated with images of men's bodies as passive, masochistic and desired. Narcissism, the desire to be desired, once regarded as a feminine quality *par excellence*, seems, in popular culture at least, now more often associated with men than with women.

(Simpson, 1994: 4; original emphasis)

The display of the female body is of course traditional and familiar. Historically, the representation of that body has been intended for men's consumption (see, for example, Berger, 1972). Although there is the argument that the complementary spectacularization of the male body is, in a sense, an equal-opportunities move to satisfy women's desire for visual pleasure, it is by no means evident that the motivation is so simple. Given the tendency of late capitalism to commodify everything, the increasing prominence of women and women's issues has served to offer merely a further opportunity for commodification, in this particular instance the male body, produced by the media as "desire-worthy" on the part of women. This assumes, of course, that women desire in the same way as men, something that is by no means self-evident.

It is worth observing that media techniques for representing the male body tend to construct it as heroic, sculptural, even when in repose. These bodies are not merely muscular and powerful. Through their strong definition and the consequent hardness of the lines and planes of the body, these male forms become self-contained, the corporeal fortresses that Antony Easthope sees in the muscular bodily ideal (Easthope, 1986: 35–44). Such bodies thus assert themselves *as objects of the gaze*, something that has traditionally been associated, through art, film, photography, and advertising, with female bodies.

It is significant that the physical type reiterated across countless representations is one seemingly important to *men's* notion of *themselves*. At least, it is marketed to men as much as to women, as a glance through many a men's magazine demonstrates. However, the exhibition of the male body runs the risk, as Simpson points out, not only of rendering that body passive to the gaze, as the female body has traditionally been, but also therefore of feminizing it. This may be counted gender equality, of course; but there remains some latitude for doubt as to whether such "equality" is ethically or philosophically adequate and appropriate. Nonetheless, the effect has been to create a sort of optical illusion: the male body as desirable object is *also* the male object as the ground on which is inscribed female desire.

It may also, of course, be the ground on which is inscribed *male* desire. The muscular youthful male form has dominated homosexual desire, from the time of classical Greece through Renaissance depictions of the male body to nineteenth-century homophile notions of the perfect male form and the emergence of physical culture. Whatever the reasons for the preeminence of that form, the development of a more visible gay subculture has allowed that particular kind of body again to be commodified. This body was consumed initially by gay men and, later, by popular mainstream culture. The appropriation of that body by the dominant no doubt defuses any anxieties felt by nonhomosexual men that the gay body might be perceived as more masculine than the straight one.

The effect, ironically, has been to make the idealized male body not only an object to be *imitated* by men in the culture, but also, regardless of their sexual orientations or preferences, to be *desired* by them. In this queering of both the represented male body and the male gaze that beholds it as object, there is again that shift to the body as the surface on which is inscribed a desire, this time a male one, which makes it potentially a cause for anxiety for heteronormative men in the culture.

A further factor in the flourishing of public images of the male body is the advent, in the early 1980s, of the human immunodeficiency virus (HIV)/acquired immune deficiency syndrome (AIDS) epidemic. Although the early appalling media images of emaciated patients with AIDS led briefly to a foregrounding of the *overweight* male body as demonstrably HIV-free, the muscular male form rapidly reasserted itself, now not only reclaiming its position as *the* object of male homosexual desire but also proclaiming its status as healthy – indeed, even as "unnaturally healthy," as the Australian performer and satirist Barry Humphries remarked in an interview with talk-show host Andrew Denton (Denton, 2003). The association of that body with health has also entered mainstream culture, even although the regime of diet and exercise necessary to attain and maintain such a body goes beyond what would normally be required for fundamental physical health and well-being. In this aspect the contours and form of the body become simply signs for that health.

Such bodies are often represented as hairless. The depilation of the male body has been for some time a practice in the cult of bodybuilding. It serves the purpose in competitions, together with oiling the body, of rendering the contours and musculature of the body more obvious, and more susceptible to the play of light and shadow. The entry of this practice into mainstream culture seems to have come also via gay subculture, and, partially anyway, as a result of the HIV/AIDS epidemic. In the first place, the depilated body is a *legible* body. Free of hair, the body may be scanned and read for signs of viral infection. In fact, however, this is not how the HIV virus is to be detected. Nor are the physical symptoms of the diseases that take advantage of the compromised immune system necessarily immediately visible on the body. Nonetheless, the myth is perpetuated that a healthy-*looking* body is in fact a healthy body.

In the second place, given the culture's obsession with youth and with staying young, bodily depilation creates the momentary illusion of a prepubescent or just pubescent body. The juxtaposition of that illusion with a body that is clearly not only postpubescent but often quite mature, it would seem, provides a motive for erotic desire on the part of the viewer of such a body. Moreover, the combination of depilated body and athletic or muscular physique is reminiscent of the *kouros* of early Greek sculpture and the subsequent representations of athletic youths. In this way, the depilated male body in modern times may be understood to refer to its antecedent classical model, and at the same time to be authorized by that reference.

The proliferation of images of the male body is also associated with shifts in employment patterns in the culture since the 1970s. Equal employment opportunities for women and their resulting greater presence in the marketplace, economic downturns and the consequent "downsizing" of businesses and industries, the removal offshore of the manufacturing of items, and an increasing emphasis on managerial and technological rather than physical skills: these are some of the reasons why, in late capitalism, men are no longer automatically the breadwinners in a family – nor even necessarily employable. An important definition of the masculinity of the male subject since the Industrial Revolution has thus become unstable or irrelevant. The male body thus becomes legible also in terms of its status as employed citizen, determined not only through the condition of the body itself, but also through the appurtenances (the clothing, jewelry, location, etc.) of the body.

For many men, therefore, the body may become the irreducible ground-zero of their subjectivity as masculine. It is that which (apparently, anyway) cannot be taken from them or colonized in some fashion. A number of popular cultural texts point to this development. For instance, in the 1997 British film *The Full Monty*, the unemployed former steelworkers who are the principal characters (many of whose womenfolk have found or retained employment) no longer have even the labor of their bodies to offer in exchange for wages. They are driven to simply exhibiting those bodies as objects in a striptease performance. And, as we saw in chapter 1, in the movie *Fight Club* (1999), men who are drawn to fight club use their bodies to express their frustration, rage, and despair at being not only "a generation of men raised by women," but also a generation of men unhappy and dissatisfied with their lives, seeking solace in the acquisition of material objects and the promise (rarely fulfilled) of celebrity. Fight club allows them to reconnect with their bodies through pain, and permits them to understand that at least they have power over their own bodies.

The male body as temple

In this context, the male body becomes the site of resistance against the declining power of men in the culture, often perceived (and rendered in shorthand) as the feminization of men. However, not all bodies are eligible for the public exhibition of such resistance, and Edisol Wayne Dotson, taking his cue from Naomi Wolf's *The Beauty Myth* (Wolf, 1990), articulates concern over the way that men are pressured, through media representations and advertising, to conform to and thereby to consume certain restricted notions of what it is to be male and attractive (Dotson, 1999). Dotson points out how compelling the iterated representations of that body are for men in the culture, who are urged thereby to aspire to the representations, to emulate them, and, in so doing, to homogenize their own actual bodies with those represented as the desirable ideal – or to accept rejection and ridicule as nonmen if they fail in that effort.

Laurence Goldstein remarks: "If the body is all we have, having lost the soul hypothesized by old-time religion, then making a spectacle of abundant material possessions is our era's special form of devotional piety and bourgeois vanity alike" (Goldstein, 1994: ix). However, it may be that the cult and cultivation of the male body have in effect become a *new* religion, with its own "theology" and rituals. The development of the ideal body requires a particular asceticism, involving not only, as we have seen, a rule of diet and exercise, but also and therefore a rigid self-discipline and self-surveillance. In addition, it requires an alert surveillance of others, for purposes of comparison and judgment.

In this it is consonant, first, with the dynamics of patriarchal masculinity. Masculinity, we recall from chapter 4, is conferred upon the individual male by other men, and may be rescinded by them at any time, should he be judged to have deviated from or to have fallen short of the recommended/required practices of that masculinity. Second, it is consonant also with the mutual surveillance of members of religious Christian communities, to ensure not only one's own salvation but the salvation also of one's brothers and sisters in God. The cultivation of the body thus takes on a sort of Calvinist approach to salvation, here defined as the achievement of the body to be admired and envied by others, because it is a body that has been persistently worked on and worked over. It is, therefore, possible to see it as another manifestation of the Protestant work ethic. Within the context of late capitalism, then, even ascetic practice may become something to be consumed, both by the ascetic himself and by the onlooker.

The apotheosis of the male body has also created its own temples. These are not, as one might have guessed, the gymnasium and other places of exercise – such sites are really the workshops for the creation of "man." Rather, the places of worship are the public places (the magazines, the billboards, the television programs, and so on) in which icons of the divinized male body are exhibited to the people for their visual consumption. Like a sort of communion, by exciting admiration and envy of, as well as desire for, that body, it creates and defines the community of worship of the body. For men in the culture, particularly, there is also the powerful pressure to emulate that body in one's own, in a sort of profane imitation of Christ.

However, such representations rarely show accurately what it takes to achieve such a figure. Even the wide variety of magazines that focus on exercise in its various forms frequently offer images of men who, although they may be shown using exercise machines or weights, do not appear even to have broken out in a sweat, much less grimace, with the sheer physical effort of performing the necessary movements. The represented contours of the musculature of the body thus both signify *and* conceal the effort required to gain them. The idealized male body accordingly appears to us as natural, effortlessly achieved – even when we *know* that this cannot have been the case. That body is intended to be worn with apparent ease, and to excite admiration and envy in the beholder.

The acquisition of the ideal male body, then, becomes a gesture of what in the Renaissance was called *sprezzatura*; literally, "disprizing." That is, what required a good deal of effort, skill, and technical knowledge, whether in the form of painting, sculpture, or literature, might be dismissed as a mere bagatelle, a paltry attempt of little intrinsic worth. And so it is with the representations of the ideal male body: they transform that body into a gesture that simultaneously draws attention to itself *and* pretends that it is little more than the result of youth, nature, and accident. This is one reason that older male bodies as gym-built as the more familiar youthful ones are rarely represented in widely disseminated popular cultural texts. The gesture of *sprezzatura* becomes harder to accept when the effort to achieve and maintain the ideal(ized) body of the muscular youth becomes more palpable and therefore more difficult to disguise in the body of the older man.

Dutton observes that in medieval culture, "the human body ceased to be a candidate for glorification and became rather a vessel doomed to condemnation unless supernaturally saved by God through the instruments of grace" (Dutton, 1995: 59). Accordingly, therefore, "the human body – significantly, in its naked form – is depicted in the portrayals of the Judgment of the Damned which illuminated missals and decorated cathedral facades, whilst the portrayals of the Blessed entering Paradise show them fully clothed in the raiment of glory" (Dutton, 1995: 60). This polarity appears to have reversed itself in our own time. The body fit to be exhibited in all its nakedness or near-nakedness is the "saved" body, whereas the one that fails to conform to current aesthetic standards of physique is the one better decently covered.

Even when the idealized male body is represented as clothed, there are often suggestions of the naked form beneath the garments, for instance, through gratuitous gaps in the clothing. Again, the movie *Fight Club* (1999) furnishes a useful example. We are invited continually to make comparisons between Edward Norton's slim and unremarkable body and the muscular, heroic physique of Brad Pitt, who not only persistently exposes his body to our view, but in his habitual wearing of extremely low-slung trousers, barely covering his crotch, often creates a gap between trousers and shirt that in turn invites us to imagine what lies beneath. His looks and his body allow his character Tyler Durden to wear the ugliest and tackiest items of clothing, and yet to make them appear fashion statements rather than lapses of taste. Battered and bloody, he still looks better than the narrator and the other men in fight club. "All the ways you wish you could be: that's me. I look like you want to look, I fuck like you want to fuck, I am smart, capable, and most importantly, I am free in all the ways that you are not," Durden tells Jack in the movie. Handsome, well-built and strong, intelligent, knowledgeable, resourceful, a charismatic leader, Durden is the hegemonic masculine made flesh. He therefore addresses also a sizeable number of men in the film's international audience who all want to look "saved" by their bodies as a token of their support of and engagement in that ideal(ized) masculinity.

The tendency in recent years to regard the body, and especially the male body, as plastic matter to be molded in deliberate ways (what is often called "body sculpture") bespeaks a desire to surpass the body, both in the traditional way of Christian asceticism as a contempt of the natural body, and in the way of an artist taking a formless lump and fashioning it into something of aesthetic value.

These two views are, of course, mutually contradictory. Nonetheless, they coexist almost without interrogation, as the slogan of the gymnasium makes clear: "No gain without pain." This motto implies a subordination of the body to the will of the subject, but, at the same time, a *re-creation of that body* according to that will, not the traditional disregard of the body in Christian asceticism.

In this way, representations of the male body become *self*-representations by men. The pursuit of that body by the individual male desirous of shaping his own in emulation gives the practice a certain religious intensity. It also has entailed men's disengagement from their own bodies, so that they have come to view them as objects to be re-created until they come within range of the desired ideal. In this sense, therefore, the male body has become a fashion item; and like clothing fashion, it bears both on its surface and in its depth the pressures, influences, and actions that have brought it into being. Yet at the same time it seeks to conceal and transcend them, appearing nonchalant and natural; a simple, integral given – *haute couture* (high fashion) worn as *prêt-à-porter* (ready-to-wear).

Covering the male body with distinction: the fop, the dandy, and the metrosexual

The contemporary attention to the male body and its accoutrements inevitably invites comparison with the fop of the seventeenth and eighteenth centuries, and with the dandy of the late eighteenth and nineteenth centuries. However, there are significant differences from the current state of affairs with regard to the male body. The fop may be thought of as a conspicuous consumer of fabrics, decorations, styles, and colors. Foppishness and taste were not necessarily synonymous. English Restoration drama frequently represents the fop as excessive, both in his obsession with wearing the latest and often most outlandish fashions, and in his mannerisms. Unsurprisingly, therefore, the fop is often characterized as feminized, if not in fact effeminate. The name of the character Sir Fopling Flutter in George Etherege's *The Man of Mode, or, Sir Fopling Flutter* (1676), together with the main title, in a sense says it all.

However, the dandy offers a rather different case. Rather than simply follow it, the dandy sought to lead fashion. More soberly clad than the fop, the dandy was interested in the quality of fabric, the grace and elegance of cut and fit, and appearing in public always perfectly dressed and presented. James Laver, speaking of George "Beau" Brummell (1778–1840), perhaps the most famous of the nineteenth-century English dandies, suggests that, although Brummell mixed socially with members of the aristocracy and royalty, his middle-class background never allowed him to feel completely at home with the upper class. His dandyism, which Laver characterizes as revolutionary,

> *was essentially a conspiracy against aristocracy.* Brummell saw instinctively that the day of aristocracy was over and that the day of gentility had arrived. There were to be no more peers wearing their Orders proudly on their embroidered coats, but only gentlemen in plain cloth and immaculate linen.

There were to be no more beplumed and gold-laced *tricornes* [three-cornered hats], but only well-brushed top hats. The top hat was indeed a symbol of the new dispensation. On this flat but exalted plateau, it seemed to say, all gentlemen are equal, even if one of them is called George, Prince of Wales, and the other is called George Brummell. Indeed there was nothing to distinguish them except that Brummell's cravat was more carefully tied and his coat better fitting.

(Laver, 1968: 34; original emphasis)

Where the fop intended the onlooker to be aware of the cost of his outfit (and frequently went into debt to his tailors), the dandy spent considerable sums on outfits that looked good, but did not loudly announce their monetary value. Where the fop saw his body as essentially a frame on which to hang the most modish and extravagant of garments, the dandy saw *his* body as a means to make a statement about taste, refinement, and social class.

The metrosexual, whom we encountered in chapter 1, represents yet another development in the engagement of the male body with fashion and with its own spectacularization in the public space. Although the metrosexual is of course concerned to wear the latest designer-label fashion for men, like the fop he generally is led by, rather than himself leading, fashion. However, unlike either the fop or the dandy, the metrosexual pays particular attention to his body, not only ensuring that it is fit and attractive, but also that his skin and hair are in prime condition. "Looking the best you can" is implicitly equated with "looking as natural as you can," even when that natural look has been purchased at great expense from a gymnasium, manufacturers of skin and hair products, and the like.

This seems peculiarly appropriate to a postmodern culture, which Fredric Jameson, in his influential "PostModernism, or the cultural logic of late capitalism," argues is concerned with surfaces, rather than with depth (Jameson, 2000). One might add that the postmodern is also concerned with moments, rather than with historical narratives. Thus, in Tyler Durden's statement in the movie of *Fight Club*, "I look like you want to look," we may hear the desire of the postmodern male body. Brad Pitt's is that body simultaneously idealized and enfleshed, detaching itself from the squalor, the contestations, and the uncertainties of its social context. That body resolves in its own physicality all the difficulties and ambiguities that men feel they face in our current historical moment. Thus, through movies, advertisements, TV shows, men's magazines, and the like, men are urged to make their individual bodies *the* male body, and thereby to *em*body masculinity itself.

Suggested further reading

Edwards, T. (1997) *Men in the Mirror: men's fashion, masculinity and consumer society*, London and Herndon, VA: Cassell.

Friedman, D.M. (2003) *A Mind of Its Own: a cultural history of the penis*, New York: Penguin Books.

Garelick, R.K. (1998) *Rising Star: dandyism, gender, and performance in the fin de siècle*, Princeton, NJ: Princeton University Press.

Lehman, P. (ed.) (2001) *Masculinity: bodies, movies, culture*, New York and London: Routledge.

Tuana, N., et al. (eds) (2002) *Revealing Male Bodies*, Bloomington and Indianapolis: Indiana University Press.

7 Postapocalyptic masculinities

We return, in this final chapter, to the question that began and frames this book: are we presently attending the demise of masculinity? Certainly, for many the answer is yes, and we had better do something about it. Articles in the popular media, even entire books, have been devoted to this issue, as we saw in chapter 1. Indeed, for many (the organization of the Promise Keepers, for instance), the end of masculinity (if this is in fact what we are looking at) signals also the collapse of society and the end of all things. Social chaos and barbarism await us, unless something is done to arrest and perhaps even reverse this Free-Fall of Man.

Apocalypse and postapocalypse

This dire prophecy of doom, together with the anxiety and panic it typically inspires, constitutes an apocalyptic discourse. In *After the End: representations of post-apocalypse*, James Berger offers three meanings of the term "apocalypse":

> First, it is the *eschaton*, the actual imagined end of the world, as presented in the New Testament Apocalypse of John and other Jewish and early Christian apocalypses, or as imagined by medieval millenarian movements, or today in visions of nuclear Armageddon or ecological suicide. Second, apocalypse refers to catastrophes that resemble the imagined final ending, that can be interpreted as eschaton, as an end of something, a way of life or thinking. The destruction of the temple in 70 C. E. and the expulsion from Spain in 1492 worked in that way for Jews. And in our age the Holocaust and the use of atomic weapons against Japan have assumed apocalyptic significance. They function as definitive historical divides, as ruptures, pivots, fulcrums separating what came before from what came after. All preceding history seems to lead up to and set the stage for such events, and all that follows emerges out of that central cataclysm. Previous historical narratives are shattered; new understandings of the world are generated. Apocalypse thus, finally, has an interpretive, explanatory function, which is, of course, its etymological sense: as revelation, unveiling, uncovering. The apocalyptic event, in order to be

properly apocalyptic, must in its destructive moment clarify and illuminate the true nature of what has been brought to an end.

> (Berger, 1999: 5; original emphasis)

Observing that American popular culture in the 1980s seemed to present (at least, in the movies that gained popular currency) ever more "explosive, conclusive, and repetitive" catastrophes (Berger, 1999: xiii), Berger connects these representations of apocalyptic endings with the presidency of Ronald Reagan:

> In its effort to portray a nostalgic vision of American perfection, Reaganism erected gorgeous mechanisms of amnesia. There was so much *not* to think about. It occurred to me that the most ideologically approved posture was not to think at all. Just do it, says Nike. Just buy. Perhaps "thinking" was a function of a historical epoch that was now ending ... I began trying to figure out what it was that Reaganist amnesia was trying to forget. Most immediately, it was trying to forget the 1960s or rather, to reinvent the 1960s movements for social justice and peace as destructive and infantile – to forget their content and the serious problems they addressed.
>
> (Berger, 1999: xiv; emphasis added)

It is not merely coincidental, therefore, that the anxiety around boys and men, and masculinity, began to emerge more clearly towards the end of the second Reagan presidency. As with other social and cultural aspects, the rot was deemed to have set in during the 1960s, with feminism, Gay Liberation, and the other civil rights movements, the achievements of which upset the ascendancy of white, middle-class, patriarchal, conservative American ideals and social practices.

Berger points out that annunciations of imminent or eventual apocalypse are by nature paradoxical:

> The apocalypse, then, is The End, or resembles the end, or explains the end. But nearly every apocalyptic text presents the same paradox. The end is never the end. The apocalyptic text announces and describes the end of the world, but then the text does not end, nor does the world represented in the text, and neither does the world itself. In nearly every apocalyptic presentation, something remains *after the end*. ... Something is left over, and the world after the world, the *post-apocalypse*, is usually the true object of the apocalyptic writer's concern. The end itself, the moment of cataclysm, is only part of the point of apocalyptic writing. The apocalypse as eschaton is just as importantly the vehicle for clearing away the world as it is and making possible the post-apocalyptic paradise or wasteland.
>
> (Berger, 1999: 5–6; original emphasis)

This, suggests Berger, creates paradoxes of time:

> Temporal sequence becomes confused. Apocalyptic writing takes us after the end, shows the signs prefiguring the end, the moment of obliteration, and the aftermath. The writer and reader must be both places at once, imagining

the post-apocalyptic world and then paradoxically "remembering" the world as it was, as it is. … Every action before the apocalypse is simultaneously an action after the apocalypse … The "signs of the times" are replayed as post-apocalyptic messages sent back to anticipate the apocalypse. … The narrative logic of apocalyptic writing insists that the post-apocalypse precede the apocalypse. This is also the logic of prophecy. The events envisioned have already occurred, *have as good as occurred*. Once the prophecy is uttered, all the rest is post-apocalypse. …

And yet the world, impossibly continues, and the apocalyptic writer continues to write. It is a common pattern. A disaster occurs of over-whelming, disorienting magnitude, and yet the world continues. And so writers imagine another catastrophe that is absolutely conclusive, that will end this world. The initial disaster, which distorts and disorients – which, in a sense, is not an apocalypse in that it does not reveal – requires imagining a second disaster that *is* an apocalypse and thereby gives the first disaster retrospective apocalyptic status.

(Berger, 1999: 6–7; emphasis added)

In terms, therefore, of the crisis in and foretold end of masculinity, the 1960s, together with the subversions of and upheavals in sex, gender, and sexuality of that period, become represented retrospectively as the cataclysm that both precedes and so announces the coming apocalypse, yet, at the same time, *brings it about*.

However, there is a significant difference between the apocalyptic previsions of social collapse caused by shifts in the gender system, especially around men and masculinity, and what Berger perceives as an essential element of apocalyptic writing:

Apocalypse is a semantic alchemical process; it burns and distills signs and referents into new precipitates. The study of post-apocalypse is a study of what disappears and what remains, and of how the remainder has been trans-formed. …The apocalypse would be the *definitive* catastrophe – not only final and complete but absolutely clarifying. It would unmistakably separate good from evil, true from false. The apocalypse would replace the moral and epis-temological murkiness of life as it is with a post-apocalyptic world in which all identities and values are clear.

(Berger, 1999: 7–8; original emphasis)

That is, *new* meanings and *new* values are produced in the postapocalyptic world. Or, at the very least, the old ones would be rendered clear and beyond dispute. However, in the clamor concerning the confusion felt by boys and men about what is expected of them now, the degeneration of masculinity as an expression of noble maleness, and so on, we may discern, not the realization and understand-ing of new meanings and values, but an urging to return to a status *ante quo*, a prior condition or set of practices. It is the voice of the Old Testament prophet Ezekiel, foretelling the cataclysm that will befall an entire people: "Say unto them, As I live, saith the Lord GOD, I have no pleasure in the death of the wicked, but that the wicked turn from his way and live: turn ye, turn ye from your evil ways; for why will ye die, O house of Israel?'" (Ezekiel 33:11).

Such a position suggests less the realization of a new truth or truths than an insistence upon the continuing validity of the old truth or truths; or perhaps a willful blindness to the revelation of new ones, so that the old order may continue to hold sway. This inevitably implies the continuation of the patriarchal economy, together with its familiar distributions of power between men and women, and among men. Thus, it is hoped, the apocalypse itself (in this case, the utter destruction of the old gender order) might be averted.

Activity 7.1

- In your reading of print media (newspapers, magazines, etc.) or viewing of electronic media (TV news programs, online news information services, etc.), see if you can find any statements or claims that might be categorized as postapocalyptic, in Berger's terms.

    ○ To what events or situations do such statements or claims generally refer?
    ○ What "cataclysms" are identified?
    ○ What is the nature of the postapocalypse indicated: in Berger's terms, paradise or wasteland?
    ○ What clarifications are said in those statements or claims to emerge?

- Perform the same exercises on movies, TV programs, novels, electronic games, or other types of narrative in which you identify elements of apocalypse or postapocalypse.
- To what degree do issues of gender and/or sexuality play a role in these proclamations or visions of apocalypse and postapocalypse?

    ○ For example, is the human body represented as dimorphic ("having two forms," namely, male or female) only?
    ○ Is human sexuality represented in terms of narrowness or diversity?
    ○ Are masculinity and/or femininity represented as heightened in any way?
    ○ What are the characteristics by which you recognize this?
    ○ What is the purpose or function of this emphasized set of gender traits, within the narrative world, and within the world of the assumed reader?
    ○ What are the implications of your reading of these issues of gender and/or sexuality in those visions of apocalypse and postapocalypse, and how do these affect your understanding of the meanings offered by the texts or documents in question?

We may say, then, that The End having arrived as prophesied (or, at least, as retrospectively foretold by the demonization of the 1960s at the hands of conservative elements of a post-Reaganite society), men now live in an era of postapocalyptic masculinity, with the knowledge that the end of masculinity has been (and continues to be) announced. Yet the world has not descended in flame. In these postapocalyptic times, what becomes of men's relationship to hegemonic masculinity?

Masculinity as *habitus*

The French sociologist Pierre Bourdieu offers a useful theorization of social existence.[1] He postulates the presence of multiple and often overlapping or intersecting *fields*, which we may think of as roughly (and therefore inexactly) comparable with Foucault's notion of discourse. Masculinity, then, constitutes one such field (within the broader field of gender). Bourdieu used the metaphor of a game, especially football, being played out on such social fields, a metaphor that Patricia Thomson explains:

> A football field is a boundaried site where a game is played. In order to play the game, players have set positions – when the football field is represented in visual form, it is as a square with internal divisions and an external boundary, with the set positions marked in predetermined places. The game has specific rules which novice players must learn, together with basic skills, as they begin to play. What players can do, and where they can go during the game, depends on their field position. The actual physical condition of the field (whether it is wet, dry, well grassed or full of potholes), also has an effect on what players can do and thus how the game can be played.
>
> (Thomson, 2008: 68)

The appropriateness of this metaphor to the performance of masculinity by individual males is fairly self-evident. Young males must learn the "rules" of the game of masculinity, and must also understand their positions in that game, together with the conditions under which it is to be played, and what sorts of advantages or penalties might be involved.

The idea of a game played out in a social field carries with it the notion of competitiveness, "with various social agents using differing strategies to maintain or improve their position. At stake in the field is the accumulation of *capitals*: they are both the process within, and product of, a field" (Thomson, 2008: 69; original emphasis). We may map on to this description our understanding of the patriarchal order, as discussed in chapter 4. If that order is thought of as the game, then Thomson's explanation that the various players (agents) seek "to maintain or improve their position" seems most apt. Relevant too is her comment about capitals being both "the process within, and product of, a field." We may think of masculinity as one such capital: it is required as process in order to play the game of the patriarchal order; but it is also the product of that game.

Thomson goes on to observe that

> Bourdieu nominated four forms of capital: *economic* (money and assets);
> *cultural* (e.g. forms of knowledge; taste, aesthetic and cultural preferences;
> language, narrative and voice); *social* (e.g. affiliations and networks; fam-
> ily, religious and cultural heritage) and *symbolic* (things which stand for all
> of the other forms of capital and can be "exchanged" in other fields, e.g.
> credentials). However, unlike the carefully manicured football field, there is
> no level playing ground in a social field; players who begin with particular
> forms of capital are advantaged at the outset because the field depends on,
> as well as produces more of, that capital. Such lucky players are able to use
> their capital advantage to accumulate more and advance further (be more
> successful) than others.
>
> (Thomson, 2008: 69; emphasis added)

In our terms, then, the man who most closely approaches the ideal of hegemonic
masculinity is the one with most capital, and therefore most likely to "win" the
game. Although, of course, there is no actual material prize (as there often is in a
real game), the gains in terms of what we might call phallic viability within the
patriarchal order may be considerable. Those men who lack the necessary capital
(membership in the dominant social group [normatively defined as white and
middle-class], level of education, the ideal physique, measurable prowess in
terms of profession, wealth, sexual attractiveness, and so on) are disadvantaged
in the game of masculinity. Some capital, naturally, might be acquired, which in
turn helps to advance them. However, other forms of capital may be permanently
out of reach: for example, racial or ethnic affiliation.

The combination of field and capital helps to produce what Bourdieu calls
habitus: a sense of being "at home" in a particular field. Bourdieu uses the image
of a fish in or (wholly or partly) out of water, depending on the match or mismatch
among field, capital, and habitus. Karl Maton points out that

> As "fish in water," social agents [that is, people in general] are typically un-
> aware of the supporting, life-affirming water, the match between the habitus-
> es and the fields in which they flourish or feel at ease, and how they come to
> be in these contexts. Moreover, by virtue of field-habitus match, social agents
> share the *doxa* of the field, the assumptions that "go without saying" and that
> determine the limits of the doable and the unthinkable.
>
> (Maton, 2008: 59: original emphasis)

In other words, for the fish in water, everything is as it should be, natural, inevitable. (This is, of course, also the effect of ideology, discussed in chapter 2.)
However, for those who are fish out of water, the mechanisms and processes of
the interacting elements of the field, capital, and habitus become visible and are
consequently denaturalized. This, of course, intensifies the sense of marginalization felt by those subjects. *Their* habitus does not, and cannot, match the habitus
of the dominant.

However, it also opens for them the door to a more or less radical critique of both field and capital. This, in effect, is what happened in the reviled 1960s: historical and social circumstances created the conditions under which groups that were actual minorities (people of color, gay people) or were treated as minorities (women) gained sufficient critical mass and momentum to embark on a sustained critique of the habitus of the dominant in order to demonstrate that it was neither natural nor inevitable. They sought to find strategies to change the nature of that habitus so that it became more inclusive. That process of critique, of course, continues; and so does the resistance of the dominant habitus to both critique and to the possibility of change.

It is important to understand that Bourdieu's model of the social agent or individual functioning within a social context is a dynamic one. Conditions of the field may alter, necessitating alterations in the kinds of capital best suited to it. Therefore,

> The relation between habitus and the social world is ... not always simply one of degrees of match or class – they can become "out of synch [sic]." Because its dispositions are embodied, the habitus develops a momentum that can generate practices for some time after the original conditions which shaped it have vanished. ... One can thus have situations where the field changes more rapidly than, or in different directions to, the habitus of its members. The practices of social agents can then seem anachronistic, stubbornly resistant or ill-informed.
>
> (Maton, 2008: 59)

This lag or gap between field and habitus Bourdieu calls "the hysteresis effect" (see Hardy, 2008), "hysteresis" being derived from the Greek word meaning "to be behind, come late, etc.," and defined by the *Oxford English Dictionary* as "the lagging of magnetic effects behind their causes." (We return to the notion of hysteresis later in this chapter.)

Activity 7.2

- From your own experience or observation, think of some examples of being a fish in water or a fish out of water in particular social contexts:
  - What is the "field" in each case (for example, education, gender, employment, etc.)?
  - Analyse some of the kinds of capital involved: how did these work to advantage or disadvantage you, or someone you know?

- Did this experience or observation bring into visibility and so denaturalize the habitus of the dominant?

Residual and emergent masculinities, "passing," and the schlemiel

Shifts in the social field, together with the possibility of consequent shifts in the valuation of the kinds of capital involved, may mean that hitherto subordinate masculinities begin to take a greater prominence, even if they do not displace the current hegemonic model of masculinity. Moreover, as such shifts occur, a number of models of masculinity may be in play simultaneously. In *Marxism and Literature*, Raymond Williams proposes, like Bourdieu, that a culture is constantly in dynamic movement, and that this movement derives from the complex interrelationships and interplay among what Williams calls dominant, residual, and emergent elements.

He distinguishes the *residual* from the archaic, the latter being "that which is wholly recognized as an element of the past, to be observed, to be examined, or even on occasion to be consciously 'revived,' in a deliberately specializing way," whereas the residual

> has been effectively formed in the past, but it is still active in the cultural process, not only and often not at all as an element of the past, but as an effective element of the present. Thus certain experiences, meanings, and values which cannot be expressed or substantially verified in terms of the dominant culture, are nevertheless lived and practised on the basis of the residue – cultural as well as social – of some previous social and cultural institution or formation.
>
> (Williams, 1977: 122)

The residual, Williams observes, "may have an alternative or even oppositional relation to the dominant culture," and this should be distinguished "from that active manifestation of the residual (this being its distinction from the archaic) which has been wholly or largely incorporated into the dominant culture" (Williams, 1977: 122).

Williams offers as one example the notion of "rural community." Another, more obviously American example is the Wild West, a foundational myth of the frontier that has been articulated and elaborated in many movies and novels, and the incarnation of which is to be found in the figure of the cowboy. His determination, ingenuity, and capacity for endurance and survival often inform his various representations, whether as pioneer or lawman. These include the once-popular "Marlboro Man," the advertising emblem for a brand of cigarette that associated the qualities of the Wild West with smoking. Another example is the 4-wheel drive, off-road vehicle, which, despite its initial cost and the subsequent costs of fuel and maintenance (and despite the fact that many such vehicles often never leave the confines of the urban or suburban landscape), continue to be shown as essential to American fantasies of exploring, pioneering, and ultimately conquering wild and rugged territory. Indeed, such vehicles as the contemporary

Winnebago mobile home[2] may provide, for many actual or would-be purchasers, echoes of the Conestoga wagons that once filed westward from the East Coast in the opening up of the interior of America.

Politicians, too, may hark back to this heavily mythicized era in American history in direct or indirect form, indicating the strength of this notion of an idealized past and masculinity. Indeed, President George W. Bush often seemed to represent himself as the Texas cowboy in the White House: simple, down-to-earth, full of home-spun wisdom and expressions: "President of the Wild Frontier," as Susan Faludi calls him (Faludi, 2007: 146–64). Indeed, after the events of 9/11, he took on the role of global sheriff, the world's lawman.

Another example of a residual masculinity is the Byronic hero, based as much on the life of the poet George Gordon, Lord Byron himself (1788–1824) as on characters such as Manfred, from his dramatic poem of the same name (1816–17). Typically dark and brooding, attractive and charismatic, yet deeply flawed in moral and/or emotional terms, the Byronic figure often nurses a terrible secret, which may be symbolized as a physical defect or mark. Encompassing such literary characters as Mr Rochester in Charlotte Brontë's novel *Jane Eyre* (1847) or Heathcliff in *Wuthering Heights* (1847), by Emily Brontë, and the heroes of innumerable romance novels, particularly those of a Gothic nature, the Byronic figure has reappeared recently in the form of the vampire.

Whereas, in Bram Stoker's *Dracula* (1897), which may be regarded as the ancestor of the current spate of vampire movies and novels, the vampire is a figure of dread and horror, in such series as Charlaine Harris's Sookie Stackhouse novels (also called the Southern Vampire Mysteries) (for example, Harris, 2001) and *True Blood* (2008–), the TV show based on those novels, or Stephenie Meyer's *Twilight* series of novels (Meyer, 2008) and the movies based on them (for example, *Twilight*, 2008), the central male vampire figures are represented as intense, romantic characters. The very fact that they are vampires constitutes in many such narratives the terrible secret to be discovered by other characters, especially the human heroine. Vampirism makes its subject immensely attractive and dangerous, while at the same time it is frequently defined as a physical as well as a moral *disability*. The figure of the male vampire thus coalesces and foregrounds the key features of the Byronic hero, and next to him mere mortal, human males may seem, ironically, pallid and lifeless.

Such figures, for Williams, are "predominantly residual, but ... in some limited respects alternative or oppositional to urban industrial capitalism, though for the most part [such a figure] is incorporated, as idealization or fantasy, or as an exotic – residential or escape – leisure function of the dominant order itself." Williams goes on to explain that, because "the dominant culture cannot allow too much residual experience and practice outside itself, at least without risk," it recuperates the residual through "reinterpretation, dilution, projection, discrim-inating inclusion and exclusion" (Williams, 1977: 122).

Activity 7.3

- See if you can identify the myth of the Wild West or the figure of the cowboy in material you read or view; for example, political statements, news items, magazine stories, and film or print narratives not concerned explicitly with the Wild West or frontier history.

  ○ How do such echoes or references affect your understanding of what is being said or represented?

- Can you identify other kinds of residual elements relating to representations of masculinity in your reading or viewing of various types of material? How do these affect your understanding of what is being said or represented?

The *emergent*, in Williams's terms, refers to the idea that "new meanings and values, new practices, new relationships and kinds of relationship are continually being created." However, he warns that "it is exceptionally difficult to distinguish between those which are really elements of some new phase of the dominant culture (and in this sense 'species-specific') and those which are substantially alternative or oppositional to it" (Williams, 1977: 123). An interesting example here is the figure of the schlemiel. Although this has been around for a long time and so may be considered technically a residual form of the masculine, it has moved from the margin further towards the center in contemporary culture and so may be thought of rather as an emergent masculinity. Despite the fact that the schlemiel remains a subordinate masculinity in relation to the hegemonic, his wider distribution in representations of the masculine in popular culture suggests not only that this character appeals to a broad audience but also that this form of masculinity has been culturally endorsed, to however limited an extent.

Schlemiel is a Yiddish word the origin of which is uncertain. Like many other Yiddish words and phrases, *schlemiel* offers a rich array of meanings. Leo Rosten provides seven definitions:

1. A foolish person; a simpleton. ...
2. A consistently unlucky or unfortunate person; a "fall guy"; a hard-luck type; a born loser; a submissive and uncomplaining victim. ... A Yiddish proverb goes: "The shlemiel falls on his back and breaks his nose."
3. A clumsy, butterfingered, all-thumbs, gauche type. ...
4. A social misfit, congenitally maladjusted. ...
5. A pipsqueak, a Caspar Milquetoast. ...
6. A naïve, trusting, gullible customer. ...
7. Anyone who makes a foolish bargain, or wagers a foolish bet. ...

(Rosten, 1971: 352)

The schlemiel, as defined by Rosten, then, is a sort of cosmic fool combined with cosmic victim. Accident-prone and ineffectual, he is the universe's unfortunate passive bystander, to whom life happens, especially as embarrassing circumstance, and for whom taking the initiative and seeking active agency ends almost invariably in frustration and humiliation.[3] Much has been written on the schlemiel figure in relation to Jewish masculinity (see, for instance, Stratton, 2000: 301–3). However, the schlemiel can be understood as offering a broader, more spacious and culturally inclusive meaning.

The schlemiel, as a figure that has difficulty meeting the performance and attitudinal requirements of hegemonic masculinity, has emerged in recent years as a key male identity in a number of popular movies and TV shows. Such a character is typically represented as hapless (catastrophes just seem to collect around and happen to him) and as hopeless (both in the sense that he is a bumbling, stumbling figure and in the sense that he appears to have no appreciable future except a permanent repetition or looping of the same sort of events). Despite any manifest desire and efforts to the contrary, the schlemiel may be physically awkward and socially inept, he may lack the ambition and competitive drive that characterizes many "proper" men, and so on. He is, then, an inadequately or incompetently masculine male. By "inadequately masculine male" is meant a man who seems constitutionally incapable of being masculine according to the current norms of the culture, whereas by "incompetently masculine male" is intended a man who tries to meet those norms, but fails.

Most of Ben Stiller's film *oeuvre* (for instance, *There's Something About Mary*, 1998; *Mystery Men, Meet the Parents*, 2000; *Zoolander*, 2001; *Along Came Polly*, 2004; *Meet the Fockers*, 2004; *Night at the Museum*, 2006) focuses on such characters, as do movies like *Deuce Bigalow: Male Gigolo* (1999) as well as coming (in all senses)-of-age narratives such as *American Pie* (1999). *Napoleon Dynamite* (2004) appears to be almost entirely populated by such male figures. This type appears also as the key character in many television programs. From Homer Simpson, in *The Simpsons* (1989–), to Peter Griffin, in *Family Guy* (1999–), to all the adult males in the Barone family, in *Everybody Loves Raymond* (1996–2005), masculinity is shown to be inadequately or incompetently performed. In *Everybody Loves Raymond*, for instance, both Ray and his older brother Robert (played, respectively, by Ray Romano and Brad Garrett) bear the scars of having been reared in a home in which their mother Marie (Doris Roberts) has been controlling and their father Frank (Peter Boyle) both distant and dismissive. Yet Frank, as the family patriarch, also fails to assert himself as fully masculine, being reduced to spiteful behavior and instances of a kind of guerrilla resistance against domination by his wife.

The representation of inadequate masculinities, and particularly of the male-as-schlemiel, is hardly a new development in either movies or TV. The male-as-schlemiel has been a presence since the silent movies; indeed, Charlie Chaplin's Little Tramp or Stan Laurel's antics with Oliver Hardy may be classified, at least partially, as inadequately masculine performances. Often, as Vito Russo observes in *The Celluloid Closet*, the inadequately masculine man was coded as homosexual: "Homosexuality in the movies, whether overtly sexual or not, has always been seen in terms of what is or is not masculine" (Russo, 1987: 4). Thus, for instance, in a film like *Shall We Dance* (1937), starring Fred Astaire and Ginger Rogers (Sandrich, 1937),[4] Edward Everett Horton's nervous fussiness certainly suggests more an old-maidish fluttering than a fully masculine command of the situation.

Historically, however, despite his frequent appearance in film and television narratives, the inadequately masculine male often simply provided a foil for another principal male character whose performance of masculinity was thereby shown to be more than merely competent. Jerry Lewis, for example, in the series of films he made with Dean Martin was typically represented as juvenile, foolish, socially inept, and physically awkward, whereas Martin was all maturity, intelligence, poise, and self-assurance. Similarly, Abbott functioned as a foil for Costello, and Laurel for Hardy, although in the latter case both were ultimately shown up as incompetent in the masculinity stakes. Likewise, Gilligan, in *Gilligan's Island* (1964–67), represented the nadir of masculine incompetence, but the points of comparison in this show were all themselves also representations of flawed masculinities.

However, although earlier representations of this kind may well have articulated the culture's anxiety about and scorn of the inadequately or incompetently masculine male, the persistence of this figure in later movies and television suggests something else may also have been taking place: a reevaluation of gender performance, and of the performance of masculinity in particular. The schlemiel figure may, of course, be seen simply as a failure of the individual male to achieve the masculine – to comply with the requirements of the patriarchal order and to attain success in terms of the patriarchal economy. Such a figure may be comic *because of* that failure, or he may be merely pathetic.

However, he may also be understood as *refusing* the dictates of the patriarchal order. If this is indeed the case, signaling a declining to "pass" as masculine in the system, then we may infer that such a man may be indifferent to the real or symbolic presence of an audience of his gender performance. Such a figure undoes still further the mechanisms by which the culture monitors and controls its members via gender. The representation of the schlemiel figure in film and television narratives may thus be understood as enacting *a resistance to or even a refusal of* the coercive pressure of the gender system.

We may discern several ways in which that resistance or refusal take place. The first of these is the genre of narrative in which such enactment usually takes place, namely, comedy. Dramatic genres are more likely to render the schlemiel hero pathetic or tragic, annulled as a human being because he is unable to perform up to the standards of traditional masculinity and hence successfully to sustain the narrative trajectory to its end. However, this is not to say that such a figure never appears in serious or dramatic movies or TV shows; but he is more likely to be represented in such texts as a humorous sidekick, a pitiable excuse of a man, or, at the extreme of this logic, a deserving victim.

The comedic context, moreover, allows the male viewer, no matter how incompetent at masculinity *he* may be, to feel relieved that there is someone up there on the screen who is worse than he is, or who deflects from himself any anticipated inspection and criticism. In this respect, the incompetently masculine character acts either as a reassurance of the viewer's own performance of masculinity, or as a lure to distract attention from a viewer whose own masculinity may be perceived as inadequate. Either way, such a viewer no doubt leaves such a movie or TV program feeling at least somewhat cheered.

The comedic representation of the incompetently masculine male functions also (and importantly) to establish this figure *as part of the repertoire of masculine performance*. Laughter has a way of naturalizing and accepting the object laughed at, because, in order to laugh at something, we have in the first place to accept it to some degree. This is why some comic treatments of certain topics may be regarded as dangerous, ideologically speaking. For instance, the television series *Hogan's Heroes* (1965–71), although it consciously foregrounded the wit, ingenuity, and daring of the Allied Forces even in captivity, also tended, through comedy, to naturalize and make acceptable the notion of a prisoner-of-war camp (and no doubt, in the minds of many, also of the Nazi labor and concentration camps too, because most viewers probably did not realize that these were different kinds of camps).

The structure of comedy as a genre often causes comedic narrative texts to close on a normalization of the situation that obtained at the commencement of the narrative. Often, in works that foreground the schlemiel figure, this means that the protagonist gets or keeps the girl or the job or the social circle or the social position that he desires. In other words, *the rewards of normative, "proper" masculinity remain his, even although he has not demonstrated his competence at such masculinity*. Whereas for some viewers this might signify merely the discursive protection at all costs of the male in a patriarchal system, it might also be taken to indicate a rupturing of the connection between adequacy of gender performance as a male and the rewards offered by a patriarchal order to men obedient to its performance requirements.

Thus, the schlemiel as hero may be seen as haunting the culture's gender system and especially the cultural construction of the masculine, for he both separates himself from and refuses the gender performance normatively required of his sex, yet both illegitimately and publicly enjoys the rewards normally destined for those males who are more compliant in terms of gender performance. In this respect, the central schlemiel figure need not actively or even consciously refuse or challenge normative masculinity: the narrative structure and genre do it for him.

However, in a movie like *Napoleon Dynamite* we witness a more deliberate struggle; and this constitutes another way of resisting or refusing the norms of gender. Normative masculinity is represented here chiefly by Uncle Rico (Jon Gries), a former football player who relives his past glories, and desires to return to that moment in his past when he was a hero, rather than the ethically questionable nonentity he is today. It is also represented by Don (Trevor Snarr), one of the high-school jocks who bullies and humiliates Napoleon (Jon Heder). Neither of these characterizations elicits much sympathy from the audience.

Nor, initially, do those of Napoleon and his elder brother Kip (Aaron Ruell), inadequate males both. Napoleon, a geek type, lives half in a fantasy world in which he hunts wolverines in the arctic wastes, witnesses and communicates with aliens from outer space, and is familiar with mythical beasts such as unicorns. He is physically awkward, except in the scene in which he dances on stage before his fellow students. He is, in addition, socially graceless, responding to others mostly in an aggrieved whine. Kip, awkward, nerd-like, and solitary, seeks connection, love, and a relationship through online chat rooms. He eventually comes upon LaFawnduh Lucas (Shondrella Avery), a statuesque black woman with a great deal of "bling" who at first sight seems to be a drag queen.

Although Kip achieves a certain masculinity in this new-found relationship by adopting the clothes, gestures, and attitude of a black man, his very whiteness undermines the machismo he affects. At the same time, however, that impersonation of the masculinity of the black other also demonstrates the performativity of gender itself. Napoleon, by contrast, in continuing to assert his awkwardness and lack of social grace, refuses the demands of the gender system that he conform to a particular model of masculinity if he is to succeed. His modest notion of success is measured by different indicators.

An instructive comparison may be made here with the TV series *Frasier* (1993–2004), in which, as in *Everybody Loves Raymond*, there is a triad made up of a father and two sons who are competitive, just as are Raymond and Robert. However, whereas Frank Barone is a failed patriarch, Frasier's father is a maimed one. Shot in the hip while pursuing a criminal, the ex-policeman Martin Crane (John Mahoney) represents a once-heroic and authoritative masculinity. Crippled, in need of constant therapy, he is now to some degree dependent on his son Frasier (Kelsey Grammer) for his existence. Like Napoleon or Kip Dynamite, Frasier and his brother Niles (David Hyde Pierce) want to be in with the "in" crowd. However, their attempts at it are self-conscious, snobbish, elitist, pompous, implicitly feminizing – and, ultimately, largely unsuccessful. Frasier and Niles, despite their contempt for popular culture and the common man (represented by Martin), absolutely need an audience to see them perform their version of masculinity; and when that audience denies them its attention or refuses them recognition, Frasier and Niles become comic fools.

By contrast, Napoleon and Kip interrogate the need for such an audience. Napoleon, as we have seen, is indifferent to it. Kip, in his assumption of black masculinity after the failure of his attempts at white masculinity (by confronting the martial arts teacher Rex of the Rex Kwan Do dojo, for instance, or by attempting to sell dubious merchandise to unsuspecting housewives, in the manner of his Uncle Rico), dares that audience to challenge either his performance of black masculinity or his *right* to perform it. Whereas Frasier and Niles fail dismally to be "cool" according to the norms of traditional masculinity, Napoleon and Kip are the proponents of a new "cool" that refuses those norms.

Another way of resisting or refusing the traditional masculine is to be found in those films in which the very basis of maleness itself may come under attack.

Here Ben Stiller's films provide a number of examples, although we focus chiefly on *There's Something about Mary*. Stiller's characterizations, in most of the films he has made (and particularly in those that have had the most popular appeal) present a stumbling, uncertain, sometimes overtly feminized male. In *Zoolander*, for instance, Derek Zoolander is a male model whose behavior, gestures, and gait all suggest the feminine and, by extension, the homosexual. In *Meet the Parents*, "Greg" Focker's real name is Gaylord, leading Jack Byrnes (Robert De Niro) to ask incredulously if his daughter's boyfriend's name is "Gay Focker," pointing up the potentially homosexual in the character. In *Mystery Men* we are confronted by a character, Mr Furious, who, together with his group of would-be-superhero friends, seems like a pathetic nerd who has spent far too much time reading Marvel comics. In addition to these traits, Stiller's characters are often naïve, and hence easily misled or easily led to misunderstand. In *There's Something about Mary*, for instance, as Ted Stroehmann (note the similarity to "straw man"), he is duped by the psychopathic Dom Woganowski (Chris Elliott) into behaving uncharacteristically with Mary (Cameron Diaz).

The Stiller character, moreover, often leaves a trail of damage and destruction behind him, a trail that includes animals, for instance, a cat (*Meet the Parents*) and a dog (*Meet the Fockers*), as well as a ferret (*Along Came Polly*). There is also, in *Meet the Parents*, the razing of a wedding gazebo carefully fashioned by Owen Wilson's character, Kevin Rawley. Despite the amiability of most of the characters Stiller plays, we cannot help but see them fundamentally as losers who have managed somehow to connect with the right girl, or find the right moment in which to realize themselves (as in *Mystery Men*, when Mr Furious discovers his superpower only when he really *is* furious).

There's Something about Mary proved immensely popular with younger audiences, especially males, partly because of the film's iconoclastic refusal of decorum. We are familiar with "gross-out" scenes of this sort from such movies as *National Lampoon's Animal House* (1978) and *Porky's* (1982), in which a youthful version of hegemonic masculinity, with all its roistering, drunkenness, and womanizing, is reinforced and promoted. However, two key scenes to which viewers often refer as memorable, if not, indeed, iconic, in *There's Something about Mary* make clear the film's agenda to subvert and interrogate traditional masculinity.

At the beginning of the film, the hapless, awkward, shy high-school student Ted has come to his date's house. While waiting to take her to the prom, he goes to the bathroom, where he succeeds in trapping his penis in his fly zipper. After enduring the humiliation of the assumption by his date and her family that he has been masturbating in their bathroom, he must face the even more humiliating experience of being carted out of the house on a stretcher into an ambulance, to the delight of the entire neighborhood and the amusement of the ambulance drivers. Although one could, of course, discuss this scene in terms of the male fear of castration, it can also be read, first, as exposing the penis to the public gaze, when to do so is to invite invidious comparison of the actual penis (usually small and flaccid) with the cultural symbol of the phallus (always erect and huge).

Second, this scene also exposes the physical vulnerability of the penis. Again this contrasts with the notion of the phallus as dominant, impervious, and invincible.

This scene also suggests a concern around circumcision, especially of an inadvertent or unintentional kind. This is a theme to which the Jewish Stiller returns in *Meet the Fockers*. We learn that Roz Focker (Barbra Streisand) has kept Greg's desiccated foreskin in an album marking the stages of his life, which she shows to the Byrneses, his destined parents-in-law. In his anxiety to retrieve his dried-up infantile foreskin and somehow alleviate his embarrassment, Greg manages to flip it into the fondue pot on the table. There it sinks into the hot liquid with a sizzle, suggesting that Greg thereby symbolically undergoes a second circumcision.

The other scene from *There's Something about Mary* (and perhaps the one that viewers recall the most) is the famous masturbation scene. Dom Woganowski, an acquaintance of Ted's who, we learn, is also the psychotic ex-boyfriend from whom Mary is trying to escape, informs Ted that it is essential that he masturbate before he goes on a date with Mary (or, indeed, any girl), so that he doesn't go out with, as Dom puts it, "a loaded gun," which will result in premature ejaculation and invite Mary's contempt. Dom manipulates Ted in order to destroy his fledgling relationship with Mary; his real intent, of course, is to try to ensure the reduction of Ted's libido while at the same time making him anxious about his ability to perform sexually.

Ted obligingly masturbates in the bathroom of his hotel room, but, having ejaculated, cannot find the semen in order to dispose of it. Meanwhile, Mary arrives at his hotel room door, where he greets her, as it turns out, with a glob of his semen hanging from his ear. Embarrassed, he tells Mary, who inquires about it, that it is hair product, and she promptly takes some and applies it to her own hair. We see her later with Ted in a bar, her fringe transformed into an enormous cockatoo crest.

Ted's subordinate status in this scene is accomplished and revealed, first, by his acquiescence to Dom's bidding, especially in relation to a sexual act like masturbation; there is something almost homoerotic about Dom's relish in informing Ted of this way of avoiding sexual humiliation. Second, the semen hanging from his ear when he opens the door to Mary looks at first like a pendant earring, feminizing (or, at any rate, demasculinizing) Ted still further. Third, something essentially male (his semen) is transformed into a beauty product and appropriated by a woman. It is tempting, in this connection, to read Mary's crest as signifying the transfer of the erect phallus from Ted to herself.

Ted's act of masturbation raises other possibilities of meaning. In the economy of male sexuality, masturbation has rarely been rated highly. Men have tended to see it as a preliminary, usually adolescent, exploration of sexuality, and as secondary to "real" sex, for which it is deemed a not very acceptable substitute. "Real" sex is, of course, penetrative sex, and requires a partner. However, "real sex," as a phrase, could just as easily mean *any* sexual act that ends in orgasm and ejaculation. The juxtapositioning of an act of masturbation with the possibility of "real" sex with Mary thus says something about Ted's willingness to substitute solitary sex for actual intercourse, despite masturbation being here a stratagem to avoid premature ejaculation.

Ted's perplexity about what has become of his ejaculate can be read ironically against the practice of many adolescents who engage in group masturbation (the "circle jerk") as a form of competition: who comes first, who ejaculates the most semen, who can ejaculate it the farthest, and so on. Masturbating by himself, Ted's incompetence or inadequacy with regard to masculinity is to be measured by the fact that he cannot even find his ejaculate. It has to be pointed out to him, and by a woman at that. (It is worth noting, too, that this sequence in the film reproduces the sense of competition via the rapid cutting of scenes of Ted masturbating with scenes of Mary's arrival at his hotel. The contest then becomes which of them will come first: Ted to his orgasm, or Mary to his hotel room door.)

Yet, despite these assaults on Ted's very manhood (first his penis, then his semen), he still manages to get the girl and the lifestyle he desires at the end of the film. This suggests that a displacement of the notion of masculinity takes place in the film, from the biological or anatomical to the behavioral, whereas in the cultural discourse of gender the biological/anatomical and the behavioral are indissociably connected. Moreover, this movie, like others of Stiller's work, offers, in place of traditionally masculine behaviors, new practices. For example, the taciturn, forceful patriarchal masculinity of Jack Byrnes (Robert De Niro) in *Meet the Fockers* gives way to the loquacious, playful, egalitarian masculinity of Bernie Focker (Dustin Hoffman), whom we first see, interestingly, practising *capoeira*, the Brazilian martial art that is also dance.

The reiteration of the figure of the incompetently masculine male may be a way of naturalizing him and of making him acceptable in the eyes of the audiences who watch television programs and go to see movies that include such a character as central to the narrative. Anecdotal evidence suggests that, in the case of the Ben Stiller movies, that audience consists chiefly of young men, and we might consider some reasons why this might be. At one level, of course, such movies might elicit the response "I'm not as terrible at masculinity as he is, so I feel pretty good" from this audience. However, at another, deeper level, we understand that these men have grown up in a cultural discursive and ideological context that continues to foreground traditional patriarchal masculinity and its practices as the ideal to which men must conform and for which they must strive, yet at the same time has made it largely impossible, or at any rate very difficult, for men (especially young men) to do so. Social changes around the position of women make it hard for young men to behave as their grandfathers and great-grandfathers did, without comment and criticism by women. Those same changes have also altered many young men's perspective on and attitude toward women (and, often, also nonheteronormative people), making older behaviors feel uncomfortable, if not, indeed, also unethical.

Employment, too, has reconfigured itself in particular patterns that do not systematically favor hegemonic masculinity. In any case, it has tended to become scarcer and more transitory, making it more difficult for young men to define themselves in terms of a permanent job or profession (most young people today can expect to undergo several changes of career in the course of their working lives). Moreover, late capitalism has encouraged behaviors such as extravagant expenditures on luxury items and a narcissistic concern with one's looks and body that have traditionally been marked as feminine, thereby countermanding the dictates of patriarchal masculinity.

These are just a few reasons why young men may find it difficult today to comply with the dictates of an older, "traditional" masculinity still held up as desirable. Dramatic texts, as opposed to comedic ones, for example, often still represent that masculinity: strong, powerful, silent, rugged, efficient, stoic, heroic, etc. This is where the appeal of the Ben Stiller movies, and others like these, lies. The comedic structure actually resolves the complications of the plot and characterizations in terms of the rewards and perquisites of traditional masculinity. Despite their bumbling and fumbling, Stiller's characters still get the girl, still get the career, still survive triumphant. Comedy is of course supposed to resolve things so that they end happily ever after, or at any rate with a strong promise of happy-ever-after. But, given the audience demographic of Stiller's films, it seems that the closures of these narratives are being decoded as signaling that *it doesn't matter if you are an inadequately or incompetently masculine man*: you are still going to end up in the same place and with the same benefits and privileges as a competently masculine one.

The increasing presence of the inadequately or incompetently masculine male and the bestowing of traditional male rewards upon him at the end of the narrative can be understood as suturing a growing population of young men into a familiar and, in that sense, acceptable discourse of the masculine and, especially, of the hegemonic masculine. That is, such a closure tacitly reinscribes that audience into the dominant notion of the "properly" masculine. However, such closure may also be read as expanding the notion of the masculine in order to undermine the constraints upon individual male subjects, so as to include those who do not measure up to the conservative norms of hegemonic masculinity. In that case, the schlemiel may start to look more and more like the norm.

The nerd herd

Narratives that represent the inadequately or incompetently masculine male may thus be read as signifying a form of resistive struggle, and indicating another way of being male that is not dependent on traditional notions of the masculine. An increasingly popular subset of the schlemiel narrative is the one centered on the nerd or geek. Broadly, this figure, usually male, is of an intellectual or academic bent. He obsessively focuses on particularly narrow disciplines of expertise, often computer-, engineering-, and other science-related technologies, with interests in popular-cultural fields such as science fiction, Gothic/horror narrative, or fantasy fiction. He brings to his fondness for such movies as the *Star Wars* series, or TV shows such as *Star Trek*, the same research-oriented intensity that drives his interest in computers or physics. Indeed, like *Napoleon Dynamite*, he may even partially inhabit those imaginary worlds, entering into dialogue with others of his kind not only about the merits of one another movie or TV series, or even a single episode of a TV show, but also about hypothetical (that is, not actually narrated in the original) situations and character traits.

Although the geek or nerd is often treated with scorn or contempt, however indulgent or gentle, in real life, several TV shows now center on this figure. While the geek has been around for several decades now as a masculinity subordinate to the hegemonic, he has become acceptable as another emergent form of masculinity. This has been an inevitable development as the culture has moved more and more towards dependence on computers and other information technologies. Indeed, we have all, in the developed world, become to some degree "ennerded." Computer literacy has become essential in almost all walks of life, from primary education through to international finance. Social networking media such as Facebook or Twitter are now thoroughly embedded in the lives of most young people. People who have difficulty with computer technology or refuse it entirely are often regarded as old-fashioned, if not, indeed, reactionary in the face of "progress." Thus, although we may continue to regard the computer nerd as a marginal masculinity, and as simply a helper-technician to our needs, the fact is that he has become central to our lives. Unsurprisingly, therefore, the nerd has now acquired a certain preeminence in the culture.

The British series *The IT Crowd* (2006–), for example, focuses on the adventures and misadventures of Roy (Chris O'Dowd) and Moss (Richard Ayoade), both computer technicians for Reynholm Industries, and Jen, their supervisor (Katherine Parkinson). Whereas Roy demonstrates a masculinity that is incompetent and ineffectual when compared with that of other male characters and, indeed, of men in the viewing audience, Moss's gender performance is almost surreal, given his naïveté and quirky, uncertain grip on reality. These characters are shown, in their knowledge of computer technology, as essential to the working of the large corporation that employs them. The implicit message is that although the computer geek may be a laughable identity, his knowledge and talents are now indispensable in a culture that has come to rely more and more on technology.

The American comedy TV series *The Big Bang Theory* (2007–) is almost contemporaneous with *The IT Crowd*. Here, four young male university academics (Leonard Hofstadter [played by Johnny Galecki], Sheldon Cooper [Jim Parsons], Howard Wolowitz [Simon Helberg], and Raj Koothrappali [Kunal Nayyar]) play out before the viewer their fears and sense of awkwardness (in relation to women, and to men who represent the hegemonic masculine) and obsessions (with technology, electronic and board gaming, and [perhaps ironically] women). That this series has achieved almost cult status in terms of its popularity both in the United States and abroad suggests that it speaks eloquently to a viewing audience comprising both nerds and nonnerds, and men and women, who presumably recognize themselves and others in these characters.

Hegemonic masculinity remains dominant in *The Big Bang Theory*. After all, it is what Leonard, Sheldon, Howard, and Raj both fear (having been bullied and ridiculed all their lives by other males) and desire (because to be a nonnerd is to belong to the dominant, and to enjoy such perquisites as sex with, and the companionship and love of, women, as well as the admiration of other males). The popularity of the show suggests that many male viewers, although not necessarily nerds themselves, understand and perhaps empathize with the four central male characters who, although intelligent men and high achievers in their respective fields, are generally denied, yet crave, the benefits of hegemonic masculinity. In Bourdieu's terms, they are at home chiefly in the field that comprises their interests and abilities, where they have enormous capital. Unfortunately for them, this is not the wider social field in which they must operate, something that Sheldon, at least, has difficulty coming to terms with, insisting as he does that the social field follow the same rules and dispositions that create a habitus for him in the field of science, specifically, physics.

The indispensability of the geek's technological know-how recurs in the American TV series *Chuck* (2007–), in which Chuck Bartowski (Zachary Levi), the leader of the "Nerd Herd" technicians at the Buy More store in Burbank, involuntarily becomes The Intersect, the human host of a database of critical intelligence information. The CIA (Central Intelligence Agency) and the NSA (National Security Agency) each send agents, Sarah Walker (Yvonne Strahovski) and John Casey (Adam Baldwin), to protect him (in fact, to protect the information that constitutes The Intersect; Chuck himself is disposable). Suddenly, Chuck finds himself in the spy business, and having to conceal his new occupation from his sister and brother-in-law, as well as from his still geekier colleagues at Buy More. Although, as the series unfolds over several seasons, Chuck develops better competency at being a spy, he remains essentially a nerd who is very much a fish out of water in the ruthless and often literal cut-and-thrust of espionage. Therein lies much of the humor and comedy of the program. However, we might understand *Chuck* as attempting to wed a hegemonic masculinity (the man of action who laughs at danger, demonstrates better-than-average physical as well as intellectual qualities, and possesses that heady and dangerous combination of ruthlessness and attractiveness) with a marginal one (the nerd who is unsure of himself, panics in the face of danger, and lacks the steely resolve to kill another human being).

Activity 7.4

- Consider the role of the nerd or geek in such movies as *Independence Day* (1996) or *Die Hard 4* (2007):

  ○ How do such echoes or references affect your understanding of what is being said or represented?

- Can you identify other kinds of residual elements relating to representations of masculinity in your reading or viewing of various types of material?

  ○ How do these affect your understanding of what is being said or represented?

- From your reading or viewing, are you able to identify any emergent masculinities, for example, in terms of sexuality, race, or age?

The new father

The schlemiel, nerd/geek are, of course, not the only emergent forms of masculinity to appear in popular culture. For example, there is also the comparatively novel figure of the young single father, exemplified in the TV series *Raising Hope* (2010–). Although the single father as the key character in a TV sitcom is not new (there were the characters Steve Douglas [played by Fred MacMurray], in *My Three Sons* [1960–72]), or Tom Corbett [Bill Bixby], in *The Courtship of Eddie's Father* [1969–72]), what *is* new in *Raising Hope* is the representation of a very young man, Jimmy Chance (Lucas Neff), himself constructed as a loser figure, who takes on the responsibility of raising a daughter born of a one-night stand with a woman not long afterwards executed as a serial killer. There is no shortage in the real world of young men who thoughtlessly and/or inadvertently impregnate women, and who may or may not decide to take a hand in the raising of the child born out of this union. However, representing this in a TV sitcom (rather than, say, a television or movie drama) suggests that the responsible and, especially, youthful male parent may be a new form of masculinity that interrogates the older, more familiar love-'em-and-leave-'em masculinity often represented in movies and literature as a key element of the masculine, and often practised in real social terms.

Another instance of an emergent paternal masculinity is provided in the series *Modern Family* (2009–). The older father figure (indeed, we even consider him a patriarch figure) Jay Pritchett (played by Ed O'Neill) represents hegemonic masculinity. He is successful, enjoys a second marriage with an attractive young Colombian, Gloria (Sofia Vergara), exercises authority both at work and at home, and is a competent handyman. By contrast, his son-in-law Phil Dunphy (Ty Burrell) has difficulty focusing on and successfully carrying through any project or issue, tries to be a friend to his children rather than their parent, and generally comes across as an amiable but not very competent New Age man. He thus signifies a subordinate masculinity, made clear by his scarcely concealed anxiety and discomfort when in Jay's presence.

Jay's gay son Mitchell (Jesse Tyler Ferguson) and his partner Cameron Tucker (Eric Stonestreet) offer a different model of masculinity: the gay male parenting couple. Although there is no doubt many gay men and women have reared children, whether as single parents or as members of a parenting couple, the representation of such a couple on a prime-time TV show just when there are fairly heated debates in the United States and elsewhere in the world about the issue of gay marriage (under which the matter of gay parenting is often subsumed by detractors of proposals to permit gay marriage), is surely meaningful for the show's audience. Although this may be a specifically *gay* emergent form of masculinity, it sets itself up in contrast to the images, realistic, simply stereotyped, or caricatured, of gay men as driven pleasure-seekers, pathetic lonely and possibly predatory individuals, screamingly camp, walking vectors of disease, and so on. Although there may be some element of truth in all these figurations of the gay man, they are not, taken as a whole, truly representative.

In *Modern Family* we see a positive reworking of the figure of the male homosexual. It is true that both Mitchell and Cam can act in a "girly" way; that they can panic unnecessarily in the face of an emergency; that they can descend into bitching at one another – and, indeed, that they do reflect some other aspects of gay stereotyping, such as Cam's fascination with theatre and performance.[5] However, the viewer is left in no doubt that Mitchell and Cam constitute a loving couple and are devoted parents to their adopted Vietnamese baby daughter Lily. In this way, *Modern Family* creates a space in which a new, distinctly gay masculinity is enacted.[6]

Although the single Jimmy Chance and the paired Mitchell Pritchett and Cam Tucker are all white men, Jimmy comes from a working-class background, whereas Mitchell and Cam are middle-class. What is otherwise common to all of them, aside from the fact of being fathers (whether natural or adoptive), is their confusion and helplessness when it comes to having to look after an even more helpless infant. Although no doubt many young parents and single mothers, faced with the responsibility of taking care of the baby, have also become panic-stricken, the culture's assumption has conventionally been that women are "natural" mothers, so that the whole process of childcare may be confidently left to them. What is new in the representations of young fatherhood in these two TV programs is the making explicit of men's inadequacy in the business of raising very young children; not because they are "naturally" incompetent at it, any more than the women are "naturally" maternal, but rather because infant care has not traditionally been a part of the repertoire of hegemonic masculinity. That Jimmy, and Mitchell and Cam are shown as *learning* how to become confident, competent fathers is another way in which these roles may be said to point to an emergent masculinity.

Activity 7.5

- Consider other representations of single fatherhood, for example, the Dwayne Johnson ("The Rock") vehicle, *The Game Plan* (2007): how is masculinity represented in relation to fatherhood, and especially to the single father?
- From your reading or viewing, are you able to identify any other emergent masculinities, for example, in terms of sexuality, race, or age?

  - In what types or genres of text are such masculinities typically to be found?
  - Are these, in Williams's terms, truly new masculinities or are they rather alternative or oppositional to existing, dominant masculinities?

Man up, princess: decorative masculinity and the terror dream

The development of emergent masculinities and the reworking of residual ones have taken place alongside the continuing production of action movies and dramas that foreground features and behaviors associated with hegemonic masculinity, with emphasis on such factors as physical size and strength, action rather than talk, violence rather than negotiation, and so on. Before 9/11, such narratives might have been thought to offer chiefly a nostalgic representation of the hegemonic masculine at a time when the latter was being challenged by other ways in which men could be men. Indeed, the excessive nature of the masculinity (for example, the action heroes performed by Sylvester Stallone, Arnold Schwarzenegger and others) also suggested a certain hysteria, an anxiety in the culture that the familiar form of masculinity was fading. However, the events of 9/11 and their aftermath have brought about a recentering and a new intensification of the hegemonic masculine.

The destruction of the Twin Towers in New York and the attempt on the Pentagon in Washington, DC at the hands of Al Qaeda terrorists, together with the enormous loss of life involved, have been understood as both the foretold apocalypse and the cataclysm that announces a coming apocalypse. Questions have circulated about US intelligence and its role in uncovering (or failing to uncover) the preparation for an attack on US soil, together with how and why the attacks were able to take place. Those questions were frequently infused with the implication or actual charge, not merely of failure or error on the part of the agencies concerned, but also of a "softening" of attitudes and processes.

It was felt, in short, that the US had been "unmanned," in the sense both of lacking someone in control (like an unmanned fighter jet) and of being emasculated. The commentary on the destruction of the World Trade Center in the blog of the director of mensaction.net, a former military officer, makes this latter sense explicit:

> The phallic symbol of America had been cut off … and at its base was a large smoldering vagina, the true symbol of the American culture, for it is the western culture that represents the feminine materialistic principle, and it is at its extreme in America.
>
> (cited in Faludi, 2007: 9)

Western culture and its materialism are thus defined as feminine, so that American culture, here characterized as Western, materialistic culture at its most intense, presumably has brought upon itself its own punishment: not merely castration, but feminization. (In this, the author of the blog echoes the philosophy of Tyler Durden in *Fight Club*.)

A similar kind of argument could be made about the assault on the Pentagon. Given the open structure of the building, the attack on it might be seen as the attempted rape of a symbolic national bodily orifice, whether vagina or anus. Indeed, it does not matter which: the forced entry of either could be construed as signifying the feminine nature of the body thus penetrated. The blog entry cited above might be criticized for the excessive nature of its language and imagery; but the sentiment expressed was no doubt felt by many in the United States, especially men.

An indicator of this is to be found in "To Kill A Mockingturd," a segment on Jon Stewart's satirical TV news program *The Daily Show*, broadcast on 2 May 2011, dealing with the announcement on the same day of the death of Al Qaeda leader Osama bin Laden at the hands of US Navy Seals (*The Daily Show*, 2011). Stewart's gleeful commentary scripted the event not simply as a phallic victory by the United States over Al Qaeda and bin Laden, but also as an explicitly penile one, representing the peninsula of Florida as a penis. (This symbology had already been exploited in "Map Filth," a cartoon by B. Kliban in which the North American continental landmass, sporting a rather phallic Florida peninsula, says to the European continental landmass, "Hey, Europe! Eat my Florida!" [Kliban, 1976].) In effect, then, the death of bin Laden was constructed as a recovery, if only partial, of American phallic power, and a regaining of the lost/castrated national penis.

Fears about the "failure" of masculinity, especially in the United States, already a matter of concern before 9/11, have thus inevitably intensified in the aftermath of 9/11. Figuring in the cultural imagination as an apocalyptic cataclysm, with all that this implies in terms of revealed truth and a postapocalyptic vision of society as a ruined, desolate wasteland, Susan Faludi characterizes these events as a "terror dream," a description she borrows from Alan Le May's novel *The Searchers*. She cites a passage from this as one of the two epigraphs to *The Terror Dream: fear and fantasy in post-9/11 America*:

> … His stomach dropped from under his heart, and a horrible fear filled him – the fear of a small helpless child, abandoned and alone in the night. He tried to spring up and out of that, and he could not move; he lay there rigid, seemingly frozen to the ground. Behind the ringing in his ears began to rise to the unearthly yammer of the terror-dream – not heard, not even remembered, but coming to him like an awareness of something happening in some unknown dimension not of the living world.
>
> (Faludi, 2007: ix)

The cultural response to the paralyzing terror provoked by the events of 9/11, especially in the media, as Faludi details, included (indeed, emphasized) the accusation that men had become "soft": "women's liberation had 'feminized' our men and, in so doing, left the nation vulnerable to attack" (Faludi, 2007: 23).

Faludi observes that "we kept rummaging through the past to make sense of the disaster, as if the trauma of 9/11 had stirred some distant memory, reminded us of something disturbingly familiar" (Faludi, 2007: 3). The media initially sought to redefine the attack on the World Trade Center and the Pentagon in terms of Pearl Harbor; but

No draft ensued, no Rosie the Riveters were called to duty, no ration cards issued, no victory gardens planted. Most of all, no official moral leadership emerged to challenge Americans to think constructively about our place in the world, to redefine civic commitment and public responsibility. There was no man in a wheelchair in the White House urging on us a reassessment of American strength and weakness. What we had was a chest beater in a borrowed flight suit, instructing us to max out our credit cards for the cause.

(Faludi, 2007: 3)

The Pearl Harbor analogy gave way to another invocation: the Cold War of the 1950s:

This one seemed a better fit. In the aftermath of the attacks, the cultural troika of media, entertainment, and advertising declared the post-9/11 age and era of neofifties nuclear family "togetherness," redomesticated femininity, and reconstituted Cold Warrior manhood. "Security moms" were said to be salving their fears of terrorists by sticking close to the hearth and stocking their pantries with canned goods and anthrax antidotes, while suburban dads were stockpiling guns in their families' linen closets. Scared single women, the media held, were reassessing their independence and heading for the altar; working mothers were "opting out" for the protected suburbs. The nation's men, from the inhabitants of the White House on down, were reportedly assuming a hard-boiled comportment last seen in post-World War II cinema.

(Faludi, 2007: 3–4)

The important point to grasp here is not whether people actually did these things, but rather that *they were imagined publicly, through the media, as undertaking them*. The American people were thus being called to revert to roles and behaviors that predated the 1960s and the social and cultural changes that that era ushered in.

Popular culture responded with a flood of movies, video games, and TV programs that depicted incandescent, apocalyptic cataclysms, ravaging destruction caused by aliens, gigantic robots, or by sinister forces located both within and outside the United States or, indeed, the earth itself. The superhero genre of movie was given a new lease of life; unsurprisingly, because as Tom Pollard notes in *Hollywood 9/11: superheroes, super villains, and super disasters*, the superhero narrative has, since the late 1930s, reflected the historical, social, and cultural conditions within which it has been created, from the Depression through World War II, and now to 9/11 and after (Pollard, 2011: 73–106).

In an earlier work, *Stiffed: the betrayal of the American man*, Faludi examined what had happened to American men and manhood since World War II. Rather than accusing men of having gone "soft," she argues that corporatized capitalism, with its emphasis on profit margins, cost-cutting, and other "efficiencies," such as the replacement of human labor with machines, whether computers or robots, had effectually undermined the notion of masculinity:

> The men of the new generation had not simply lost a utilitarian world; they had been thrust into an ornamental realm, and the transformation had proved traumatic. … we have changed fundamentally from a society that produced the culture to culture rooted in no real society at all. The culture we live in today pretends that media can nurture society, but our new public spaces, our "electronic town squares" and "cyber-communities" and publicity mills and celebrity industries, are disembodied barrens, a dismal substitute for the real thing. Where we once lived in a society in which men in particular participated by being useful in public life, we are now surrounded by a culture that encourages people to play almost no functional public roles, only decorative or consumer ones. The old model of masculinity showed men how to be part of a larger social system; it gave them a context and promised them that their social contributions were the price of admission to the realm of adult manhood. That kind of manhood required a society in order to prove itself. All of the traditional domains in which men pursued authority and power – politics, religion, the military, the community, and the household – were societal.
>
> Ornamental culture has no such counterparts. Constructed around celebrity and image, glamour and entertainment, marketing and consumerism, it is a ceremonial gateway to nowhere. Its essence is not just the selling act but the act of selling the self, and in this quest every man is essentially on his own, a lone sales rep marketing his own image … In an age of celebrity, the father has no body of knowledge or authority to transmit to the son. Each son must father his own image, create his own Adam.
>
> (Faludi, 1999: 34–35)

In Faludi's view, the late-capitalist corporatization of American culture has hollowed out the very concept of masculinity by removing the means by which men might demonstrate it, while at the same time requiring men to perform that masculinity in the most conventional and traditional of ways.

This is a theme to which she returns in the later work, and which is encapsulated in the second of the epigraphs to *The Terror Dream*, a quotation from Richard Slotkin's *Regeneration through Violence*:

> A people unaware of its myths is likely to continue living by them, but the world around that people may change and demand changes in their psychology, their world view, their ethics, and their institutions.
>
> (Faludi, 2007: ix)

The problem, then, is not that men as a class have become soft, but rather that social and cultural conditions have changed, such that the familiar and recognizable forms of masculinity may no longer be viable, no matter how desirable people may find them.

This is closely akin to Bourdieu's idea of the hysteresis effect: the lag between, on the one hand, the change of conditions in the field and the capital required to negotiate and thrive in those new conditions and, on the other, a habitus based on older conditions and capital that is made to continue to function as though it were still workable in the new context. This hysteresis produces the effect of a sense of crisis, together with the rhetoric that, as Sally Robinson points out (Robinson, 2000: 11), helps to consolidate the idea that there *is* a crisis.

Williams's conceptualization of culture as consisting of dominant, residual, and emergent elements can be productively applied here to the perception of a crisis in masculinity. We may reformulate this idea as centered around a conflict between dominant forms of the masculine and emergent ones, a conflict made all the more salient and bitter because of the dominant's refusal to acknowledge that masculinity (like femininity) is discursive, and hence historically and culturally contingent – and therefore flexible, changeable.

There is therefore within the dominant forms of masculinity an imperative to *patrizate*, an obsolete and rare term that the *Oxford English Dictionary*, dating its first recorded use as 1623, defines as "To take after, imitate, or follow the example of one's father (or ancestors)." The residual is thus appropriated and refunctioned by the dominant, so that its present constellation appears to be a seamless and unproblematic continuation of a uniform and integral past masculinity. That fiction of a lineal masculinity (singular, although with some latitude for variation, and relatively fixed) reaching back from the present into the mists of antiquity,[7] underlies claims of a crisis in masculinity, and sees any emergent contestatory or alternative form as both hostile and traitorous to the dominant masculine. Yet emergent forms there must inevitably be, if only as discursive resistance, in the Foucauldian sense, to the dominant.

Moreover, we should understand that the dominant form of masculinity was authorized by a patriarchal order that itself resulted as a response to historical and social circumstances. Accordingly, therefore, as historical and social circumstances change, it is likely that new forms of the masculine will come into being, although no doubt slowly and tentatively, and in competition with residual and dominant forms.

Creolized masculinities

We noted in chapter 1 that the movie *Fight Club* has inspired men, particularly young men, to set up their own fight clubs, although whether they have also adopted Tyler Durden's antimaterialist, antiestablishment philosophy is open to question. Certainly, many young males have responded to Durden's notion that they are a generation raised by women, that they are the "middle children of history," and that they have been deprived in some measure of their birthright. However, we should be cautious about the movie's adaptation of Palahniuk's novel. For example, whereas the novel ends with the unnamed narrator in a mental institution, the movie concludes on a semiromantic note, with Jack and Marla holding hands as they watch the buildings around them implode when the explosives set by the "space monkeys" of Durden's Project Mayhem ignite. One of the key ironies in the movie is that Durden, like Jack's father, has franchised his "business" in a number of cities across the United States (early in the movie, Jack describes as a "franchise" his traveling salesman father's practice of moving from city to city, establishing new families in each). In seeking to free himself from the influence of his worthless father under Durden's guidance, then, Jack has merely turned to another figure cut from the same cloth, albeit more dangerously.

If Durden is indeed the embodiment of hegemonic masculinity, as we suggested in chapter 6, we need to look a little more closely at what that implies, in relation to the movie's narrative. If we bracket out the qualities of Durden that we have already noted, such as his charisma, leadership qualities, resourcefulness, and the like, and if we exclude Brad Pitt's personal charm of good looks and enviable body, we find a character who is, fundamentally, a bully. Remembering that Durden is simply a projection of Jack's mind, we might choose to read the physical fights between Jack and Durden, particularly towards the end of the movie, when Jack is severely beaten by Durden, as an externalization of the internalized violence directed toward the male subject by hegemonic masculinity, represented and enfleshed by Tyler Durden.

This helps us to understand better the CCTV footage as well as the camera point of view of several of the minor characters that show Jack apparently hitting himself extremely violently: taken at face value, such action seems most improbable, even although earlier we saw Jack brutalize himself in his superior's office, in order to blackmail his boss. However, read as a symbolic representation of the violent imposition of hegemonic masculinity on the individual male subject, scenes of this kind in the movie seem to make more sense. Such a reading suggests that what young men find alluring in this movie is its promotion precisely of the hegemonic masculine, characterized as premodern by Durden in his description of his New Jerusalem as an urban wasteland inhabited by people living as though in a premedieval village. However, this is a fantasy: short of a singular global cataclysm, it is unlikely that we could revert to so early a stage of social development. Whether or not young male viewers of the movie embrace Durden's anticapitalist, antimaterialist philosophy along with his idea of fight club, the liberation that he offers them is simply another form of servitude, in this case to a renewed and strengthened hegemonic masculinity, together with the patriarchal order and economy of which it is an integral part.

The kinds of masculinities that we have explored in this chapter as emergent ones may be considered alternatives to hegemonic masculinity. Although still only subordinate to the latter, their growing presence, attested by their movement from marginal to central roles in much popular-cultural narratives, suggests their viability as competitors with hegemonic masculinity. They may therefore be regarded as in some degree postapocalyptic masculinities, challenging the hegemonic as possible ways for men to be men in a twenty-first-century culture in which social, economic and political conditions are very different from those of the pre-1960s. If there *is* a crisis in masculinity, if men *are* confused about their roles and what is expected of them, then we must look for a solution, not in the reversion to an earlier set of attitudes and practices that evolved under different conditions and out of a different history, but rather in the adaptation of men and boys to current conditions and a presently developing history. Besides, as Fintan Walsh observes in *Male Trouble: masculinity and the performance of crisis*,

> It is interesting to note ... that discourses of crisis rarely concede to the condition's *reconstitutive dimension*. In place of this presumption of stasis, or failure, I suggest that crisis is not an end in itself but a period of disorder that precedes and precipitates a longer period of productivity, restructuring, and redevelopment, which may even lead to the reestablishment of the temporarily agitated norm. In fact, crisis is to be seen as a constitutive element of all social, political, and economic systems, a fact that seems pertinent during the current global recession. Further to this, indeed following on from it, *we should appreciate that certain kinds of crises are also constitutive of subjectivity*.
>
> (Walsh, 2010: 8–9; added emphasis)

Crisis, then, is not always a bad thing: it can be productive and, as Walsh suggests, central to subjectivity, to a sense of the self.

It may be that, especially for young males today, we are dealing, to borrow a term from linguistic, sociological, and colonial/postcolonial studies, with a *creolized masculinity*. Eve Stoddard and Grant H. Cornwell observe:

> It is agreed that the immediate antecedent [for the word *creole*] is the Spanish *criollo*, meaning born locally though ancestrally from elsewhere. The Spanish *criollo* is believed to derive from the verb *criar*, meaning to breed (*OED*, 1989), from the Latin *creare*, meaning to create.
>
> (Stoddard and Cornwell, 1999: 336)

In such a context, the Creole belongs *racially or ethnically* to one group (the Spanish, say) whose ethnic identity is dictated by the colonial metropolitan center (Madrid or, more generally, Spain, in this case). However, such a subject, having been born outside that center itself, feels a certain pressure to ally her/himself *culturally* with the group into which s/he has been born (Central or South American, or Caribbean, for instance), adopting its language, customs, foods, and so on. Thus a certain divided subjectivity may emerge, so that the individual finds her/himself with a double set of allegiances and influences.

This explains in part why, as Stoddard and Cornwell point out, "Creole" spelled with a capital "C" and with a lower-case "c" may have different significations:

> If "Creole" is a proper name, then creolisation is less a general process and more an acculturation into a specific society, such as the white

French-descended people of Louisiana. If it is a generic lower-case term, then it describes a state or process...

(Stoddard and Cornwell, 1999: 336)

If young males today are dealing with a creolized masculinity, then at the level of "Creole," with a capital "C," we may understand them as having inherited a certain patriarchal ancestry (the current constellation of hegemonic masculinity as the notional or symbolic metropolitan center) that is serving them less and less well in the context of a culture that has seen many revolutionary changes since the 1960s.

At the same time, these males must seek to integrate themselves into the culture into which they have been born, in which those changes are taken for granted, naturalized, and rendered mostly invisible. Accusations of "softness," of the failure to perform a "proper" masculinity, are thus exhortations to return to an earlier form of masculinity, however imaginary or historically inaccurate. They function, therefore, as an urging to adhere to the hegemonic masculinity that is a general metropolitan "ethnicity," as it were, of a culture whose history and conditions are on the point of receding into the past, if, indeed, they have not already done so. Those accusations either do not take account of the radical social and cultural changes that often form the real context of the individual young male's life, or ignore them in the interests of preserving a familiar ideology of gender and gender relations.

However, "Creole" spelt with a lower-case "c" offers a different set of possibilities: Stoddard and Cornwell observe,

> the process of creolisation is credited with producing persons uniquely equipped to be open, adaptive, agile, and especially adept with nuance, language, ambiguity contradiction, and irony. Creole cultures are fixed in a state of openness, primed to appropriate, incorporate, synthesize, and play with cultural forms whatever their source.
>
> (Stoddard and Cornwell, 1999: 338)

This is a description almost of postmodern culture itself. And perhaps this is the place to begin thinking of the possibility of a new masculinity, one that (unlike the conservative masculinities with which we are familiar or like the nostalgic one advocated by Bly and Biddulph) is capable of continual shifts and alterations, now adapting parts of more traditional masculinities and blending them with new feminisms, now with new notions of male–male relations, and so on, so that new constellations of what may count as hegemonic *masculinities* may be given the chance to come into being. In such circumstances, we may feel free enough to abandon the idea that men *must* conform to a certain model of the masculine if they are to be counted as men, and come to recognize that "masculinity" is simply the totality of how *all* men might choose to enact socially the fact of their maleness.

Activity 7.6

- Revisit your responses to the first activity in chapter 1.

    ○ Have your ideas about masculinity changed in any way after reading this book?
    ○ What aspects of your initial responses have been confirmed?
    ○ Are there any ideas about or areas of research in that you would like to pursue? Why do these interest you?

Suggested further reading

Barker, G.T. (2005) *Dying to Be Men: youth, masculinity and social exclusion*, London and New York: Routledge.

Ducat, S.J. (2004) *The Wimp Factor: gender gaps, holy wars, and the politics of anxious masculinity*, Boston: Beacon Press.

Pfeil, F. (1995) *White Guys: studies in postmodern domination and difference*, London and New York: Verso.

Seidler, V.J. (2006) *Young Men and Masculinities: global cultures and intimate lives*, London and New York: Zed Books.

Trice, A.D. and Holland, S.A. (2001) *Heroes, Antiheroes and Dolts: portrayals of masculinity in American popular films, 1921–1999*, Jefferson, NC and London: McFarland and Company, Inc.

Watson, E. and Shaw, M.E. (eds) (2011) *Performing American Masculinities: the 21st-century man in popular culture*, Bloomington and Indianapolis: Indiana University Press.

Webb, J., Schirato, T. and Danaher, G. (2002) *Understanding Bourdieu*, Los Angeles: Sage.

Notes

3 Doing/undoing gender

1 We explore the notion of abjection in chapter 5.
2 "Queer" and queer theory are addressed in chapter 5.

4 Regarding patriarchy

1 Connell has published under several variations of his name, for example, R. W. Connell, Bob Connell, Robert W. Connell, and so on. More recently, as a transgender woman, she publishes under the name of Raewyn Connell.
2 In Roman culture, which had other words for "penis" ("tail," in Latin), "phallus" more often signified an image or a carving of the penis, to be found in both profane and sacred contexts, such as a brothel and a religious procession, respectively.
3 The need for a man to find a best friend has become something of a theme in recent movies; for instance, the French film *Mon meilleur ami* (*My Best Friend*) (*My Best Friend* [*Mon meilleur ami*], 2006.
4 One does not need to travel very far in cultural history to see a connection between Hermione's efforts to make Harry and Ron more mature and sensible, and the tendency during the nineteenth century to regard woman as a civilizing influence on man, a theme that recurs in many movie westerns, for example. This is the positive counterpart of and complement to the contemporaneous view of woman as only partially evolved, which we touch on in the next chapter.

5 Troubling patriarchy

1 I use this hyphenated term in order to distinguish it from "the" male homosexual as a social and sexual identity. Like "the feminine," it signifies an attribute that functions as an abstract quality.
2 It is generally argued that the Deuteronomical and Levitical prescriptions and proscriptions were intended to maintain the purity of the Hebrew people, and especially of the priestly castes, against defilement, in this instance, by garments made of a mixing of two kinds of fiber: plant and animal. However, the same law might be invoked today in relation to, say, blends of silk (from an insect source) and cotton (from a plant), or silk (insect) and wool (animal) blends, or of polyester-cotton fabrics (which mix artificial and natural fibers). Were Deuteronomy 22:11 to be applied in a manner consistent with the way in which the biblical injunction against homosexual practices is continually cited, much of the clothing which we wear daily ought also to be prohibited.

3 In *Epistemology of the Closet*, Eve Kosofsky Sedgwick speaks of

> the contradiction between seeing homo/heterosexual definition on the one hand as an issue of active importance primarily for a small, distinct, relatively fixed homosexual minority (what I refer to as a minoritizing view), and seeing it on the other hand as an issue of continuing, determinative importance in the lives of people across the spectrum of sexualities (what I refer to as a universalizing view).
>
> (Sedgwick, 1990: 1)

That is, both the difference and contradiction lie in whether nonheteronormative subjects should be thought of as a distinct group, separate and different from the majority ("others" to the dominant) or rather as both part of and integral to the range of sexualities available to people in the culture.

6 (Em)Bodying masculinity

1 Of course, women also work out in gyms. However, this motto appears to have emerged specifically in relation to men's activity in such a context. Accordingly, women's use of their bodies in workouts may be understood by some as a form of masculinization of those bodies, the extreme example of which is that of the female bodybuilder, whose muscular physique is often regarded as unfeminine and "unwomanly."
2 "Virtue" should here be understood not simply as chastity, a meaning that came to be attached later to the term (so that "a woman's virtue" signified her status either as virgin or as chaste wife), but rather as a complex of ethical principles and behaviors appropriate to living in a civil society.
3 It should be noted that in later Greek art these conventional representations became conflated, so that satyrs were shown with youthful athletic bodies. However, they could be distinguished from the *kouroi* proper by various attributes, for example, pointed ears, diminutive horns, or vestigial tail, all pointing to the animal (savage) nature of the satyr.
4 However, as is typical with Montaigne, the essay ends with the ironic and ambiguous comment, "All this is not too bad – but what's the use? They don't wear breeches" (Montaigne, 1971: 159). Here are a few possible meanings: (1) the achievements of the cannibals amount finally to nothing, because they have not learned even to clothe themselves; (2) no one in Europe will pay attention to the achievements of these exotic people, because they lack the technology of clothing and are naked; (3) from the perspective of European culture, the "cannibals" are immoral, rather than merely innocent; (4) in the end, they are simply savages.
5 The complete title of the play is *Almanzor and Almahide, or The Conquest of Granada by the Spaniards, a Tragedy*. Almanzor speaks the following lines:

> No man has more contempt than I of breath,
> But whence hast thou the right to give me death?
> Obeyed as sovereign by thy subjects be,
> But know, that I alone am king of me.
> I am as free as nature first made man,
> Ere the base laws of servitude began,
> When wild in woods the noble savage ran.
> (Dryden, 1808: 40)

6 In his book *Rabelais and His World*, Bakhtin suggests that the grotesque is frequently linked, in medieval and early Renaissance culture, with carnival, defined as a period in which official sanctions and rules were lifted, the usual hierarchies inverted, and the

common people permitted to vent feelings in parody and play. In the example given here, the night out with the boys might be considered a moment of carnival in an otherwise controlled and disciplined existence (Bakhtin, 1984).

7 Kenneth R. Dutton draws attention to the Roman convention in art of the *cuirasse esthétique* (literally "aesthetic breastplate"). This breastplate, originally made of washed and molded leather (*cuir* is French for "leather") and later of steel, was decorated with garlands, scenes of military triumph and so on, in the same material as the breastplate itself, and was used to enhance and ennoble sculptures of notable Romans (for instance, the Emperor Augustus, various generals, and so on). Dutton points out that this cuirasse was itself modeled on the ideal muscular male upper body, irrespective of the actual physique of the man represented (Dutton, 1995: 49–51). Until at least the eighteenth century, this remained a convention in visual images (painting as well as sculpture) of warriors and soldier-heroes – this, despite the fact that such a breastplate, if fashioned in reality for use on the battlefield, would have been impractical, because it would have offered too many contours and crevices where a lance, sword, or pike could catch and so inflict damage, if not also actually penetrate. Here, too, the male body subtly merges into strapping, pads, and, in this instance, leather and/or metal plating. The armor of the American footballer and of his Roman antecedent serves, in fact, not only to protect the male body within the plating (notionally so, in the case of the *cuirasse esthétique*) but also to fix an ideal masculine form in the cultural consciousness, a form that includes the occupation of space.

7 Postapocalyptic masculinities

1 Bourdieu developed and elaborated his theory over many years, and across multiple works. Given the complexity of his thought (and of his writing), and given the scope of the present work, what follows is necessarily only a brief and partial presentation of that theory. Moreover, because of that same complexity, I rely here on the useful synoptic view offered by the various chapters in *Pierre Bourdieu: key concepts* (Grenfell, 2008).

2 "Winnebago" refers to the former name of a Native American people of the mid-West of the United States; the connection with the Wild West is thus inscribed in the brand name itself.

3 There seems in Yiddish to be grammatically no feminine form of "schlemiel," suggesting that this figure is essentially always male, although there have been a few attempts at constructing a female schlemiel: in recent years, notably Sandra Bullock's character in *Miss Congeniality* (*Miss Congeniality*, 2000), in which the female schlemiel commences as a masculinized character, and has to learn how to be feminine, although, it is suggested, this remains only provisional at the end of the film.

4 This is not to be confused with the similarly titled 2004 movie starring Jennifer Lopez and Richard Gere (*Shall We Dance?*, 2004).

5 This trait of Cameron's no doubt allows the thoughtful viewer to reflect on masculinity itself as a form of performance, if not precisely on Judith Butler's notion of gender performativity. For example, although Jay's masculinity is periodically put in question, he is usually represented as performing his gender as though it were unproblematic. By contrast, Phil struggles perpetually to meet his gender "obligations" as a man, especially in trying to win Jay's approval, but is torn between identifying with hegemonic masculinity and embodying a new, gentler masculinity that remains nonetheless heterosexual. Cam periodically asserts temporarily aspects of hegemonic masculinity, such as his experience as a member of the football team while in college.

6 Although the earlier TV sitcom *Will and Grace* (*Will and Grace*, 1998–2006) also sought to naturalize the figure of the gay man (and occasionally that of the lesbian) in mainstream popular culture and thought, the series in general tended to work with *types*

of gay, Will (Eric McCormack) in general representing the "straight" (or "straight-acting") gay man, Jack (Sean Hayes) the camp gay individual. Although the two principal characters may have interchanged these roles from time to time, in general this sitcom did not offer an emergent masculinity in the same way as *Modern Family* does. However, it should be noted that Will and Jack's friends Rob (Tom Gallop) and Larry (Tim Bagley) are another gay couple who adopt a baby daughter, Hannah. Nevertheless, their roles are fairly minor in the entire series.

7 This is, of course, exactly the assumption underlying the writings of Robert Bly and Steve Biddulph, discussed in chapter 1.

References

Films/TV programs/online video

Along Came Polly. (film, 2004) directed by J. Hamburg, USA, Universal Pictures.

American Pie. (film, 1999) directed by P. Weitz, USA, Universal Pictures.

Better Off Ted (TV, 2009–10) directed by M. Fresco et al., USA, American Broadcasting Company.

Chuck (TV, 2007–) directed by R. D. McNeill et al., USA, NBC Universal Television Distribution.

Deuce Bigalow: Male Gigolo (film,1999) directed by M. Mitchell, USA, Buena Vista Pictures.

Dexter (TV, 2006–) directed by K. Gordon et al., USA, Showtime Networks.

Everybody Loves Raymond (TV, 1996–2005) directed by M. Lembeck et al., USA, Columbia Broadcasting System (CBS).

Family Guy (TV, 1999–) directed by P. Shin et al., USA, Fox Film Corporation-20th Century Fox Home Entertainment.

Fight Club. (film, 1999) directed by D. Fincher, USA, Twentieth Century Fox Film Corporation.

Frasier (TV, 1993–2004), directed by D. Lee et al., USA, National Broadcasting Company (NBC).

Gilligan's Island (TV, 1964–67) directed by J. Arnold et al., USA, CBS Television.

Harry Potter and the Chamber of Secrets. (film, 2002), directed by C. Columbus, USA, Warner Bros. Pictures.

Harry Potter and the Deathly Hallows: Part 1. (film, 2010) directed by D. Yates, USA, Warner Bros. Pictures.

Harry Potter and the Deathly Hallows: Part 2 (film, 2011) directed by D. Yates, USA, Warner Bros. Pictures.

Harry Potter and the Goblet of Fire. (film, 2005) directed by M. Newell, USA, Warner Bros. Pictures.

Harry Potter and the Half-Blood Prince. (film, 2009) directed by D. Yates, USA, Warner Bros. Pictures.

Harry Potter and the Order of the Phoenix (film, 2007) directed by D. Yates, USA, Warner Bros. Pictures.

Harry Potter and the Philosopher's Stone. (film, 2001) directed by C. Columbus, USA, Warner Bros. Pictures.

Harry Potter and the Prisoner of Azkaban (film, 2004) directed by A. Cuarón, USA, Warner Bros. Pictures.

Hogan's Heroes (TV, 1965–71) directed by G. Reynolds et al., USA, Columbia Broadcasting System (CBS).

How I Met Your Mother (TV, 2005) directed by P. Fryman et al., USA, 20th Century Fox Television.

I Love You, Man (film, 2009) directed by J. Hamburg, USA, DreamWorks SKG.

Laverne and Shirley (TV, 1976–83) directed by Tom Trbovich et al., USA, American Broadcasting Company (ABC).

Mad Men (TV, 2007–) directed by P. Abraham et al., USA, Lionsgate Television.

Meet the Fockers (film, 2004) directed by J. Roach, USA, Universal.

Meet the Parents (film, 2000) directed by J. Roach, USA, Universal Pictures.

Miss Congeniality (film, 2000), directed by D. Petrie, USA, Warner Bros.

Modern Family (TV, 2009–) directed by J. Winer et al., USA, American Broadcasting Company (ABC).

My Best Friend (Mon meilleur ami) (film, 2006) directed by P. Leconte, France, The Weinstein Company.

My Three Sons (TV, 1960–72) directed by F. De Kordova et al., USA, American Broadcasting Company (ABC)/Columbia Broadcasting System (CBS).

Mystery Men (film, 1999) directed by K. Usher, USA, United International Pictures.

Napoleon Dynamite (film, 2004) directed by J. Hess, USA, Fox Searchlight Pictures.

National Lampoon's Animal House (film, 1978), directed by J. Landis, USA, Universal Pictures.

Night at the Museum (film, 2006) directed by S. Levy, USA, Twentieth Century Fox Film Corporation.

Orlando (film, 1992) directed by S. Potter, USA, Sony Pictures Home Entertainment.

Porky's (film, 1982) directed by B. Clark, USA, Twentieth Century Fox Film Corporation.

Raising Hope (TV, 2010–), directed by E. Gordin et al., USA, Fox Network.

Shall We Dance (film, 1937) directed by M. Sandrich, USA, RKO Radio Pictures Inc.

Six Feet Under (TV, 2001–5) directed by A. Ball, USA, Home Box Office (HBO).

The Big Bang Theory (TV, 2007–) directed by M. Cendrowski et al., USA, Columbia Broadcasting System.

The Courtship of Eddie's Father (TV, 1969–72) directed by H. Cooper et al., USA, American Broadcasting Company (ABC).

The Full Monty (film, 1997) directed by Peter Cattaneo, UK, 20th Century Fox.

The IT Crowd (TV, 2006–) directed by G. Linehan et al., UK, Channel 4 Television Corporation.

The Simpsons (TV, 1989–) directed by M. Kirkland et al., USA, 20th Century Fox Television-Gracie Films.

There's Something about Mary (film, 1998) directed by B. Farrelly and P. Farrelly, USA, 20th Century Fox.

"To Kill a Mockingturd" *The Daily Show* (2011). J. Stewart. Online. Available at <http://www.thedailyshow.com/watch/mon-may-2-2011/to-kill-a-mockingturd> (accessed: 9 May 2011).

True Blood(TV, 2008–), directed by M. Lehmann et al., USA, Home Box Office (HBO).

Twilight (film, 2008) directed by C. Hardwicke, USA, Summit Distribution.

Two and a Half Men (TV, 2003–) directed by A. Ackerman et al., USA, Columbia Broadcasting System.

Will and Grace (TV, 1998–2006) directed by James Burrows et al., USA, NBC Universal Television Distribution.

"Wodaabe" (online video, n.d.) *National Geographic Kids, National Geographic*. Online. Available at <http://video.nationalgeographic.com/video/player/kids/people-places-kids/nigeria-wodaabe-kids.html> (accessed: 15 June 2011).

Zoolander (film, 2001) directed by B. Stiller, USA, Paramount.

Articles/books

Aboim, S. (2010) *Plural Masculinities: the remaking of the self in private life*, London and Burlington, VT: Ashgate Publishing Limited.

Althusser, L. (1976) "Ideology and ideological state apparatuses (notes towards an investigation)," in L. Althusser, *Essays on Ideology*, London and New York: Verso: 1–60.

Anderson, B. (2006) *Imagined Communities: reflections on the origin and spread of nationalism*, London and New York: New Left Books–Verso.

Bakhtin, M. (1984) *Rabelais and His World*, trans. Hélène Iswolsky, Bloomington: Indiana University Press.

Barber, R. (1999) *Bestiary, being an English version of the Bodleian Library, Oxford M. S. Bodley 764, with all the original miniatures reproduced in facsimile*, Woodbridge: The Boydell Press.

Barthes, R. (2009) *Mythologies*, London: Vintage-Random House.

Belsey, C. (1980) "Constructing the subject: deconstructing the text," *Critical Practice*, London: Methuen: 103–95, revised and reprinted in J. L. Newton and D. Rosenfelt (eds) (1986) *Feminist Criticism and Social Change*, New York: Routledge, 45–64.

Berger, J. (1972) *Ways of Seeing*, London: BBC; Harmondsworth: Penguin.

Berger, J. (1999) *After the End: representations of post-apocalypse*, Minneapolis and London: University of Minnesota Press.

Biddulph, S. (1995) *Manhood: an action plan for changing men's lives*, Sydney: Finch Publishing.

Bly, R. (1991) *Iron John: a book about men*, Shaftesbury, Dorset and Rockport, MA: Element.

Bordo, S. (1999) *The Male Body: a new look at men in public and in private*, New York: Farrar, Straus and Giroux.

Boswell, J. (1980) *Christianity, Social Tolerance, and Homosexuality: gay people in Western Europe from the beginning of the Christian era to the fourteenth century*, Chicago and London: University of Chicago Press.

Bovin, M. (2001) *Nomads Who Cultivate Beauty: Wodaabe dances and visual arts in Niger*, Uppsala: Nordiska Afrikainstitutet.

"Boy-girl learning differences" (April/May 2001), *Scholastic Parent & Child*. 8.5: 18. Online. Available at ProQuest Central <http://proquest.umi.com.dbgw.lis.curtin.edu.au/pqdweb?did=71457691&sid=1&Fmt=4&clientId=22212&RQT=309&VName=PQD> (accessed: 30 June 2011).

Bray, A. (1982) *Homosexuality in Renaissance England*, London: Gay Men's Press.

Brickner, B.W. (1999) *The Promise Keepers: politics and promises*, Lanham, MD: Lexington Books.

Buchbinder, D. (1989), "Some engendered meaning: reading Shakespeare's sonnets," *Works and Days 14: essays in the socio-historical dimensions of literature and the arts*, 7: 2, 7–28.

—— (1994) *Masculinities and Identities*, Melbourne: Melbourne University Press.

Butler, J. (1990) *Gender Trouble: feminism and the subversion of identity*, New York and London: Routledge.

—— (1993) *Bodies That Matter: on the discursive limits of "sex"*, New York & London: Routledge.

—— (2004) *Undoing Gender*, New York and London: Routledge.

Carrigan, T., Connell, B. and Lee, J. (1985), "Toward a new sociology of masculinity," *Theory and Society*, 14: 5, 551–604.

Cixous, H. (1994) "The Newly Born Woman (La Jeune Née)," in S. Sellers (ed.) *The Hélène Cixous Reader*, London and New York: Routledge: 35–46. Reprinted from "Sorties: Out and Out: Attacks/Ways Out/Forays," in H. Cixous and C. Clément (1986), *The Newly Born Woman*, trans. Betsy Wing, Minneapolis: University of Minnesota Press: 63–129.

Clare, A. (2000) *On Men: masculinity in crisis*, London: Chatto and Windus.

Cohen, M. (1998) "'A habit of healthy idleness': boys' underachievement in historical perspective," in D. Epstein, J. Elwood, V. Hey and J. Maw (eds) *Failing Boys? Issues in gender and achievement*, Buckingham and Philadelphia: Open University Press: 19–34.

Connell, R.W. (1983) *Which Way Is Up? Essays on sex, class and culture*, Sydney: Allen and Unwin.

—— (1987) *Gender and Power: society, the person and sexual politics*, Sydney: Allen & Unwin.

—— (1995) *Masculinities*, St Leonards, NSW: Allen and Unwin.

—— (2000) *The Men and the Boys*, St Leonards, NSW: Allen and Unwin.

Connell, R.W. and Messerschmidt, J.W. (2005), "Hegemonic masculinity: rethinking the concept," *Gender and Society*, 19, 829–59.

de Brito, S. (2008) *Building a Better Bloke*, Camberwell, Victoria: Penguin.

de Montaigne, M. (1971) "Of cannibals," *The Complete Essays of Montaigne*, Stanford: Stanford University Press, 150–59.

Demetriou, D.Z. (2001), "Connell's concept of hegemonic masculinity: a critique," *Theory and Society*, 30: 3, 337–61.

Denton, A. (2003), "Barry Humphries," *Enough Rope with Andrew Denton*, 26 May 2003. Online. Available at <http://www.abc.net.au/tv/enoughrope/transcripts/s864967.htm> (accessed: 17 October 2011).

Derrida, J. (1976) *Of Grammatology*, trans. Gayatri Chakravorty Spivak, Baltimore and London: The Johns Hopkins University Press.

Dijkstra, B. (1986) *Idols of Perversity: fantasies of feminine evil in fin-de-siècle culture*, New York and Oxford: Oxford University Press.

Dotson, E.W. (1999) *Behold the Man: the hype and selling of male beauty in media and culture*, New York and London: Harrington Park-Haworth Press, Inc.

Doty, A. (1993) *Making Things Perfectly Queer: interpreting mass culture*, Minneapolis and London: U of Minnesota P.

Dryden, J. (1672) "Almanzor and Almahide, or The Conquest of Granada by the Spaniards, a Tragedy," in W. Scott (ed.) *The Works of John Dryden, Now First Collected in Eighteen Volumes. Illustrated with Notes, Historical, Critical, and Explanatory, and a Life of the Author, by Walter Scott, Esq*. Vol. IV. London: William Miller, reproduced in J. Ingram, F. Robinson and the Online Distributed Proofreading Team (eds) (2007) *The Works of John Dryden, Volume 4*. Online. Available at <http://www.munseys.com/diskfour/dryfo.htm> (accessed 14 May 2012).

Dutton, K.R. (1995) *The Perfectible Body: the western ideal of male physical development*, New York: Continuum.

Dyer, R. (1985) "Male sexuality in the media," in A. Metcalf and M. Humphries (eds) *The Sexuality of Men*, London and Sydney: Pluto Press, 28–43.

Dynes, W.R. and Johansson, W. (1990) "Homosexual (term)," in W. R. Dynes (ed.) *The Encyclopedia of Homosexuality*, New York and London: Garland Publishing: 555–56.

Easthope, A. (1986) *What A Man's Gotta Do: the masculine myth in popular culture*, London: Paladin-Grafton.

Edwards, J. (2009) *Eve Kosofsky Sedgwick*, London and New York: Routledge.

Encyclopædia Britannica (2010) "Orléans, Philippe I de France, duc d' ", *Encyclopædia Britannica Ultimate Reference Suite*, Chicago: Encyclopædia Britannica.

Epstein, D., Elwood, J., Hey, V. and Maw, J. (1998) "Schoolboy frictions: feminism and 'failing' boys," in D. Epstein, J. Elwood, V. Hey and J. Maw (eds) *Failing boys? Issues in gender and achievement*, Buckingham and Philadelphia: Open University Press: 3–18.

Faludi, S. (1999) *Stiffed: the betrayal of the American man*, New York: Perennial-HarperCollins Publishers.

—— (2007) *The Terror Dream: fear and fantasy in post-9/11 America*, Melbourne: Scribe Publications Pty Ltd.

"Fight club draws techies for bloody underground beatdowns" (29 May 2006) *USA Today*. Online. Available at <http://www.usatoday.com/tech/news/2006-05-29-fight-club_x.htm > (accessed: 29 May 2006).

Forth, C.E. (2008) *Masculinity in the Modern West: gender, civilization and the body*, Basingstoke and New York: Palgrave-Macmillan.

Foucault, M. (1977) *Discipline and Punish: the birth of the prison*, New York: Vintage-Random House.

—— (1981) *The Will to Knowledge: the history of sexuality, volume 1*, translated by Robert Hurley, London: Penguin.

Girard, R. (1972) *Deceit, Desire, and the Novel: self and other in literary structure*, Baltimore: Johns Hopkins University Press.

Goldstein, L. (1994) "Introduction", in L. Goldstein (ed.) *The Male Body: features, destinies, exposures*, Ann Arbor: University of Michigan Press, vii–xiv.

Graham, S. (2001) "Sulawesi's Fifth Gender," *Inside Indonesia* 66. Online. Available at <http://www.insideindonesia.org/edition-66-apr-jun-2001/sulawesi-s-fifth-gender-3007484> (accessed: 20 November 2011).

Greenberg, D.F. (1988) *The Construction of Homosexuality*, Chicago and London: University of Chicago Press.

Grenfell, M. (ed.) (2008) *Pierre Bourdieu: Key concepts*, Durham: Acumen Publishing Ltd.

Hall, P. (29 August 2003) "Boys undone by cultural attitude to education," *Regeneration & Renewal*. 14. Online. Available at ProQuest Central <http://proquest.umi.com.dbgw.lis.curtin.edu.au/pqdweb?did=405841191&sid=1&Fmt=3&clientId=22212&RQT=309&VName=PQD> (accessed: 29 August 2003).

Harding, S. (1988) "Introduction: is there a feminist method?", in S. Harding (ed.) *Feminism and Methodology: social science issues*, Bloomington and Indianapolis; Milton Keynes: Indiana University Press; Open University Press, 1–14.

Hardy, C. (2008) "Hysteresis," in M. Grenfell (ed.) *Pierre Bourdieu: key concepts*, Durham: Acumen Publishing Ltd, 131–48.

Harris, C. (2001) *Dead until Dark*, New York: Ace Books.

Hartley, J. (1994a) "Hegemony," in T. O'Sullivan et al. (eds) *Key Concepts in Communication and Cultural Studies*, London and New York: Routledge, 133–35.

—— (1994b) "Subject/subjectivity," in T. O'Sullivan et al. (eds) *Key Concepts in Communication and Cultural Studies*, London and New York: Routledge: 309–10.

Hill, D. (1997) *The Future of Men*, London: Phoenix.

Hoch, P. (1979) *White Hero, Black Beast: racism, sexism and the mask of masculinity*, London: Pluto Press.

Horrocks, R. (1994) *Masculinity in Crisis*, New York: St Martin's Press.

Jameson, F. (2000) "Postmodernism, or the cultural logic of late capitalism," in M. Hardt and K. Weeks (eds) *The Jameson Reader*, Oxford, UK, and Malden, MA: Blackwell, 188–232.

Jardine, L. (1983) *Still Harping on Daughters: women and drama in the age of Shakespeare*, New York: Harvester Wheatsheaf.

Jones, A. (28 June 1998) "Love me do," *Sunday Times*. 1. Online. Available at ProQuest Central <http://proquest.umi.com.dbgw.lis.curtin.edu.au/pqdweb?did=30875727&sid=4&Fmt=3&clientId=22212&RQT=309&VName=PQD> (accessed: 15 June 2011).

Kahn, J.S. (2009) *An Introduction to Masculinities*, Chichester: Wiley-Blackwell.

Kinsey, A.C., Pomeroy, W.B. and Martin, C.E. (1948) *Sexual Behaviour in the Human Male*, Philadelphia and London: W.B. Saunders & Co.

Kinsey's Heterosexual-Homosocial Rating Scale (1996–2011), *The Kinsey Institute for Research in Sex, Gender, and Reproduction*. Online. Available at <http://www.kinseyinstitute.org/research/ak-hhscale.html> (accessed: 30 August 2011).

Kliban, B. (1976) *Never Eat Anything Bigger Than Your Head and Other Drawings*, New York: Workman Publishing Company.

Kristeva, J. (1982) *Powers of Horror: an essay on abjection*, New York: Columbia University Press.

Kroeger, B. (2003) *Passing: when people can't be who they are*, New York: Public Affairs.

Laqueur, T. (1990) *Making Sex: body and gender from the Greeks to Freud*, Cambridge, MA, and London: Harvard University Press.

Laver, J. (1968) *Dandies*, London: Weidenfeld and Nicolson.

LeGuin, U.K. (1969) *The Left Hand of Darkness*, London: Futura.

Leo, J. (2 February 1999) "Gender wars redux," *US News and World Report*. 126.7: 24. Online. Available at ProQuest Central <http://proquest.umi.com.dbgw.lis.curtin.edu.au/pqdweb?did=38977427&sid=5&Fmt=2&clientId=22212&RQT=309&VName=PQD> (accessed: 30 June 2011).

Levy, D.P. (2007) "Hegemonic masculinity," in M. Flood et al. (eds) *International Encyclopedia of Men and Masculinities*, London and New York: Taylor & Francis Group-Routledge, 253–54.

Lindsay, J. (2004) *Darkly Dreaming Dexter*, London: Hachette Livre UK-Orion.

—— (2005) *Dearly Devoted Dexter*, London: Hachette Livre UK-Orion.

—— (2007) *Dexter in the Dark*, London: Hachette Livre UK-Orion.

—— (2009) *Dexter by Design*, London: Hachette Livre UK-Orion.

—— (2010) *Dexter Is Delicious*, New York: Doubleday.

MacInnes, J. (1998) *The End of Masculinity: the confusion of sexual genesis and sexual difference in modern society*, Buckingham and Philadelphia: Open University Press.

McKeon, M. (2005) *The Secret History of Domesticity: public, private and the division of knowledge*, Baltimore: The John Hopkins University Press.

McMillan, P. (1992) *Men, Sex and Other Secrets*, Melbourne: The Text Publishing Company.

Malkin, B. (25 November 2008) "Boys start real-life fight club in Australia," *The Telegraph*. Online. Available at ProQuest Central <http://www.telegraph.co.uk/news/worldnews/australiaandthepacific/australia/3518831/Boys-start-real-life-fight-club-in-Australia.html> (accessed: 25 November 2008).

Marcus, S. (1969) *The Other Victorians: a study of sexuality and pornography in mid-nineteenth-century England*, London: Corgi Books.

Maton, K. (2008) "Habitus," in M. Grenfell (ed.) *Pierre Bourdieu: key concepts*, Durham: Acumen Publishing Ltd, 49–65.

Meyer, S. (2008) *The Twilight Saga Collection*, London: Little, Brown.

Middleton, Nick (19 June 2004) "Winning smiles, face-paint and feathers make for a role-reversing African beauty contest," *FT Weekend Magazine – First Person, Financial Times*. 7. Available at ProQuest Central <http://proquest.umi.com.dbgw.lis.curtin.edu.au/pqdweb?did=653109431&sid=6&Fmt=3&clientId=22212&RQT=309&VName=PQD> (accessed: 15 June 2011).

Mills, S. (1997) *Discourse*, London and New York: Routledge.

Moore, G. (1966) *Am I Too Loud? Memoirs of an accompanist*, Harmondsworth, Middlesex: Penguin.

Morgan, D. (1993) "You too can have a body like mine: reflections on the male body and masculinities," in S. Scott and D. Morgan (eds) *Body Matters: essays on the sociology of the body*, London and New York: Taylor and Francis, 69–88.

Mort, F. (1988) "Boy's Own? Masculinity, style and popular culture", in R. Chapman and J. Rutherford (eds) *Male Order: unwrapping masculinity*, London: Lawrence and Wishart, 193–224.

Muggeridge, A.R. (Spring 2003) "The war against boys: boys should be boys," *The Women's Quarterly*. Issue 34: 21. Online. Available at ProQuest Central <http://proquest.umi.com.dbgw.lis.curtin.edu.au/pqdweb?did=506121461&sid=8&Fmt=3&clientId=22212&RQT=309&VName=PQD> (accessed: June 30, 2010).

O'Beirne, K. (1 June 1998) "Let's hear it for the boys," *National Review*. 50.10: 28. Online. Available at ProQuest Central <http://proquest.umi.com.dbgw.lis.curtin.edu.au/pqdweb?did=29588692&sid=10&Fmt=3&clientId=22212&RQT=309&VName=PQD> (accessed: 30 June 2011).

Palahniuk, C. (1996) *Fight Club*, New York: W. W. Norton and Company, Inc.

"Police, D203 officials break up Jefferson 'fight club'" (10 May 2011) *NapervilleSun*. Online. Available at <http://napervillesun.suntimes.com/news/5295261–418/police-d203- officials-break-up-jefferson-fight-club.html> . Updated: 28 September 2011 (accessed: 19 November 2011).

Pollard, T. (2011) *Hollywood 9/11: superheroes, supervillains, and super disasters*, Boulder, CO: Paradigm Publishers.

Po[ole], R. (1999) "Deconstruction", in A. Bullock and S. Trombley (eds) *The New Fontana Dictionary of Modern Thought*, London: HarperCollins, 202–3.

Rich, A. (1980) "Compulsory heterosexuality and lesbian existence," in H. Abelove, M. A. Barale and D. M. Halperin (eds) (1993) *The Lesbian and Gay Studies Reader*, New York and London: Routledge: 227–54. Originally published in *Signs: Journal of Women in Culture and Society* 5 (Summer 1980): 631–60.

Richardson, S. (2004) *Clarissa, or The History of a Young Lady*, London: Penguin.

Robinson, S. (2000) *Marked Men: white masculinity in crisis*, New York: Columbia University Press.

Rosten, L. (1971) *The Joys of Yiddish: a relaxed lexicon of Yiddish, Hebrew and Yinglish words often encountered in English, plus dozens that ought to be, with serendipitous excursions into Jewish humour, habits, holidays, history, religion, ceremonies, folklore and cuisine; the whole generously garnished with stories, anecdotes, epigrams, Talmudic quotations, folk sayings and jokes – from the days of the Bible to those of the beatnik*, Harmondsworth, Middlesex: Penguin.

Rowling, J.K. (1997) *Harry Potter and the Philosopher's Stone*, London: Bloomsbury.

—— (1998) *Harry Potter and the Chamber of Secrets*, London: Bloomsbury.

—— (1999) *Harry Potter and the Prisoner of Azkaban*, London: Bloomsbury.

—— (2000) *Harry Potter and the Goblet of Fire*, London: Bloomsbury.

—— (2003) *Harry Potter and the Order of the Phoenix*, London: Bloomsbury.

—— (2005) *Harry Potter and the Half-Blood Prince*, London: Bloomsbury.

—— (2007) *Harry Potter and the Deathly Hallows*, London: Bloomsbury.

Rubin, G. (1997) "The Traffic in Women: notes on the 'political economy' of sex," in L. Nicholson (ed.) *The Second Wave: a reader in feminist theory*, New York and London: Routledge: 27–62. Reprinted from Raina R. Reiter (ed.) (1975), *Toward an Anthropology of Women*, New York: Monthly Review Press: 157–210.

Russo, V. (1987) *The Celluloid Closet: homosexuality in the movies*, New York: Harper and Row.

Santagati, S. and Cohen, A. (2007) *The Manual: a true Bad Boy explains how men think, date and mate – and what women can do to come out on top*, Crows Nest, NSW: Allen and Unwin.

Sedgwick, E.K. (1985) *Between Men: English literature and male homosocial desire*, New York: Columbia University Press.

—— (1990) *Epistemology of the Closet*, Berkeley and Los Angeles: University of California Press.

Seidman, S. (1996) "Introduction", in S. Seidman (ed.) *Queer Theory/Sociology*, Cambridge, MA, and Oxford: Blackwell, 1–29.

Shakespeare, W. (1969) *Macbeth*, A. Harbage (ed.), in A. Harbage (gen. ed.) *William Shakespeare: the complete works*, Baltimore: Penguin Books, 1107–35.

Simpson, M. (1994) *Male Impersonators: men performing masculinity*, London: Cassell.

—— (2011) *marksimpson.com*. Online. Available at <http://www.marksimpson.com/> (accessed: 17 May 2011).

Stinson, B. and Kuhn, M. (2008) *The Bro Code*, New York: Fireside-Simon and Schuster, Inc.

Stoddard, E. and Cornwell, G.H. (1999), "Cosmopolitan or mongrel? *Créolité*, hybridity and 'douglarisation' in Trinidad," *European Journal of Cultural Studies*, 2: 3, 331–53.

Stratton, J. (2000) *Coming Out Jewish: constructing ambivalent identities*, London and New York: Routledge.

Stryker, S. (2004) "Berdache," *glbtq: an encyclopedia of gay, lesbian, bisexual, transgender, and queer culture*. Online. Available at <http://www.glbtq.com/social-sciences/berdache.html> (accessed: 17 November 2011).

Thomson, P. (2008) "Field," in M. Grenfell (ed.) *Pierre Bourdieu: key concepts*, Durham: Acumen Publishing Ltd, 67–81.

Turner, B.S. (2008) *The Body and Society*, Los Angeles: SAGE.

Updike, J. (1994) "The disposable rocket", in L. Goldstein (ed.) *The Male Body: features, destinies, exposures*, Ann Arbor: The University of Michigan Press, 8–11.

Walsh, F. (2010) *Male Trouble: masculinity and the performance of crisis*, Houndmills, Basingstoke: Palgrave Macmillan.

Warner, M. (1993) "Introduction", in M. Warner (ed.) *Fear of a Queer Planet: queer politics and social theory*, Minneapolis and London: University of Minnesota Press, vii–xxxi.

Williams, R. (1977) *Marxism and Literature*, Oxford: Oxford University Press.

Williams, R.H. (2001) "Promise Keepers: a comment on religion and social movements", in R. H. Williams (ed.) *Promise Keepers and the New Masculinity: private lives and public morality*, Lanham, MD: Lexington Books, copublished with the Association for the Sociology of Religion: 1–10.

Winterson, J. (1994) *Written on the Body*, New York: Vintage Books. Originally published in 1992 by Vintage Books.

Wolf, N. (1990) *The Beauty Myth*, London: Chatto and Windus.

Woolf, V. (1992) *Orlando: a biography*, Oxford: Oxford University Press.

Index

24240654R00120

Printed in Great Britain
by Amazon